Dear Ed & Margaret,

I cherish the many blessings that have come from the Ingles-Isaksen Connection. They mean the world to me!

I hope this book can provide you an update on some of what we've been busy with over the years.

Lots of Love,
kat

FACILITATIVE LEADERSHIP

Making a Difference with Creative Problem Solving

Edited by Scott G. Isaksen

Creativity Research Unit
Creative Problem Solving Group — Buffalo

CREATIVE PROBLEM SOLVING GROUP - BUFFALO ®

Copyright © 2000 by Creative Problem Solving Group — Buffalo

ISBN 0-7872-6703-1

Printed in the United States of America
10 9 8 7 6 5 4 3 2 1

FOREWORD

In my 30 years of experience as a creativity and leadership researcher, trainer and consultant, I have come to know Scott Isaksen as a colleague and friend. Our work together at the Center for Creative Leadership and other settings around the globe allowed me to observe Scott's ability to perceive adult learners' needs and his capability to design and deliver programs that have assisted leaders interested in creativity and innovation. *Facilitative Leadership: Making a Difference through Creative Problem Solving* builds on Scott's years of unique experience using creative problem solving as a basis for a new and effective form of facilitative leadership.

Alex Osborn, Sid Parnes, George Prince and William J. J. Gordon were the pioneers whose ideas required a focused adherence to their processes. In contrast, Scott's descriptive approach to process has led him and his colleagues to take many risks. These risks include combining various elements from a variety of processes, leading to new elements and insights, to help us look outside any one particular paradigm. With this in mind, I would describe Scott as a leader in this new generation of problem solving professionals.

This book could only have been edited and written by "thought leaders" who have a broad understanding of what it means to facilitate the creative process in real organizations. With this understanding and experience, they have been able to assemble the many valuable success stories that appear within this book. Scott Isaksen brings to this work years of academic rigor and applied experience inside global organizations.

Facilitative Leadership: Making a Difference through Creative Problem Solving is a book experienced professionals will find useful in their efforts to promote creative leadership in today's organizations. In addition, I think those of you who have an interest in organizational change and improvement, with an eye towards the learning and application of creative problem solving, will be particularly pleased.

Stanley S. Gryskiewicz, Ph.D.
Vice President and Senior Fellow
Creativity and Innovation
Center for Creative Leadership
Greensboro, North Carolina
USA

CONTENTS

ACKNOWLEDGEMENTS

First, I want to dedicate this book to Ruth B. Noller, for her constant support and mentoring. She has been a role model for so many as to what it means to be a good teacher and facilitative leader.

There are so many people that need to be recognized for their input, guidance and assistance in making this book a reality. I truly believe that those of us who are pursuing this line of work are standing on the shoulders of many giants.

To start, Ruth Noller and Sid Parnes provided the early exposure and experiences in creative studies. Without Sid's work and commitment I would have never initiated my career-long mentorship with Ruth. Without their partnership, I would have missed meeting and working with so many people who had contact with the Creative Education Foundation, the Annual Creative Problem Solving Institute and the Center for Studies in Creativity. I have been very lucky to meet and work with so many great people from among all three of these contexts, but I need to particularly thank Jerry Accurso for his sponsorship and Michael Johnson for his colleagueship (and excellent edits and quotes). I have learned a great deal from both of these men.

The close collaboration and colleagueship with Don Treffinger and Brian Dorval has been instrumental in helping me learn and become more explicit about our practice. Their friendship means a great deal to me, and has been a source of strength as we have moved beyond the original paradigm and worked at the edge of our comfort zones.

My friends and colleagues at the Center for Creative Leadership have really helped me see the value of creativity and facilitative leadership within organizations. Particular thanks go to Stan Gryskiewicz, Anne Faber, Ken and Mim Clark, David Campbell and David Hills. I was very stimulated by participants and presenters at the Targeted Innovation Courses, Creativity Week Conferences and the Leadership Education Conferences. I will particularly remember my interactions with John Gardner.

The entire Creative Problem Solving Group — Buffalo network of reflective practitioners who have committed to high standards of certification and the ongoing exchange of learning and insights has been a source of inspiration and support. In particular, those who were students, and have now become close colleagues, include; John Gaulin, Glenn Wilson and Luc De Schryver. Others who have expanded my perspectives include Marianne Tempelaar, Barbara Babij, Gretchen Bingham, Gwen Sperrazini, Sue Besemer, and Doug Reid.

Our clients have been, by far, the main reason for needing to become more explicit and clear about our practice. The original invitation to work with Procter and Gamble by Bill Lambert has continued through the very able professional efforts of Mary Wallgren (yet another student turned colleague)! The early invitations to work with Alcoa by Tom Carter, with DuPont by David Tanner, Charlie Prather and Peter Lyons, and with Exxon by Don Taylor, opened my eyes to the importance of our work to organizations.

Our learning continues through working with other organizations like: Armstrong World Industries (Mary Boulanger and Nancy Hann); PricewaterhouseCoopers (Frank Milton, Trevor Davis, Alan Arnett, Jean-Marc le Tissier and Wayne Lewis); International Masters Publishers (Alf Tönnesson, Mikael Paulsson, Debbie Clarke-Nilsson, Samantha Stead, Greg Dziuba, and Rolf Nilstam); IBM (Rita Houlihan, Bruce Esposito, Will Husta and Ed Lynch); Indiana State University's Bloomberg Center for Interdisciplinary Special Education (Bill Littlejohn, Priscilla Wolfe, and Bonnie Buddle); and David Dunkelman and colleagues from the Wienberg Campus (formally the Rosa Copeland Home).

Creativity Research Unit Fellows: Michael Kirton, Göran Ekvall, Geir Kaufmann, Ken McCluskey, Ruth Noller, Guido Prato-Previde and Don Treffinger, have been wonderful colleagues and scholars who continue to teach me important lessons. I have also been influenced by other scholars including: Teresa Amabile, John Feldhusen, Pros Vanosmael, Istvan Maygari-Beck, Mary McCauley and Rita Dunn. I must acknowledge the formative influence of J.P. Guilford, Donald MacKinnon, E. Paul Torrance and Moe Stein.

For their help in stimulating my cross-cultural learning, I am indebted to; Herloff Trolle, Per Groholt and Guttorm Floisted; graduate students Alex Britz, Patrick Colemont, Marjorie Parker and Remko van der Lugt; and my colleagues from the Santiago, Spain graduate program — especially Lillian Dabdoub and Helena Gilda Costa.

Support from the staff of CPS-B including Matt, Brad, Erik, Keith, Kristin, Ken, Brian and Marves has been instrumental in making this book a reality.

Rev. Harry Grace, Marves, Kristin and Erik have kept their eyes and prayers on my family front for the entire time I was busy with the details of this book. Thanks for your support, faith and love — for helping me learn the most important lessons in life!

——— ABOUT THE CONTRIBUTORS ———

LUC DE SCHRYVER

Luc is currently the director of the Creativity and Innovation Center — Europe (CIC). Luc is also a faculty member at a university college in Belgium where he is responsible for developing a curriculum on creativity and problem solving. Luc initiated the associate program with the Creative Problem Solving Group — Buffalo and has worked to translate CPS into Dutch and French. He currently manages the liaison between CIC and CPS-B. Luc is a CPS-B Certified Facilitator and currently working toward his trainer certification. His work has been published in Dutch, French and English in various conference proceedings, edited collections and the popular press.

Luc has conducted presentations, workshops and training programs for-profit and not-for-profit organizations, such as: The Chamber of Commerce, L'Ecole des Parents, Plato, The Young Economic Chamber, the "Vlaamse Ingenieurskamer" (the Flemisch Chamber for Engineers) and several Quality Centers. Clients Luc has worked with include Belgacom, Kluwer, Oasis and Zwan. He also works with small organizations to link quality initiatives with creativity.

He is a member of various professional organizations including The Center for Development of Creative Thinking (COCD) and The Chamber of Commerce. He is president of the Young Economic Chamber Haspengouw. He is a lecturer at The Center for Total Quality Management.

Luc has earned his M.Sc. degree in Creativity and Innovation from Buffalo State College (1992). He also earned a M. A. in Business Administration from the University of Antwerp (UFSIA - 1988), and an M.Sc. (candidate) in Total Quality Management from the University of Diepenbeek, Belgium. He is a certified user of the Kirton Adaption Innovation Inventory.

Luc is interested in traveling, chess and wine. Whenever he gets a chance, he tries to combine at least two of those three interests.

Luc can be reached at:

Creativity and Innovation Center — Europe
Steenweg 286
B-3570 Alken, Belgium
Tel/Fax: (32) 11-59.21.62

K. Brian Dorval

Brian Dorval is the Director of Programs at the Creative Problem Solving Group-Buffalo (CPS-B). He was Coordinator of Special Services and adjunct faculty member of the Center for Studies in Creativity at Buffalo State College from 1988-1992. In his role as Director of Programs, Brian is responsible for managing the programs and services activities of the group including the development and coordination of agreements with organizations to license and use CPS-B intellectual property. He also manages the facilitator and trainer certification programs. He is responsible for managing relationships with CPS-B's customers and group members.

In addition to this role, Brian is also involved in research and development activities on the topics of creativity and mental imagery. His work has been published in academic journals like *Imagination, Cognition and Personality,* popular publications like *Creative Learning Today,* and *the Communiqué,* and in edited collections like *Understanding and Recognizing Creativity: The Emergence of a Discipline.* He has co-authored a number of books including *Creative Approaches to Problem Solving (1994), Creative Problem Solving: An Introduction (1994), and Toolbox for Creative Problem Solving: Basic Tools and Resouces (1998).*

Since 1988, Brian has provided over 300 training programs, workshops and presentations as well as facilitation sessions for dozens of fortune 100 companies and educational institutions in eleven countries.

Brian is a member of the Board of Directors of the Center for Creative Learning, Inc. He is also an accomplished tennis player and coach, working as assistant and head professional at multiple resorts and training facilities. Many of his players have gained national recognition ranking.

He has earned a Bachelor's Degree in Psychology from Rhode Island College (Magna Cum Laude, 1986) and a Master of Science Degree from Buffalo State College in Creativity and Innovation. He received the John E. Hetherman Award for outstanding student/athlete achievement from Rhode Island College and the Director's Award from the Center for Studies in Creativity (Buffalo State College) for service excellence.

Brian can be reached at:

Creative Problem Solving Group — Buffalo
1325 North Forest Road - Suite F-340
Williamsville, NY 14221-2157 USA
Phone: (716) 689-2176 • Fax: (716) 689-6441
e-mail: cpsb@cpsb.com • web: www.cpsb.com

Scott G. Isaksen

Dr. Isaksen is the President of the Creative Problem Solving Group — Buffalo and the Senior Fellow of its Creativity Research Unit. He has been a professor and director of the Center for Studies in Creativity at Buffalo State College from 1981 to 1997 — a teacher for more than twenty-five years. Scott has published over 120 books, articles and chapters and has conducted more than 800 programs and courses by working with over 200 organizations and groups in more than 27 states or provinces and fourteen different countries.

Scott is the second editor with D. J. Treffinger and R. L. Firestien of the *Handbook of Creative Learning* - published in 1982 by the Center for Creative Learning; author with D. J. Treffinger of *Creative Problem Solving: The Basic Course* - published in 1985 by Bearly Limited; editor of *Frontiers in Creativity Research: Beyond the basics* – published in 1987 by Bearly Limited; editor with M. C. Murdock, R. L. Firestien, and D. J. Treffinger of *Nurturing and Developing Creativity: The Emergence of a Discipline* – and *Understanding and Recognizing Creativity: The emergence of a discipline* published in 1993 by Ablex Publishing; author with K. B. Dorval and D. J. Treffinger of *Creative Approaches to Problem Solving* – published in 1994 by Kendall/Hunt Publishing; second editor with M. Joyce, F. Davidson, G. J. Puccio, C. Coppage and M. A. Maruska of *An Introduction to Creativity* – published in 1995 and 1997 by Copley Publishing; and author (with K. Brian Dorval and D. J. Treffinger of *Toolbox for Creative Problem Solving: Basic tools and resources* – published by the Creative Problem Solving Group — Buffalo in 1998. Scott is currently working on an updated and revised edition of *Creative Approaches to Problem Solving* (with K. B. Dorval and D. J. Treffinger) and *Leading Creative Change: A systems approach* (with R. B. Noller).

Scott serves on the educational advisory board of the National Invention Center as well as the American Creativity Association and has been a visiting faculty member to various universities. He has been on the faculty of the Creative Problem Solving Institutes and a Senior Adjunct Trainer with the Center for Creative Leadership. He has been on the editorial boards of the *Creativity Research Journal* and the journal of *Creativity and Innovation Management* and currently serves as a consulting editor for the *Journal of Creative Behavior*.

He is the recipient of the Service and Commitment Award and the Distinguished Leader Award from the Creative Education Foundation, as well as the State University of New York Chancellor's Award for Excellence in Teaching.

Scott earned a Bachelor of Science degree in Education (Cum Laude, 1974) from Buffalo State College, the Master of Science degree in Creative Studies from the Center for Studies in Creativity (1977), and the Doctor of Education degree in Curriculum Design from the University of Buffalo (1983).

Scott can be reached at:

The Creative Problem Solving Group — Buffalo
1325 North Forest Road – Suite F 340
Williamsville, NY   14221-2143   USA
Phone: (716) 689-2176 • Fax: (716) 689-6441
e-mail: sgi@cpsb.com • web site: www.cpsb.com

KENNETH MCCLUSKEY

Dr. McCluskey has more than 25 years experience as a teacher, special educator, psychologist, and senior administrator in the public school system. Currently, he is an Associate Professor of Education at The University of Winnipeg. Ken has authored, co-authored, or edited more than 70 professional articles and chapters, as well as a dozen books, including *Mexico: Behind the Sombrero* (1980), *The Doubtful Gift: Strategies for Educating Gifted Children in the Regular Classroom* (1986), *Challenge: Sourcebook for gifted Education* (1989), *Lost prizes: Talent Development and Problem Solving with At-risk Students* (1995), *Butterfly Kisses: Amber's Journey Through Hyperactivity* (1996), and *Teaching for Talent Development: Current and Expanding Perspectives* (1998).

In private practice, Ken has been President of Winnipeg Educational Consultants, Inc. since 1979. In 1996, he assumed the same role with Associates for Creative Education. His work with Indian and Northern Affairs Canada and local bands has taken him to more than 50 native communities and schools throughout Manitoba and other Canadian provinces. As well, Ken has done extensive work in educational and vocational planning (federally for Human Resources Development Canada, and provincially with Employment Services, Workers Compensation, and the Department of Corrections).

Dr. McCluskey earned his Bachelor of Arts (Honors), Master of Arts, and Doctor of Philosophy degrees in Psychology from the University of Manitoba. He has conducted workshops or given invited addresses throughout Canada, the U.S., Mexico, and Trinidad and Tobago. Ken is a recipient of the *Reclaiming Children and Youth Journal*'s Spotlight on Excellence Award (1996), the Manitoba Council of Exceptional Children's Outstanding Achievement Award (1996), and the Canadian CEC's Joan Kershaw Publications Award (1997).

Ken can be reached at:

Bachelor of Education Program
the University of Winnipeg
515 Portage Avenue
Winnipeg, Manitoba, Canada R3B 2E9
Phone: (204) 786-9470 • Fax: (204) 772-7980;
e-mail: k.mccluskey@u.winnipeg.ca

Donald J. Treffinger

Dr. Treffinger is the President of the Center for Creative Learning, Inc. He is Professor Emeritus of Creative Studies in the Center for Studies in Creativity at Buffalo State College. Don has published more than 250 articles or chapters in a variety of academic journals, popular publications, books, and monographs. He has authored, co-authored, or edited *The Handbook of Creative Learning* (1982), *Creative Problem Solving: The Basic Course* (1985), *Creative Thinking and Problem Solving in Gifted Education* (1985), *Bringing Out the Giftedness in Your Child* (1992), *Identifying and Recognizing Creativity: The Emergence of a Discipline* (1993), *Nurturing and Developing Creativity: The Emergence of a Discipline* (1993), *Creative Problem Solving: An Introduction* (1994), and *Creative Approaches to Problem Solving* (1994).

Dr. Treffinger has previously served as Professor of Educational Psychology and Chairman of the Educational Psychology and Research Department at the University of Kansas (1972-1978), and as Associate Professor of Educational Psychology and Research at Purdue University (1968-1972). He is a Fellow of the American Psychological Association, and a Life Member of the National Association for Gifted Children. He received NAGC's Distinguished Service Award in 1984, and the NAGC E. Paul Torrance Creativity Award in 1995. Don served as Editor of the *Gifted Child Quarterly* from 1980—1984, and has been a member of the editorial board of several other professional journals.

Since 1968, Don has conducted workshops and programs or given invited presentations in forty-nine states in the U.S., seven Canadian provinces, and five countries outside North America.

Don earned a Bachelor of Science degree in Education (Cum Laude, 1961) from Buffalo State College, and the Master of Science (1967) and Doctor of Philosophy (1969) degrees in Educational Psychology from Cornell University.

Don can be reached at:

Center for Creative Learning, Inc.
Post Office Box 14100 NE Plaza
Sarasota, FL 34278-4100 USA
Phone: (941) 351-8862 • Fax (941) 351-9061
e-mail: cclofc@gte.net • http://www.creativelearning.com

ABOUT THE CREATIVE PROBLEM SOLVING GROUP — BUFFALO (CPS-B)

Buffalo, New York has been a major center for the understanding and developing of creativity for more than 50 years. Alex F. Osborn, the inventor of brainstorming, founded the Buffalo-based Creative Education Foundation in 1954. He was joined by Sidney Parnes and other colleagues who then founded the Center for Studies in Creativity (CSC) at Buffalo State College in 1967.

The results of over 55 years of work have included the establishment of an academic journal, an international annual conference, undergraduate and graduate course work leading to the Master of Science degree, the establishment of a unique library collection and a literature data base on creativity, among many others. Hundreds of articles, books and other resources have been produced and thousands of people internationally have attended conferences, courses and have visited the facilities.

Buffalo has also been the intellectual home of creative problem solving. In fact, more than a dozen different versions of the systematic framework have been developed and tested. The work of Alex Osborn established creative problem solving, and the research efforts of Sid Parnes and Ruth Noller provided evidence that deliberate courses could help develop creative potential.

CPS-B was formed to respond to the many requests being made by organizations from business, industry, government (and others) for up-to-date information and help with their interests in creativity. The not-for-profit organizations were simply ill-equipped to deal with the expanding requests for information, training, and a variety of kinds of support external organizations demanded.

Scott Isaksen joined the faculty of the University and assumed the directorship of the CSC in the early 1980's. He provided a variety of services to outside organizations. In 1982, he formed SGI Associates to respond to the demand and soon found that the growth in interest had exceeded the capability of the faculty and staff to provide programs and courses. Organizations were beginning to request real-life applications of CPS on new product development, strategy, and a variety of change-management challenges.

In 1991, CPS-B was formally established with a growing international network of associates to help meet the demand for services across North America and Europe. Scott was joined by Brian Dorval as Director of Programs and Ken Lauer as Director of Research. Marves Isaksen came aboard as Director of Administration and Finance. In 1997, Scott assumed the full-time Presidency of CPS-B. Keith Kaminski joined the full-time core team in 1998. A number of additional support-team members help to provide courses, manage databases, and assist in meeting our customers' needs.

CPS-B has developed an international network of more than 50 highly-qualified professionals that help to conduct courses, programs and consulting services for our clients. We use a defined and well-researched skillbase to develop and certify these professionals and maintain the highest standards for planning, providing and following through on the services we provide.

The services we provide are supported by the Creativity Research Unit within CPS-B. This unique center for basic and applied creativity research involves numerous Research Fellows from other major academic centers in conducting studies, translating measures and writing scientific articles, books and reports. Some Fellows also assist CPS-B in writing and developing up-to-date learning resources to help others learn and apply our unique version of CPS, as well as a variety of other practical tools.

THE STORY BEHIND THIS BOOK

Facilitative Leadership:
Making a Difference with Creative Problem Solving

Leadership is an awesome responsibility, and it becomes particularly challenging when you need to help others learn and use new ways of thinking and behaving. If you look to the literature, dozens of books offer helpful ways of looking at leadership. Many focus on the leader and what he or she is like and accomplishes. This book connects two areas of concern: what we know about facilitative leadership; and our work with a broad and inclusive method for making change happen.

This book is for those of you who have an interest in helping others become better able to learn about and apply their creative talents. If you already facilitate meetings and change within organizations, you should find many of the insights and resources within this book of value. The book is designed to assist those who use methods and tools to manage change and who seek to make a positive difference.

The purpose of this introduction is first, to tell you about my story and some of the key events that shaped my own understanding of facilitative leadership. My understanding has been shaped by thirty years of reading, research, development, and experience. Second, I will share key general insights from those years of learning that outline the philosophy upon which facilitative leadership is based. Finally, each chapter will be overviewed and introduced.

GROWING UP WITHIN THE OSBORN-PARNES TRADITION

The story behind this book starts with the early development of the instructional program in creative studies at Buffalo State College. The academic program had been moved to the College in 1967, and the Creative Studies Project was launched in 1969, in a pilot version. Sid Parnes and Ruth Noller, along with an internationally renowned panel of advisors, received the approval for their research project to experimentally study the effects of an educational program designed to teach creativity. It was impressive to see that the research had the support of so many scholars, the US Office of Education, the Creative Education Foundation (CEF) and the College president. I received an invitation to join the project and I opted to participate, and was assigned to the experimental group. In short, I was to receive the full treatment: to enroll in four semesters of undergraduate coursework in creativity.

As an experimental subject in the courses and program, I learned the Osborn-Parnes approach to CPS. In addition, we were exposed to courses on Synectics, Synectics Educational Systems, and Creative Analysis. In addition to attending formal courses, we were required to do a great deal of reading (and writing reaction papers), conduct outside application projects and participate in regular assessment sessions that also involved the control-group subjects. It was an eclectic series of courses. I met some very interesting people in the program and also met Marves (now my wife) during the testing sessions, as she was in the control group.

On the basis of my early participation in the courses, I had an uneasy feeling about the value or usefulness of the program. The first class meeting we had to sit in a circle and introduce ourselves, we were introduced to "Ruth" and "Sid" rather than Dr. Noller and Dr. Parnes. We were listened to and requested to provide input regarding the course requirements. Sid and Ruth made a deliberate effort to learn our names and we all wore name tags. All in all, this was a very different course from the others I was experiencing at Buffalo State College! It all felt just a little too "warm and fuzzy" for me, particularly in comparison with my other courses. It wasn't until I had to apply what I was learning in the courses, within my management position, that the value of the tools and material became more clear.

My formal education was enriched by being invited by Ruth Noller to lead the student aides during the Annual Creative Problem Solving Institute (CPSI) in 1971. In order to attend, I had to take a short leave from my management position at Mountain Haven Resort in the Lake George region of New York. I jumped at the honor of being invited by one of my professors to function in such a role. It didn't hurt that I learned about Ruth's background in mathematics and her involvement in programming the Mark I computer with Grace Hopper at Harvard! Ruth's credibility and integrity along with her love for the subject encouraged me.

Little did I know that I had been given a unique gift along with the responsibility of leading the logistical support group for an international conference. The gift was that I was on the inside of an important series of conferences held each summer at Buffalo State College. Hundreds of people came from all over the world to learn about CPS and creativity. CPSI was indeed a unique environment filled with energy and excitement. During the early 1970's the entire world of creativity seemed interested in the Creative Studies Project! I was also invited to be on a panel during each institute to tell stories about the courses and program. There was immense interest in the work being done at Buffalo State College by the CEF, and I was proud to be playing a small supportive role.

The CPSI's also gave me the chance to attend sessions and meet more personally with the "big names" in the field. I will never forget meeting J. P. Guilford, Don MacKinnon, E. Paul Torrance, John Gowan, Moe Stein, Charlie Clark, Don Treffinger and many others. The readings I had been assigned in the academic program gave me the chance to decide whom I wanted to meet, which sessions I should attend and which leaders I should seek out for answers to questions. It was surprising to me that these main and important figures within the field would be so generous with their time and expertise. Each gave time and attention to an eager undergraduate student and even sent materials following our meetings. I often refer to these years as the "Golden years of CPSI." It was the central meeting ground for everyone interested in the deliberate development of creative potential, and most leaders shared a common understanding of the Osborn-Parnes creative problem solving process.

After completing my degree in 1974, I was able to obtain a teaching job in a local school district and began taking courses in the Master of Science degree program. The district was very progressive and challenging and provided me the opportunity to work with consummate professional educators like Don Oglivie, Mary Jo Shafer, Carol Pratt, Carol Wittig, and so many others. I was also offered an Administrative Internship with the CEF during the summer. I was able to travel with my colleagues to the extension CPSI's held at Macalester College, University of California and Southern Connecticut State College – New Haven. Each institute provided the unique opportunity to team-teach with new and interesting leaders and meet other leaders who were not able to participate in the Buffalo CPSI.

Graduate coursework started that summer. Joette, Lynn, Tom, Ang and I had the undivided attention of both Ruth and Sid for all our courses. They were tough courses with many challenging requirements, and there was no opportunity to hide. We really had to pay attention and come prepared. The program was challenging, especially as I was just starting my teaching career and became a married man! I was able to finish my Masters thesis in 1977, as the fourth graduate with the unique Master of Science in Creative Studies degree.

With a few years of teaching behind me, Ruth invited me to join her and redesign the Leadership Development Program at CPSI. We had the chance to work with a large group of diverse professionals who shared an interest in becoming leaders at CPSI and developing their facilitative leadership skills and knowledge. This provided a six-year opportunity for deliberate study, learning, and development of the literature and programs on leadership and facilitation.

The next major opportunity to become grounded within the Osborn-Parnes tradition was my selection as a faculty member to work with Ruth for a year and then take her position, when she retired, the following academic year. This was a great honor for me. As a result of actually joining the full-time faculty at Buffalo State College there were many opportunities and challenges. I realized how unique and valuable the academic program was, and how challenging it was going to be to keep such a program alive and well.

I feel good about many of the events and outcomes accomplished during my tenure as a professor and director of the Center for Studies in Creativity. These results could not have been accomplished without the involvement and support of many faculty colleagues and students. The following list provides a "top-ten list" (not in order of importance) of those results for which I feel some responsibility. Namely:

✦ Strengthening the Center to a point of more than doubling the faculty support, acquiring a State budget for the program, securing appropriate space and logistical support, and many other concrete ingredients so important for a unique program and scarce resources in a shrinking State University system.

✦ Continuing to grow the Creative Studies Collection at E. H. Butler Library so that there would be a comprehensive collection dedicated to the emerging field of creativity inquiry and practice.

✦ Founding the Creativity Based Information Resources (CBIR) project to assemble and make available the corpus of creativity literature to those who have a serious interest in knowing what has been done.

✦ Establishing the Alex F. Osborn Visiting Professorship program in association with the Creative Education Foundation, and the cooperative doctoral program with the University of Bergen.

✦ Establishing and providing the initial funding for an endowment with the Buffalo State College Foundation to provide ongoing supplementary support for the academic program and library. The effort was focused on finding funds and opportunities to acquire and utilize supplementary resources to help the program grow.

✦ Bringing major international visibility to the Center's work by qualifying to host the International Creativity and Innovation Networking Conference in 1990.

✦ Designing and hosting the 1990 International Conference on Creativity Research, in conjunction with the networking conference, and bringing over 30 of the most prominent creativity researchers to Buffalo and in contact with my colleagues and students.

✦ Designing and hosting a follow-up Working Conference on Creativity Research that resulted in the explicit reformulation of an ecological approach for creativity research.

♦ Working with my colleagues and staff to obtain the internal designation as an International Center of Excellence and a State University of New York Academic Program of Distinction.

♦ Growing the number of students who: successfully achieved their Master of Science degrees in Creative Studies (nearly 120 when I left!); obtained Graduate Certificates by completing a concentration in creative studies; and completed the undergraduate minor in creative studies.

Pursuing these accomplishments taught me a great deal about leadership, facilitation, and teamwork. In the unique academic environment of the center, I also learned a great deal about transitions. The first team with whom I had the pleasure to work included: Roger Firestien, Sharon McGrath, John Moffat, and Ed Zilewicz. The team that was there when I left included: Roger Firestien, Debi Johnson, Marie Mance, Gerard Puccio, and Mary Murdock. Great things can be accomplished when there is a shared vision and a commitment to work toward its fruition.

As a result of my academic position at the Center, and my role within the Osborn-Parnes tradition, I was invited to serve on the editorial boards of all three established creativity journals (Creativity and Innovation Management, the Creativity Research Journal and the Journal of Creative Behavior), numerous Creativity organizations (e.g. Inventure Place and American Creativity Association), and serve as a representative of the Buffalo tradition in creative problem solving at numerous international conferences. I was often seen as a spokesperson and advocate of the Osborn-Parnes Buffalo-based tradition of creative problem solving.

Stepping Outside the Paradigm

Another key theme of the story starts with the opportunities to work first-hand with and obtain a deeper exposure to alternative creative problem solving frameworks. I had been exposed to formal training in other methods and approaches within the courses I took at Buffalo State College, as it was an eclectic program by design. Other than short sessions offered through CPSI, the courses were mainly taught by Sid or Ruth. In 1983, the faculty of the Center launched a project to compare alternative methods. My colleagues went to obtain training in Kepner-Tregoe, Synectics®, and other methods. Don Treffinger and I decided to go to Cambridge for some training in Gordon's method called Synectics Educational Systems. It is based on metaphor and the intrapersonal process of generating valued novelty from analogy.

Although I had been exposed to alternative methods through my training in the Creative Studies Project and CPSI, it was a unique experience to be on someone else's home ground and learn their method directly from them. Bill Gordon and Tony Poze challenged Don and me in many ways. We were able to provide rich stories and insights upon our return and to compare notes with our colleagues.

The second in-depth exposure to an alternative framework came from the Center for Creative Leadership (CCL). During one of the CPSI's held during the early 80's, I had the chance to meet Stan Gryskiewicz of CCL in Greensboro, North Carolina. Don MacKinnon had mentioned Stan's name to me and suggested that I connect with him. I was very impressed with Stan's doctoral research on Targeted Innovation. Following a conversation with him, I decided to attend the world-renowned Leadership Development Program (LDP) offered by CCL in May of 1983. Not only did this course relate to my role within CPSI, it had a profound impact on me personally and professionally. During the course I had the additional bonus of meeting Anne Faber, who worked with Stan in the Creativity Division.

Following the LDP, I chose to attend the Creativity Week Conferences and the Targeted Innovation Course hosted at CCL in 1984. It was during these events that I met Teresa Amabile, Dean Simonton, and Michael Kirton. Stan invited me to join their adjunct faculty and I began yet another journey within my quest. This time I was charged to improve the existing courses as well as assist in offering them off site. I had to work within an alternative framework and with a new group of colleagues. The big insight for me was that other frameworks seemed to work pretty well. Even more importantly, the kind of work I had been doing exclusively with young students and college undergraduates and graduates seemed to be of value for professionals within some of the biggest and most important organizations in the world.

As a result of these contacts, I designed a Frontiers of Creativity Research Conference as a part of the 1984 CPSI and invited Teresa, Dean, and Michael to attend, among other scholars. I believe this had a profound effect on the work of many leaders within CPSI and particularly my academic colleagues and students. It was very productive to invite accomplished scholars from outside the Buffalo tradition to attend and share their ideas and research with others who share a common interest in the deliberate development of creativity. Some of the ideas, results, and approaches met with some resistance and discomfort from the established camps, but I am glad I persisted.

While I was working with CCL, the CEF suddenly moved off campus and created some big challenges for me in terms of support and internal politics on campus. It was in this context that a number of organizations started making requests of me to go off campus and help them with some of their challenges needing creativity. The very first major request came from Bill Lambert from Procter and Gamble in 1984, and has resulted in a long-term working relationship with many within the company. Requests also came in from Armstrong, Alcoa, and Exxon, and the income from this work provided valuable supplementary support for the work of the Center.

Another series of events to support the break with the Osborn-Parnes tradition came as I was beginning to take on leadership responsibility for the Center for Studies in Creativity. Following the first comprehensive internal academic evaluation of our program, I interviewed all the deans on campus. They asserted that no groundbreaking research was being done within the center. They indicated that the Creative Studies Project was a great start, but that they were disappointed with the current state of affairs. As a result, I realigned some personal priorities, initiated the Cognitive Styles and Climate Projects, and launched a series of impact studies to determine what the needs were. The aim of this new thrust of research was to better determine what was working for whom and under what circumstances.

This new direction in research was readily combined with the work that organizations were asking me to provide. The biggest insight was that people were not using CPS the way it had been presented to them. They were using bits and pieces as they needed. This basic insight caused my colleagues and me to question the Osborn-Parnes method and make some improvements along the way (see Chapter 2 on the History of CPS for more information). Aside from the insights about the nature of use and needs for improvement of the Osborn-Parnes CPS model and approach, we were beginning to uncover many important facets for future research and development.

The final "break" with the Osborn-Parnes tradition came gradually as a result of pursuing reflective practice. As you can see, the earlier experiences provided exposure to diverse models and frameworks. My initial reaction to these was to attempt to influence the prevailing paradigm. I worked to update courses and curricula, wrote updated texts and articles to share the incremental improvements we were making. We designed and delivered short courses that would provide updates to communicate our new approaches. In all this work, our efforts were aimed at keeping the prevailing paradigm alive, well and growing.

Our attempts to improve the prevailing paradigm were generally met with disinterest, resistance, and anger. As we became more and more active with the newer approaches with those who faced real challenges within organizations, our learning curve increased, and that's when the breakthroughs came. The transformation came when we started to realize that it was more about making a difference and less about preserving a method or model. It became more important to see the method as only one ingredient in the larger system.

As a result of this experience and research, we have come to an improved understanding of the importance of the role of facilitation. It was clear to us that it took more than a surface understanding of the tools and techniques within the Creative Problem Solving method in order to make an enduring difference. The process-oriented leadership role seemed to be very important in making the method work. The following insights provide a foundation for those of you who have chosen to pursue the journey of learning how to develop the skills and attitudes of facilitative leadership.

KEY INSIGHTS ABOUT FACILITATIVE LEADERSHIP

Working with groups can be challenging. Anyone who must regularly attend meetings and work with committees can attest to frequently experiencing feelings of frustration and boredom, and having the general impression that very little is being accomplished. There are many reasons for the lack of productivity within groups. Group members can start offering solutions for ill-defined problems, resulting in the selection of an answer that does not resolve the real challenge. Members of groups can be reluctant to participate or share ideas or alternatives for a variety of reasons. Decisions can be made, and actions committed to, based more on someone's personal influence rather than on the basis of clear criteria.

The reason for the development of so many tools like Nominal Group, Delphi or Brainstorming was to help groups function more effectively (Delbecq, Van de Ven & Gustafson, 1975; Osborn, 1953). These tools have been found to be very effective when they are used appropriately. One of the best ways to ensure that tools are used to obtain the best value is to include a facilitator. The facilitator who is skilled with the tools and with managing groups can provide significant added value to meetings and group interactions of all sorts.

One of the best things I have learned from the Osborn-Parnes tradition is the importance of the role of the facilitator. I really like Sid Parnes' definition of a facilitator:

> *The leader who draws out, reinforces, and thus facilitates the creative learning, development, and problem solving of the people with whom he or she is working. The person facilitating creative behavior is aware of the creative process and first understands it in himself or herself, and then is able to help others see and strengthen it in themselves. (Parnes, 1997, p. 111)*

This approach to leadership is aligned with Greenleaf's (1991) view of servant leadership. Greenleaf asserted that the servant leader starts with a feeling to serve first, rather than one who is leader first. He offered a series of criteria to assess the degree to which someone was a servant leader. They included:

+ Did those served grow as persons?

+ Did they, while being served, become healthier, wiser, freer, more autonomous, more likely themselves to become servant leaders?

+ What is the effect on the least privileged in society? Will they benefit or at least not be further deprived?

These definitions provide a glimpse of an approach to leadership entirely different than the prevailing view. The "everyday view" of leadership is that it only exists at the very senior levels of the organization. I wish I had a nickel for every time I heard someone say, "You have to start at the top!" There is also a view that leaders are heroic. So, it's also very lonely at the top. They accomplish nearly superhuman tasks with miraculous energy, tireless dedication, and the unique gifts of charisma and insight.

Power and competition are also linked strongly to the prevailing view of leadership. Greenleaf offers the perspective that building and growing strong institutions for the long term will take large amounts of voluntary action in support of the goals of the organization. The corruption caused by abusive or coercive use of power or the distortion of priorities by intense and destructive competition stand in stark contrast to the ideas promoted by Greenleaf (1998). He indicated:

> *I believe that caring for persons, the more able and the less able serving each other, is what makes a good society. Most caring was once person to person. Now much of it is mediated through institutions — often large, powerful, impersonal; not always competent; sometimes corrupt. If a better society is to be built, one more just and more caring and providing opportunity for people to grow, the most effective and economical way while supportive of the social order, is raise the performance as servant of as many institutions as possible by new voluntary regenerative forces initiated within them by committed individuals: servants. (p. 17)*

Facilitative leadership is more in line with the ideas of Greenleaf. The longer term view of what's good for the organization is developing the skills and motives of those who will take future leadership roles. Rather than playing as though the leader is on the elite all-star team, time and energy are invested in developing the talent pool for a much larger and more inclusive sense of team. There is a deeper sense of service linked with facilitative leadership. A commitment to serve individuals, groups, and the longer-term purposes of the organization offsets the preoccupation with self interest and self promotion.

Facilitative leadership is the kind of leadership that focuses on service, providing help and assistance to others in ways that build strong consensus and shared commitment. The aim of facilitative leadership is the development and strengthening of others. This kind of leadership can be applied on everyday and incremental challenges and opportunities as well as for special and disruptive changes. Our work within organizations of all kinds has reinforced the value of this kind of leadership as an imperative for the building and maintaining of healthy institutions. It also provides the philosophical base for our work to develop facilitators of CPS, as these are individuals who are learning and applying a powerful framework for exploring possibilities and releasing creative talents.

Facilitation is more than just tools and techniques. It takes more than just a full toolbox to assist individuals, groups and organizations in releasing creative human talent. Of course, the facilitator must have numerous tools and frameworks at his or her disposal. The process is understood to be the servant of the content and the valued outcomes being pursued. Mindful choices must be made on the basis of both content and process (Langer, 1989). These choices must also take into account the people involved and the context within which the decisions are being made.

Taking on any leadership role in an emerging field takes courage and unwavering commitment. It's as much about giving things up as it is about taking things on. Those individuals who have pursued learning and applying CPS, and its facilitation, have faced and overcome many challenges and concerns. They have come to their learning with many ideas, assumptions, feelings and relationships that may have been dominated by the prevailing view of leadership. As they have been a part of an experiential learning community they have found new ideas and assumptions, and have often had the courage to leave the old ones behind.

As a result of our work with dozens of organizations, conducting regular public courses and our work within academic programs and courses, we often ask participants and students to share their major insights about facilitation. There are clear themes from their comments over the years. The following ten major insights have often been shared by participants following our facilitator development courses.

- ✦ **Distinguishing process and content.** One core insight they frequently share is their learning of the importance of maintaining a distinct focus on both process and content. Many of the participants with whom we work are consultants and trainers. They are often concerned about sharing information and expertise in the content area within which they work. During the facilitation training they learn that there is a whole new world surrounding process. They are often surprised how much there is to learn about how tools work, how language can affect behavior, and generally how to manage the many dynamics associated with the facilitator role.

  The content that is involved during a creative problem-solving session is often interdisciplinary, crossing functional boundaries within organizations, and usually at the frontiers of what is agreed and common knowledge. Problems and opportunities that require creativity do not often pay attention to neat disciplinary borders. Given this particularly "messy" content, it is helpful to have a clear process structure to keep it all within "bounded instability."

- ✦ **The power of choosing tools.** Newly trained facilitators often mention how powerful it is to make deliberate choices from among a set of tools to promote creative thinking and problem solving. This includes knowing the tool and how it works.

- ✦ **The dynamic balance between generating and focusing.** Being deliberate about bringing together two very different forms of thinking requires specific guidelines, language and diverse tools. These resources require different forms and amounts of energy. Extending effort during generating and focusing may be different for people who have diverse preferences and will be affected by the needs of the task. Novelty results from the act of generating and needs to be preserved and developed during focusing. This dynamic balance results in valued novelty.

Each kind of thinking requires careful managing of judgment. During generating, it is suspended or deferred. During focusing, it is applied affirmatively to develop and strengthen novel options.

✦ **The importance of preplanned flexibility.** Participants are often surprised about the level of productivity gained from having a detailed structure and time invested in up-front planning. They are often equally surprised to find that their plans are changed and modified before the meeting or application even starts!

Facilitators often share the insight that it's more about being able to think on your feet and being ready for the unexpected, rather than attempting to plan for every contingency. This personal flexibility is assisted by seeing the value of preparation. The living interaction then provides the opportunity for ongoing clarifying and contracting on expectations.

✦ **The value of diverse perspectives.** They learn that with an improved structure and increased clarity of language and purpose, there is real power in having people with diverse styles, expertise, and experiences, work on tasks that require valued novelty. This diversity can create new challenges and tensions, but the increased clarity and structure provided by using a common framework can maintain a productive focus and help obtain the needed results.

✦ **The effect of the facilitator on climate.** Many participants have been surprised to learn about the powerful effect that the facilitator's language and behavior has on the climate created within the group or situation.

✦ **Facilitating creativity rather than creative facilitation.** Within the growing field of creativity and innovation, there are many who sell their services by providing creative facilitation. They put a great deal of their energy into making their sessions and meetings creative exercises. These providers take extreme delight in putting their energy into making their events and performances as creative as possible. The focus is more on the facilitators demonstrating their own creativity while designing the meeting, the interaction, and the environment or design. It is often less about creating opportunities for others to demonstrate or develop their creative talents.

Facilitative leadership is more about having a long-term intention to strengthen others so that they are more independent and able to use their creative talent.

✦ **Not needing to have the answer for every problem or challenge.** Many consultants believe that their value lies in providing answers and content expertise to their clients. It is helpful for facilitators to have enough knowledge to be able to communicate about the task under consideration and make adjustments in the language and approach. It is not necessary for the facilitator to have sufficient knowledge in the domain or to be identified as a content expert. As a facilitator, you do need to believe in:

The people — You can ensure that there is sufficient ownership for the task and, if needed, you can assemble the right people who can share and develop new solutions for the benefit of the client(s) and sponsor(s).

The place — You can create the right environment to help establish the conditions for coming up with appropriate solutions.

The process — You can trust the process, especially if you have learned your lessons well.

The outcome — You can have faith that the effort will be worth the investment.

✦ **Yielding impressive results.** Many of those who are new to facilitation and using a deliberate process framework are amazed about the speed and level of productivity that can often come from short but focused meetings and interventions.

Sometimes the results come after a simple yet important interaction between the client (challenge owner) and the facilitator who is planning for some interaction or session. Some of my own significant insights about facilitation have come from working on personal and professional challenges and opportunities where the stakes were not very high. Other insights have come from:

■ Helping an internationally renowned entertainment organization consider and develop alternatives for growth, beyond building more theme parks.

■ Helping a consumer products organization develop fundamentally new and testably different consumer needs to leap-frog the competition.

■ Preparing a global information and computer company to improve its new product development process and drastically cut time to market, as well as generate millions of dollars in revenue from new services.

■ Helping a manufacturing organization improve the quality of its internal operations and win the Baldridge Award.

- Helping an educational organization work with social service agencies to significantly improve their capacity to provide wraparound support for families and children in need.
- Helping the senior management team of a research and development organization transform itself from a single line of service to multiple business units; thus saving 650 jobs.
- Helping a government information security agency develop procedures to handle novel data that assisted in Operation Desert Storm.
- Helping churches, symphony orchestras, and other public service organizations transform themselves.
- Helping an international publishing company increase the customer retention rate 65% in four months.
- Helping a senior management team of a major division from a global manufacturing organization reach consensus on criteria for research and development projects.
- Helping an entire rural school district successfully plan and implement strategic goals for school improvement and community involvement.
- Helping a petroleum company significantly reduce the costs associated with stopping and preventing environmental hazards.

✦ **The workings of a revised flexible structure.** There are many versions of CPS (see Chapter 2 on Understanding the History of CPS). Our version rejects the idea that a creative process can be reduced to a simple and prescribed series of steps. We do not believe in a simple recipe for creativity. As a result of more than a decade of deliberate development within the Osborn-Parnes tradition, we have taken some steps forward to help open up the framework to make it more flexible and amenable to deliberate design. We call this a descriptive or ecological approach to the creative process.

We do not feel totally alone in moving toward this approach. Research from a variety of sources (metacognition, learning strategies, cognitive science, etc.) as well as many practical experiences provide support for a more open and flexible approach to the creative process.

THE PURPOSE OF THIS COLLECTION

The purpose of this book is to assemble and synthesize what we know about the many factors and dynamics of facilitative leadership. Although the main framework we share has been our current approach to CPS, much of what is included will be useful for anyone who has to work with others to solve problems creatively.

The first chapter is entitled *Conceptual Foundations of Creative Problem Solving* (CPS) and is aimed at digging deeper into the basis for linking creativity and problem solving. Many people have questions about the name Creative Problem Solving. This chapter explains that our approach includes and synthesizes problems and possibilities. This chapter provides an academic background and theoretical information for those interested in what's underneath our practice. One practical outcome from a reading of this chapter is a better understanding of why certain tasks are more appropriate than others for CPS.

The second chapter is called *Understanding the History of CPS*. Don Treffinger has documented the unique developments of our current approach to CPS. One of the interesting features of this chapter is the inclusion of the actual graphics that have been used to depict the models over fifty years of development. Reading this chapter will help you understand and appreciate the dynamic nature of CPS and to be more aware of the different versions that are in current use.

The first two chapters will provide you with a foundation and understanding of the unique context within which facilitative leadership operates. Should you wish to obtain the most current and comprehensive statement of our current approach to Creative Problem Solving you should read:

- ✦ Isaksen, S. G., Dorval, K. B., & Treffinger, D. J. (2000). *Creative approaches to problem solving* (Revised Second Edition). Dubuque, IA: Kendall/Hunt Publishing.

- ✦ Treffinger, D. J., Isaksen, S. G., & Dorval, K. B. (2000). *Introduction to Creative Problem Solving* (Third Edition). Waco, TX: Prufrock Press.

The third chapter is entitled *Facilitating Creative Problem Solving*. It is written by Brian Dorval and me to describe the role of the facilitator as well as what the facilitator needs to know, do and believe. The chapter is based on our varied experiences and the research we have conducted with many groups. We refer to this as the skillbase associated with effective facilitation of CPS.

Setting the Stage for Creative Problem Solving is the fourth chapter. Ken McCluskey brings his expertise as a clinical psychologist together with his years of practical application of CPS. He provides insights about some of the many "other" factors that are important to consider when facilitating others.

One of the key challenges facing facilitators is dealing effectively with the other roles with which they must interact. Within the context of applying CPS, they must interact with the client(s) and the resource-group members. Chapter five deals with *Managing Clients and Resource Groups*. It contains information about the characteristics associated with each role and a model to help facilitators manage group development.

When groups are managed well they will take on characteristics of teamwork, avoid tripwires, and work within appropriate goal structures. Chapter six deals with the topic of *Encouraging Teamwork in CPS Groups*. It provides the facilitator with useful information, supporting the view that making a difference with CPS requires teamwork. Teamwork is an essential ingredient within the philosophy of facilitative leadership.

Chapter seven, entitled *Exploring Group Dynamics*, is a primer for those interested in group dynamics and interpersonal climate. The chapter provides the facilitator with a checklist to assist in observing group behavior as well as suggestions on how to establish a working climate that supports creativity.

Although all the resources contained in this book are aimed at preparing you for taking a facilitative leadership role, the only thing that is certain is that you will face unexpected challenges. Chapter eight provides you with some ideas for *Planning for the Unexpected*. Some likely challenges are identified and some suggestions and guidelines for intervening are provided.

The best way to learn CPS is through experience. Facilitators must often encourage and allow people to experience the tools, language and method before putting deliberate labels on things. Every experience people have with CPS provides a unique opportunity for creative learning. Chapter nine helps the facilitator when *Guiding the Experiential Learning of CPS*. It contains resources to assist the entire experiential learning process. You will find this chapter helpful if you share a concern about continuous learning and the power of reflective practice.

Chapter ten, *Making a Difference with CPS: A Summary of the Evidence*, summarizes the published support for CPS. Luc De Schryver and I have made an initial (and certainly imperfect) attempt to gather every published piece of literature that provides evidence about making a difference with CPS.

I hope you find the book to be a valuable resource. It is intended to be the best cumulative set of writings to help guide the effective facilitation of CPS. We are certain that it will not contain all of the answers, but it should help you with your reflective practice. If you have suggestions or feedback, please feel free to send them to me. We are all continuing to learn from our experience.

The bottom line is that while facilitative leadership may rely on many different tools, be explained in many different words, and may be seen in a variety of forms, it is mostly about an attitude. This attitude and frame of mind has a great deal to do with service and building community. Best of luck with all your creative pursuits!

REFERENCES

Delbecq, A. L., Van de Ven, A. H., & Gustafson, D. H. (1975). *Group techniques for program planning: A guide to nominal group and delphi processes*. Glenview, IL: Scott, Foresman and Company.

Greenleaf, R. K. (1991). *Servant leadership: A journey into the nature of legitimate power and greatness*. New York: Paulist Press.

Greenleaf, R. K. (1998). *The power of servant leadership.* San Francisco: Berrett-Koehler.
Langer, E. (1989). *Mindfulness.* Reading, MA: Addison-Wesley.
Osborn, A. F. (1953). *Applied imagination.* New York: Scribners.
Parnes, S. J. (1997). *Optimize the magic of your mind.* Buffalo, NY: Bearly Ltd.

CHAPTER ONE

CONCEPTUAL FOUNDATIONS OF CREATIVE PROBLEM SOLVING

Scott G. Isaksen
Creativity Research Unit
Creative Problem Solving Group — Buffalo

> "Begin at the beginning," the King said, very gravely, "and go on till you come to the end: then stop."
>
> **Lewis Carroll, *Alice in Wonderland, c. XII***

INTRODUCTION

When I ask groups to give me words to describe their first reactions to the word creativity they often respond with words such as: new, exciting, wacky, open, fuzzy, different, unique, unconventional, imagery, art and music. Then I ask for words they associate with problem solving. They share words like: root cause, closing the gap, analysis, science and mathematics, overcoming difficulties and finding useful solutions. They see creativity as generally very focused on fundamentally new opportunities; as something aspirational. They see problem solving as more focused on day-to-day challenges; something more reactive. Most people indicate that they feel tension between the two concepts.

An earlier version of this chapter was published in: G. Kaufmann T. Helstrup & K. H. Teigen (1995). (Eds.). *Problem solving and cognitive processes: A festschrift in honour of Kjell Raaheim* (pp. 145 - 181). Bergen, Norway: Fagbokforlaget Vigmostad & Bjørke AS.

So why do we call our approach Creative Problem Solving (CPS)? After all, for some, problem solving has such a negative connotation, especially the "problem" part! Well, there are a number of reasons why we have deliberately chosen to stick with CPS as opposed to "Creative Opportunity Finding" or something else. One reason is that it's the name that I originally learned when first exposed to the method. It was its given name. The name refers to a concept with a long and rich tradition of research and practice (see Chapter 2 on its history and Chapter 9 on its impact).

Another reason for linking these two concepts is the inherent, and potentially productive, tension between novelty and usefulness. Novelty for its own sake may or may not be useful. Putting these two concepts together attempts to deliberately introduce the power of possibilities when facing challenges and opportunities. The full spectrum of change implies the full diversity of leadership behaviors from day-to-day improvements to more fundamental and strategic changes.

I have an optimistic attitude toward problem solving. I believe that some of the most important human achievements have come about because of the need to accomplish goals and overcome gaps without a well-defined or rehearsed script.

Linking these two concepts provides a powerful synthesis for those who wish to better understand or deliberately develop creativity. This synthesis brings together the ideas surrounding problem solving (insight, heuristics, meta-cognition) with ideas relevant to creativity (intuition, imagery, imagination). The current and broad domain within which these concepts can be addressed is cognitive science. This chapter will present the case for linking creativity and problem solving by presenting CPS as a unique opportunity to make a bridge between practical application and conceptual or theoretical issues. The current approach we take with CPS will also be outlined.

CREATIVITY AND COGNITIVE SCIENCE

Cognitive science has been defined as a contemporary field that tries to answer questions about the nature of knowledge, its development and deployment (Gardner, 1985). Cognitive science is an interdisciplinary inquiry including psychology, philosophy, linguistics, anthropology, artificial intelligence, and the neurosciences (Gardner, 1985; Lakoff & Johnson, 1999; Matlin, 1989; Miller, Polson & Kintsch, 1984). Problem solving has always been a central concept within cognitive science. More recently, creativity has become an important construct within this field (Boden, 1991; Johnson-Laird, 1988; Schank & Childers, 1988; Sternberg, 1994 & 1999; Sternberg & Davidson, 1995; Ward, Smith & Vaid, 1997; Weisberg, 1988). Given the complexity of these constructs, careful thinking and inquiry will be necessary in order to develop useful and valuable applications and implications of them for future research and practice.

Some scholars have sought to draw creativity apart from problem solving (Raaheim, 1984). Others have found these two constructs to be closely related (Kaufmann, 1988; 1995). The purpose of this chapter is to outline some current thinking on the relationships which exist between creativity and problem solving. In order to accomplish this, it will first be necessary to carefully define both creativity and problem solving, and then draw appropriate distinctions between these two constructs.

By improving our understanding of the connection between these two important constructs, the conceptual foundation for Creative Problem Solving (CPS) can become more clear. CPS is a method or framework designed to assist problem solvers with using creativity to achieve goals, overcome obstacles and increase the likelihood of enhancing creative performance (Isaksen, Dorval & Treffinger, 1994). CPS has been developed over the past fifty years (Parnes, 1992) and offers a unique opportunity to bridge practical application with conceptual and theoretical issues. The basis for CPS comes from the broad areas of cognition, semantics and the study of thinking and problem solving, as well as from the areas of imagination, imagery, and studying acts of creation (the theoretical and historical foundation is described in more detail in Chapter 10 CPS Makes a Difference: A Summary of the Evidence.)

THE CASE FOR CREATIVITY AND CREATIVE THINKING

There are many definitions and approaches to understanding creativity (Arieti, 1976; Getzels & Jackson, 1962; Hallman, 1981; Runco & Albert, 1990; Treffinger, Isaksen & Firestien, 1983; Welsh, 1973). There are also many reviews of creativity literature and research (Anderson, 1959a; Boden, 1994; Glover, Ronning, & Reynolds, 1989; Grønhaug & Kaufmann, 1988; Isaksen, 1987; Isaksen, Murdock, Firestien & Treffinger, 1993a & b; Kuhn, 1985; Parkhurst, 1999; Sternberg, 1988 & 1999; Taylor & Getzels, 1975; Tuerck, 1987; Welsh, 1975). On the basis of most of this literature, it is most productive to view creativity as a multi-faceted phenomenon rather than as a unitary construct capable of a single precise or limited definition.

Guilford (1950) provided an impetus for increased research into creativity. As the creativity literature began to expand so did the number and variety of definitions used for the concept. Only nine years after Guilford's presidential address to the American Psychological Association, Taylor (1959) found in excess of one hundred definitions of creativity in the literature.

Despite the apparent confusion and contradictions implied by many of the definitions, there does appear to be some agreement on a few of the basic themes or strands. For example, a number of writers have pointed out the need to differentiate the kind of creativity associated with radical novelty and major significant breakthroughs from the more common notions of personal creativity. Stein (1987) has offered the solution of big "C" to describe the creativity of the genius and little "c" for the more widely available type. Boden (1991) has offered P-creative to describe psychological creativity, referring to ideas that are fundamentally novel to the individual mind, and H-creative for novelty applying to the whole of human history. Both writers (and others) have apparently identified the need for a very similar definitional distinction made by Maslow (1976) who identified two very different kinds of creativity: special talent and self actualizing. Kaufmann (1993) concluded that the major creativity concepts should be seen as a coherent conceptual complex, and that even if the domain were empirically immature, there is a clear conceptual basis for creativity research.

After reviewing twenty-two definitions of creativity, Welsch (1980) found significant levels of agreement on the key attributes of these definitions. She proposed the following definition from her review of the literature:

> *Creativity is the process of generating unique products by transformation of existing products. These products, tangible and intangible, must be unique only to the creator, and must meet the criteria of purpose and value established by the creator. (p. 97)*

Rhodes (1961) set out to find the single best definition of creativity and, in the process, assembled more than fifty-six different definitions. Despite the profusion of those definitions, he reported that they were not mutually exclusive. When analyzed, the content of the definitions formed four overlapping and intertwining strands. Although each strand has a distinct conceptual identity, the four strands functionally operate in unity. Similar conceptual approaches have been identified by a number of other scholars (Gowan, 1972; MacKinnon, 1970; Mooney, 1963).

I have chosen to illustrate these four strands in a Venn diagram to emphasize the nature of their relationship (Isaksen, 1984 & 1987). As Rhodes and others have suggested, it is most beneficial to think of these four strands as operating together (see Figure 1). For example, the most comprehensive picture of the creative person can be drawn by considering not only the characteristics or traits of the person, but also the kind of environment or context in which the person is working, the kinds of mental operations being used, as well as the nature of the desired outcomes or products. Attempting to consider all four of these strands while defining creativity supports a more ecological or systems approach to understanding and recognizing creativity (Harrington, 1990; Woodman & Schoenfeldt, 1999).

It is also quite possible that various researchers and writers emphasize certain facets of creativity in their definitions because of the focus of their work. Some, for example, have determined that product was the cornerstone for creativity research (MacKinnon, 1975). Others selected the creative personality as their central concern (Barron, 1990; Eysenck, 1993). The internal and external climates for creativity have been the central focus for other researchers (Amabile, 1990; Ekvall, 1987; 1996).

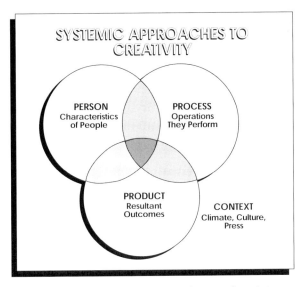

Figure 1: Systemic Approaches to Creativity

Others have chosen a process focus for their research and development. Torrance (1993) provided a number of reasons for taking a process orientation, including the fact that he is an educational psychologist concerned with learning, thinking, teaching and creative problem solving. Torrance and Torrance (1973) illustrated the close conceptual link between problem solving and creativity by emphasizing the process of:

> ...becoming sensitive to problems, gaps in knowledge, missing elements, disharmonies, and so on; identifying the difficulty; searching for solutions; making guesses or formulating hypotheses about the deficiencies; testing and retesting these hypotheses and possibly modifying and retesting them; and finally communicating the results. (p. 6)

Torrance (1993) argued that one of the desired outcomes for those who take a process orientation is to translate their definitions of creative processes into instructional models to guide teaching and learning.

Stein's (1974) orientation to creativity also took a process focus, but included a deliberate consideration of the individual and the social context surrounding the person. He stated:

> Creativity is a process that results in a novel work that is accepted as useful, tenable, or satisfying by a significant group of people at some point in time. As a process it consists of overlapping stages - hypothesis formation, hypothesis testing, and the

communication of results - all of which follow a preparatory or educational stage which is not always uniquely part of the creative process. In each stage one may see the effects of intrapersonal and interpersonal factors. All these factors reflect the fact that creativity occurs in a social context and it is a function of the transactional relationships between the individual and his environment - the creating individual is both affected by and affects his environment. (p. xi-xii)

For the purposes of this chapter, I will use the following definition of creativity: Creativity is the making and communicating of meaningful new connections to help us: think of many possibilities; think and experience in varied ways and use different points of view; think of new and unusual possibilities; and to guide us in generating and selecting alternatives (Isaksen & Treffinger, 1985). These new connections and possibilities must result in something of value for the individual, group, organization or society at some point in time.

There are many aspects of creativity which will be of interest for those involved in the cognitive sciences. The most salient aspect includes the emphasis on understanding and nurturing the creative process. This focus includes consideration of mental operations, heuristics, and problem-solving strategies. This does not mean that characteristics of the creative person are irrelevant, for individual differences in mental representations and functioning are included on the agenda for cognitive science.

Gardner (1985) argued that the aspects of emotion, context, and culture are generally de-emphasized within the mainstream of cognitive science. This suggests that some aspects of the creative person and the creative place may not be as prominent as the creative process for study within this area of inquiry. Interest in creative products or outcomes would be primarily focused on providing a sorting mechanism to discriminate individual level, capacity or style by considering the results of mental processing. It is for these reasons that Creative Problem Solving (CPS) has been chosen as a major linking construct between the broader field of creativity studies and the field of cognitive science.

THE CASE FOR PROBLEM SOLVING

Problem solving has also been defined and approached in a variety of ways (Sternberg, 1994). In summarizing the problem-solving literature, Voss (1989) outlined five distinct viewpoints. The descriptive approach exemplified by Dewey (1910) and Wallas (1926) involved describing problem solving as a stepwise process. The second theoretical framework is that of the Gestalt (Kohler, 1947; Wertheimer, 1959) and neo-Gestalt (Duncker, 1945; Maier, 1940) psychology, emphasizing the perception-like process of restructuring the problem and gaining insight. A third approach, developed by Piaget (1954), used problem solving as a means to study the mental growth of the child. Stimulus-response psychology provided a fourth view of problem solving. This approach, developed by Maltzman (1955) emphasized problem solving as the occurrence of a response that initially had a low probability of happening. A fifth approach to researching problem solving is the information processing framework (Selz, 1922; Newell, Shaw and Simon, 1958).

Voss (1989) concluded that since there exists such a variety of viewpoints, problem solving should not be considered apart from other psychological processes. He indicated that:

> *...problem solving is highly interrelated with those processes usually referred to as thinking, learning, memory, transfer, perception and motivation. (p. 255)*

The topic of problem solving has been approached and reviewed in a variety of ways. Some have attempted to raise issues relevant to the teaching-learning process (Tuma & Reif, 1980). Others have been concerned with improving our understanding of thought processes engaged in problem solving (Johnson, 1972). Mayer (1983) suggested that a general definition of thinking included three basic ideas:

> *1. Thinking is cognitive, but is inferred from behavior. It occurs internally, in the mind or cognitive system, and must be inferred indirectly. 2. Thinking is a process that involves some manipulation of or set of operations carried out on knowledge in the cognitive system. 3. Thinking is directed and results in behavior that "solves" a problem or is directed toward a solution. (p. 7)*

Essentially, thinking is what happens when a person solves a problem or produces behavior that moves the individual from the given state to the goal state; or at least tries to achieve this change.

Mayer (1983) indicated that any definition of "problem" should consist of three elements. First, the problem exists in some state with certain givens such as conditions, objects, or pieces of information. Second, the desired or goal state of the problem requires thinking to transform the given to the terminal state. Finally, there is no direct, obvious way to solve the problem. Although certain ways to change the current state to the goal state exist, the thinker does not have at hand the correct answer or the correct sequence of behaviors that will solve the problem.

Researchers and practitioners alike often use the term problem solving as though everyone holds the same definition. I would like to offer the following definition of problem solving for this chapter. Problem solving is:

◆   The process of closing the gap between what is and what is desired;

◆   The process of answering questions, clearing up uncertainties, explaining that which was not understood or known, or removing perplexity;

◆   A process that includes perceiving, thinking (cognition), feeling and behaving.

Although this particular approach to defining problem solving may be too broad for many scholars involved in the cognitive sciences, I believe that it adequately captures at least most of the conceptual breadth assigned to the terms. The inclusion of problem solving as an important area of human activity is well explicated and accepted by those within the cognitive sciences (Gardner, 1985; Matlin, 1989).

With such a broad definition of problem solving and the definition of creativity offered earlier there is tremendous potential for confusion and opportunity for clarification. From one end of the spectrum, creativity can be seen as a subset of the larger domain of problem solving. It is also possible that only parts of the domain of creativity are pertinent to problem solving and others may not be relevant. For example, the study of the creative personality may contain some elements which are within the domain of problem solving and others which would not be of concern. Specifically, Simonton (1991) found that the traits of intelligence and aggressiveness have linear positive effects on attained eminence and that these are constant across the historical period covered in his study (1642-1872). Although intelligence would clearly be related to the area of problem solving, the aggressiveness trait may fall outside that domain but within the broad area of examining the creative personality. In short, there would be limited relationships between the domains of problem solving and understanding the characteristics of creative people.

Another example of the relationship between the problem solving and creativity domains comes from the area of inquiry into creative products. If they were being understood and treated as mental representations of task outcomes or results, they would be of interest to those within the domain of problem solving. If we were more concerned with the diffusion of these new products or some objective measurement of the criteria which distinguish them from more mundane outcomes, we would be working outside the concern or interest of most problem solving researchers and within an area for creativity researchers (Besemer, 1998; Besemer & O'Quin, 1993; Firestien, 1993).

Within the broad area of understanding the creative environment or situation, if the focus were upon the conditions surrounding the task, then there would be a clear connection to problem solving. If the major concern were with cultures, work groups, and psychological climates conducive to innovation and productivity, then creativity researchers would be involved (Burnside, Amabile & Gryskiewicz, 1988; Ekvall, 1987 & 1996; VanGundy, 1984). Research and inquiry into aspects of the creative situation have been referred to as "press" and include the examination and understanding of the interaction between intra-individual and external forces.

Press is not the only creativity research facet involving interactions. Each of the four strands of creativity inquiry can be analyzed and identified separately, but they operate and function together. People interact within situations on various outcomes using a variety of processes. What makes this even more complex are the many different interactions that are possible within and among these areas of inquiry (Isaksen, Puccio & Treffinger, 1993). Each of the four creativity strands also offers potential interaction and conceptual relationship with the broad domain of problem solving. The one remaining creativity facet upon which the remaining parts of the chapter will focus is the creative process itself.

In attempting to relate creativity to problem solving, this review will include the concepts of the creative process, creative thinking, and creative learning. This review will precede the description of Creative Problem Solving (CPS) as a potentially valuable framework for improving our understanding and application of the cognitive sciences. In particular, this framework of creative problem solving would necessarily shift the conceptual focus to problem solving, which also deals with problems needing new definitions, methods which need new perspectives or modification, and outcomes which are new, useful and valuable. The following section provides conceptual support for this assertion.

RELATING CREATIVITY AND PROBLEM SOLVING

Questions surrounding the relationships between creativity and problem solving have been appearing in the behavioral science literature for nearly fifty years. Many writers have attempted to outline conceptual and operational distinctions and relationships between these two constructs. Vinacke (1952) proposed that:

> *Creative thought really seems to be intermediate between problem solving and imagination, occurring in special situations involving nearly indistinguishable problem-solving behavior and imagination.* (p. 160)

Russell (1956) differentiated between creative and critical thinking by stating:

> *Creative thinking involves the production of new ideas whereas critical thinking...involves reactions to others' ideas or to one's own previous ideas. Critical thinking can be creative in that it creates new insights for the individual, but these insights are concerned with previously established conditions. Creative thinking is very close to the problem solving process....It may be described as problem solving plus. Whenever the child or adult puts isolated experiences into new combinations or patterns we may say that creative thinking has taken place and this process does not take place in problem solving.* (p. 306)

Although Russell (1956) indicated that creative thinking and problem solving are very closely related, he also mentioned that there are some very important distinctions which need to be made. He stated:

> *The differences between problem solving or reasoning and creative thinking is that problem solving is more objective, more directed toward some goal, which is usually external. Problem solving must be more constant with the facts. Creative thinking is more personal, less fixed. It achieves something new rather than coinciding with previously determined conditions. It also tends to involve more intuition and imagination than does the more objective problem solving, though this difference is clearly a matter of degree rather than kind. The special insights of the scientist, poet, or artist differ only in degree from the insights which all persons use in solving their problems. (p. 306)*

As Russell (1956) pointed out, there may be a relationship between creative thinking and problem solving, but they are not precisely the same thing. Something that can be implied by all the literature cited above is that much learning involves a creative type of problem solving. Hilgard (1959) discussed creativity in relation to problem solving in this manner:

> *There have been two major types of approaches to problem solving and creativity. The first of these relates problem solving to learning and thinking, as a type of higher mental process or cognitive process, to which problem solving certainly belongs. The second approach, supplementary rather than contradictory to the first, sees creative problem solving as a manifestation of personality and looks for social and motivational determinants instead of (or in addition to) the purely cognitive ones. It is not surprising that these two approaches deal also with somewhat different topics. The approach via learning tends to emphasize problem solving in which a high-order product emerges, although not necessarily a highly original one, whereas the approach via personality tends to seek out somewhat more the elements of creative imagination and novelty. (p. 163)*

Maltzman (1960) also supported the closeness of the relationship when he stated:

> *There is no fundamental difference in the behavioral principle determining originality and problem solving behavior...both involve the evocation of relatively uncommon responses, otherwise the situation would not be called a problem or the behavior original. (p. 232)*

Newell, Shaw and Simon (1962) drew distinctions within the context of an information processing approach when they indicated that:

> *Creative activity appears...simply to be a special class of problem-solving activity characterized by novelty, unconventionality, persistence, and difficulty in problem formulation. (p. 63)*

Rugg (1963) found himself in agreement with the position that much of what is called learning is also creative and pointed out that learning, problem solving and perception appear to be inextricably linked to the individual's creative process. In other words:

> We look for the factors involved in precept-formation in both of the perceiver's worlds – in his inner system of stress and in the external culture. Each individual sees and feels the world in his own way, because each has built a unique body of traces in his organism by having lived his life and interpreted objective events in his own individualistic way throughout infancy, childhood and youth. This amounts to saying the precepts which are traced in the unconscious electrochemistry of the cerebral cortex have been molded by the individual's response to the culture in which he grew up, by the cumulative temperamental and physical development of body and mind which we call life style, and by the dominant wants, purposes, and needs which his individual life history has evolved. Thus perception is much more than imprinting. It is a creative process in itself. The perceiver creates the field from which his precepts, signs and symbols emerge. (p. 77)

The idea that all learning is creative remains an issue to be debated. Certainly, some types of problem solving appear to be more creative than others. In discussing the intellectual nature of creativity, Smith (1966) concluded that:

> The research and literature in this area do seem to point to some accepted conclusions regarding the creative learning process. It can be safely concluded that creative learning is not a stimulus-response type of learning. It is rather a cooperative-experiencing relationship where communication of both thought and feeling is essential. It is also safe to say that creativity is a type of problem solving stretched along a continuum from very simple thinking and learning to very complex thought processes....In creative problem solving the solution offers tremendous satisfactions, not only because a problem has been solved and a job completed, but because the product has aesthetic qualities and the creator has given himself to the project–something of himself has emerged in a form which he recognizes (and which others recognize) as his own unique contribution to the solution. (p. 57)

Guilford (1977) also believed that there was a close relationship between creativity and problem solving. He hinted that creative thinking was a subset of the more broad conceptual field of problem solving. He indicated that:

> ...problem solving and creative thinking are closely related. The very definitions of those two activities show logical connections. Creative thinking produces novel outcomes, and problem solving involves producing a new response to a new situation,

which is a novel outcome. Thus we can say that problem solving has creative aspects. (p.161)

MacKinnon (1978) outlined the creative process in relation to problem solving. He stated:

> *The creative process starts always with the seeing or sensing of a problem. The roots of creativeness lie in one's becoming aware that something is wrong, or lacking, or mysterious. One of the salient traits of a truly creative person is that he sees problems where others don't, and it is this that so often makes him unpopular. He insists on pointing out problems where others wish to deny their existence. A constantly questioning attitude is not an easy one to live with, yet in its absence many problems will not be sensed, and consequently creative solutions of them will not be achieved. It has been said of Einstein that a part of his genius, like that of all great creative thinkers, was his inability to understand the obvious. (p. 47)*

This link points to another level of conceptual relationship with problem finding and creativity (Moore & Murdock, 1991; Runco, 1994). Problem finding has been defined as the way problems are envisaged, posed, formulated, or created. It has more to do with the creative formulation of the creative problem to which the solution is one response (Getzels & Csikszentmihalyi, 1976). Placing less emphasis on achieving a known solution and more importance on constructing a new configuration of the problem is key to the cognitive aspects of problem finding. Even though a great deal of work on thinking, problem solving and creativity focuses primarily on the rational elements, those concerned with problem finding point out the importance of emotional tension. Getzels & Csiksentmihalyi (1976) indicated:

> *To be sure, art (or science, literature, religion, and other forms of symbolic activity) has its source in tensions. But the tensions that underlie the creative work are not already structured problems. To obtain meaning and substance, the initially ambiguous tensions must be embodied and formulated as problems. The crucial task of the creative person is precisely that of transforming potential into actual problems. Creative work is the concrete statement of existential problems which previously were experienced only as diffuse tensions...the aim of the creative activity is not to restore a previous equilibrium, but to achieve an emergent one. (p. 243)*

It appears that although creative thinking and problem solving are two distinguishable types of activity, there is a significant overlap of abilities, skills and outcomes. In fact, Kneller (1965) stated, "That some problem solving is creative is obvious to anyone. That all creativity is problem solving is an unwarranted presupposition." He further specified that:

...creativity seems to involve certain mental abilities. These include the ability to change one's approach to a problem, to produce ideas that are both relevant and unusual, to see beyond the immediate situation, and to redefine the problem or some aspect of it. (p. 13)

Many writers have provided explanations of the reciprocal relationship between creativity and problem solving. In order to better understand creative problem solving, it is necessary to draw some distinctions and clarify even further the relationships between creativity and problem solving. Some writers, including Covington (1987), Getzels (1964) and Van Gundy (1988), have offered taxonomies of problem solving which identify types of problems which require creativity. In examining the variety of problem-solving skills, Greeno (1980) offered a typology rather than a taxonomy because many kinds of problems involve combinations of the different types of skills. Figure 2 outlines one way the distinctions and relationships between these two important cognitive constructs might be identified.

There are three dimensions to be considered: the problem or task definition, the solution or method, and the desired outcome.

Problem or task definition. The first dimension includes the environment of the problem or task definition. The actual content or domain of the challenge can be either well-defined and clearly structured or fuzzy, ill-defined and ambiguous. A

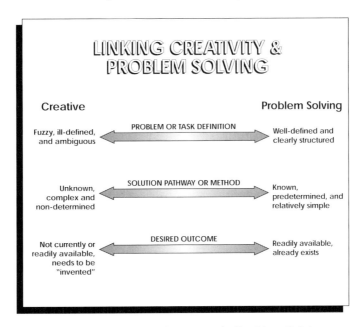

Figure 2: Linking Creativity & Problem Solving

task like writing a research report on the history of the American presidency may offer the typical high school student quite a challenge, but it is fairly well-defined and clearly structured. This would be identified as more of a problem-solving task. The problem of determining key characteristics for successful global leadership is much more fuzzy, rather ill-defined and somewhat ambiguous. This challenge requires much more definition and investment in thinking which would be characterized as original or novel. What is meant by successful? What is global leadership? How might we actually determine these key characteristics?

Although the distinction may be clear between the two tasks outlined above, it is equally feasible that creativity can be applied to the writing of a research report on the American presidency. The writer could find some creative ways to illustrate the report or to add some humorous elements to the text. It is also possible that we could apply very traditional problem solving strategies to the question of successful global leadership. However, the challenge of determining the characteristics for future global leadership clearly requires a greater investment of time and energy in defining the problem space and in problem representation.

Solution or method. Another dimension focuses on the methodology, process, or strategies needed to solve the problem. This describes the nature of the pathway toward the solution. On the one hand, a method can be well-known, a clear and standard approach is available, and the pathway is determined and simple. A sample task for this side of the dimension would be a mathematical problem like $2 + X = 4$, for which a simple method can be applied to obtain the solution. This kind of task calls for a simple rule or heuristic that can be called algorithmic - calling for a straight-forward procedure that is guaranteed to work every time (Martinez, 1998).

On the other side of the dimension are problems for which there is no known or determined method, or for which the approach is extremely complex. Determining the economic, social and psychological costs for not maximizing the productivity from the full spectrum of human talent within organizations throughout the world is an example of a problem solving task requiring this kind of method. This kind of task requires the application of more general heuristics or rules of thumb that are useful for a variety of problems or situations and are usually free of specific content.

Desired outcome. The third dimension to consider focuses on the nature of the desired outcome or the results to be obtained from problem solving. This dimension describes the goal state or future end state for the problem solver. Some tasks require outcomes that are readily available or already exist. The challenge for the problem solver is to discover them. An example of this type of task would be the need to purchase a new but existing home already available in a new community. Other tasks require the invention or active construction of the outcome. Here, the needed outcome is not currently or readily available. An example of this kind of task would be designing the learning center for a future space station.

These three dimensions summarize much of the literature describing the relationships between problem solving and creative thinking. The dimensions can help to draw distinctions regarding the relative focus on problem solving or a more creative kind of problem solving. Knowing that we are talking about a task, process or content that is more oriented toward problem solving or a more "creative" kind of problem solving can clarify our own thinking. It also makes room for an appropriate consideration of creativity within the broad field of cognitive psychology. The three-dimensional approach illustrated in Figure 2 illustrates at least some of the major conceptual linkages between these two important constructs.

Defining Creative Problem Solving

Creative Problem Solving (or CPS) was first deliberately introduced as a problem solving method by Osborn more than fifty years ago. My colleagues and I currently see CPS as a broadly applicable process that provides an organizing framework for specific generating and focusing tools or heuristics to help design and develop new and useful outcomes for meaningful and important challenges, concerns and opportunities (Isaksen, Dorval & Treffinger, 1994; 1998; 2000; Treffinger, Isaksen & Dorval, 2000). CPS is an operational model for a particular kind of problem solving where creativity is applicable to the task at hand. As such, it is a dynamic model that continues to grow and change. The model is comprised of three main cognitive components: Understanding the Challenge, Generating Ideas and Preparing for Action. The current model also includes a fourth, meta-cognitive component called Planning your Approach which includes Appraising Tasks and Designing Process. The following description of CPS previews the language we will be using in future descriptions of the framework.

Understanding the Challenge

One of the major components in this operational model is called Understanding the Challenge, which includes a systematic effort to define, construct, or formulate a problem. Although many researchers have focused on problem finding as a process separate from problem solving, such a distinction may be arbitrary, especially within the context of a flexible or descriptive approach (rather than a prescriptive approach). It is not necessarily the "first" step in CPS, nor is it necessarily undertaken by all people in every CPS session. Rather than prescribing an essential problem-finding process, Understanding the Challenge involves active construction by the individual or group through analyzing the task at hand to obtain an improved focus on constructing and implementing solutions.

The Understanding the Challenge component of CPS includes the three stages of Constructing Opportunities (Objective or Mess-finding), Exploring Data (Data or Fact-finding) and Framing Problems (Problem-finding). An opportunity is a general statement of a goal or direction. Statements of opportunity can be constructed as broad, brief, and beneficial. The opportunity generally describes the basic area of need or challenge on which the problem solver's efforts will be focused; it remains broad enough to allow many perspectives to emerge as one person (or a group) looks more closely at the situation. Exploring Data includes the generating and answering of questions to bring out key data (information, impressions, observations, feelings, etc.) to help the problem solver(s) focus more clearly on the most challenging aspects and concerns of the situation. Framing problems includes the seeking of a specific or targeted question (problem statement) on which to focus subsequent effort. Effectively worded problem statements invite an open or wide-ranging search for many, varied and novel options. They are stated concisely and are free from specific limiting criteria.

Generating Ideas

The Generating Ideas component includes the generating of options in answer to an open-ended or invitational statement of the problem. This component has only one stage. This stage (Idea-finding) has two phases: generating and focusing. During the generating phase of this stage, the person or group produces many options (fluent thinking), a variety of possible options (flexible thinking), novel or unusual options (original thinking), or a number of detailed or refined options (elaborative thinking). The focusing phase of Generating Ideas provides an opportunity for examining, reviewing, clustering and selecting promising options. Although the Generating Ideas stage includes a converging or focusing phase, its primary emphasis is divergent or generative. These two alternating phases of generating and focusing is most clearly experienced in this stage, but are also present in all the other stages of CPS.

Preparing for Action

The Preparing for Action component of CPS is appropriate when a person or group recognizes a number of interesting or promising options which may need strengthening, refining or developing. Novel or intriguing options may not necessarily be useful, valuable or valid without extended effort and productive thinking. The prime need may be to make or develop effective choices, or to prepare for successful implementation and general acceptance. The two stages in the component are called Developing Solutions (Solution-finding) and Building Acceptance (Acceptance-finding).

During the Developing Solutions stage of CPS, promising options may be analyzed, refined or developed. If there are many options, the emphasis may be on compressing or condensing them so that they are more manageable. If there are only a few promising options, the challenge may be to strengthen each as much as possible. There may be a need to rank or prioritize a number of possible options. Specific criteria may be generated and selected upon which to evaluate and develop promising options or to select from a larger pool of available alternatives. Although there may be some generating in this stage, the emphasis is primarily on focusing.

The Building Acceptance stage of CPS involves searching for several potential sources of assistance and resistance to possible solutions. The aim is to help prepare an option or alternative for improved acceptance and perceived value. This stage helps the problem solver identify ways to make the best possible use of assisters and avoid or overcome possible sources of resistance. From considering these factors a plan of action is developed and evaluated for implementation.

Using CPS Descriptively

Although the primary emphasis of CPS is within the process dimension of creativity, it is most fruitful to also consider the people who are using the process, the situation or environment within which it is being used, and the nature of the product or outcome of the problem-solving efforts. Isaksen, Puccio & Treffinger (1993) have referred to this as taking an ecological approach to CPS.

The practical implication of taking an ecological perspective on CPS is the development of Appraising Tasks and Designing Process (Isaksen, 1996). Appraising Tasks is about determining if CPS is appropriate, given the desired outcomes, the people involved, the situation or context. Once the use of CPS is qualified, the information generated during task appraisal is used to help determine where to enter and how to approach CPS. Rather than walking through all the stages and components (taking a prescribed approach), the users of CPS need to think about what they need from the model and design an appropriate pathway customized on the basis of the need, people, and situation. This is a descriptive approach to applying CPS and requires the users to be mindful and deliberate about planning their approach. Using CPS descriptively means that the framework is fully described and that choices are made for any particular journey through the process. Descriptive use of CPS implies much more flexibility than taking a predetermined and prescriptive approach.

Although CPS can be taught and learned on unreal or realistic tasks, it is best suited for the solution of real-life problems requiring creativity. Renzulli (1982) identified a set of parameters for determining whether or not a problem was "real." He asserted that since a real problem involves an emotional or affective commitment as well as an intellectual or cognitive one, it must have a personal frame of reference. Second, it must not have an already existing solution. Third, merely naming something a "real" problem does not necessarily make it so for a particular individual or group. Finally, the purpose of a "real" problem is to contribute something new or bring about some form of change to the sciences, the arts or the humanities. Thus, there may be a continuum from unreal, realistic, to real kinds of problems.

Isaksen & Treffinger (1985) identified a parallel concept of ownership as being important for selecting challenges for CPS. Ownership can occur on a variety of levels, including those that are like sole proprietorships, partnerships or corporations. For example, challenges owned by a single individual are like sole proprietorships. Other challenges may have corporate or global ownership and be shared with many others.

Ownership of a challenge means that the problem solver has some degree of influence, authority, and decision-making responsibility for implementing the solutions. It also means that the problem owner is motivated and willing to submit the challenge to systematic problem-solving efforts and is interested in following through on the results. Finally, in order for someone to have ownership of a challenge for CPS, there must be a deliberate and explicit search for something new. In short, in order for ownership to exist, there must be influence, interest and imagination.

Defining CPS this way offers an important extension to most standard academic conceptions of problem solving. In particular, this extends Raaheim's (1984) orientation to problem solving that relies on utilizing past knowledge and experience to close the current gap or decrease ambiguity in the present. The main emphasis on reconciling the present with the past ignores the potential importance of the future. An anticipatory goal state which focuses thinking toward a possible and desired future can be a powerful motivator and initiative for problem solving done by humans.

Raaheim, like a few other scholars, opposes the very concept of creative problem solving, suggesting that if the task is entirely novel, the only appropriate mental strategy is trial and error. This position ignores the wealth of information from introspective and biographical accounts which indicate the importance of intuition generally (Anderson, 1959b), in the sciences (Eyring, 1959) in art (Polanyi, 1981), in mathematics and psychology (Gardner & Nemirovsky, 1991) and in basic research (Selye, 1988). This is an important issue from a practical point of view in light of recent evidence that managerial decision making in new task environments calls upon intuition (Blattberg & Hoch, 1990; Mitchell & Beach, 1990; Taggart & Valenzi, 1990) and despite challenges presented to a rationally-oriented information processing model of cognition (Kaufmann, 1988; Russ, 1993).

Simply dumping the construct of creative problem solving off the deep end of trial and error is inconsistent with the argument that Schank and Childers (1988) put forth regarding the importance of asking questions about new tasks in order to actively construct explanations and generalizations. In fact, they suggested that by acknowledging the existence of scripts, the key to creative thinking is making an analogical leap to recall another event explained in a similar way. Similar arguments for the existence and importance of this analogical kind of thinking have been called Janusian (Rothenberg, 1971), magic synthesis (Arieti, 1976) and bisociation (Koestler, 1964). Finally, Boden (1991) dismissed trial and error as a reasonable explanation for creativity by asserting that these random kind of mental processes generally produce only first time curiosities, rarely radical surprises which account for major discoveries, inventions and creative works.

In addition, the nature of the tasks within the research paradigm proposed by Raaheim (1976) may not really have a good fit with a more creative mode of problem solving. The tasks used in research following this approach (Raaheim & Kaufmann, 1972; Kaufmann & Raaheim, 1973; Raaheim, Kaufmann & Kaufmann, 1979; Raaheim, Kaufmann & Bengtsson, 1980) may be unfamiliar, but lack the features of interest and influence.

The emphasis on using the past to adjust intelligently to the present misses another important aspect of creativity. There is also a strong theme in the creativity literature which supports the use of the unfamiliar to provide insight and bring novelty into a task (Koestler, 1964). These insights are not necessarily produced by trial and error. Gardner & Nemirovsky (1991) described thematic components which operate tacitly to provide generative schemes for learning, thinking and creative work. These robust frameworks function as "unarticulated intuition" in guiding the creator's thinking in a variety of content domains. Rather than being outside our present knowledge and thinking power, creativity in problem solving extends the threshold of efforts to understand human adjustment and change.

We can now find a rightful place for the more opportunity-oriented focus that the future image can provide than the close the gap orientation. Thinking and dreaming about the future provides a powerful "pull" for problem solving. CPS can also provide both a practical framework within which to examine possible tasks and mental activity as well as an applied research context for studying different kinds of mental representations and activities.

THE CURRENT APPROACH TO CPS

Despite the organization of CPS into components and specific stages and continued admonitions to the contrary, the use of the model by many has still followed a predetermined pathway. Furthermore, the previous graphic depictions of the model sent the message that the problem solver started at the top, with the Mess-Finding stage, and ended at the bottom with the Acceptance-Finding stage. However, when Pershyn (1992) analyzed over 150 drawings by individuals who successfully met creative challenges, he found that they were able to be organized and classified on a continuum ranging from linear, orderly, and targeted processes at one end to random, spontaneous, and complex processes at the other. Most individuals chose to construct their graphic representation of natural creative process by means of a flow-chart. Some could be characterized as utilizing a step-by-step approach, while others used a more hop-skip-step and re-step process. Others were somewhere in between.

Further, these observed differences in graphic depictions of natural creative problem solving were related to individual differences in cognitive style (Isaksen &

Pershyn, 1994). For example, we found that Kirton's innovators (Kirton, 1987) more frequently described their process as non-linear, more complex, random and contiguous. Their processes contained more stages and multiple end points. In a few cases, innovative processes contained infinite iterations with no perceivable end points. Adaptors were more likely to draw processes that were linear, orderly and targeted. They also tended to have fewer stages as well as fewer end points.

These findings suggested that effective Creative Problem Solving took on a variety of forms and that the graphic depiction of CPS we used needed to take this into consideration. As a result, the graphic depiction of CPS was altered in its representation. Given the dynamic nature of natural CPS, it was important that the new depiction be more representative of a wider array of problem-solving approaches. Isaksen & Dorval (1993a) broke the prescriptive view of CPS into a descriptive graphic to show the approach that provides for different pathways through the process (see Figure 3).

Isaksen, Dorval & Treffinger (1994) replaced the prescriptive model with a graphic depiction to specifically include Appraising Tasks and Designing Process in order to respond to the need for conscious decision making regarding when to use CPS, where to enter and exit the process, and what to do next. This development helped to resolve the content versus process argument.

Many constructivists have claimed that the only way to construct process is from within a particular domain of knowledge (Brooks & Brooks, 1993). Others have criti-

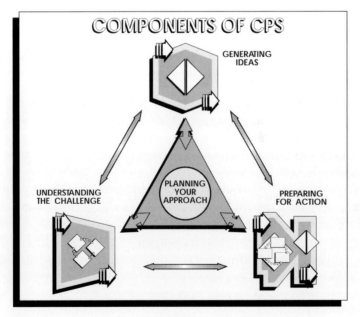

Figure 3:   Version 5.3 of CPS

cized the search for or use of general all-purpose creativity heuristics and have suggested narrowing the search for creativity skills to particular tasks within specific domains (Baer, 1991). The current view of CPS offers a compromise position in that knowledge, information and other data surrounding the task is instrumental for effective planning and application of process strategies as well as useful within the process itself. This compromise position is consistent with Simon's (1980) idea of heuristics and knowledge being "two blades of the same scissor."

The recent development of Appraising Tasks and Designing Strategies as deliberate mechanisms of CPS relates very well with the emerging concern of meta-cognitive and learning strategies (Duell, 1986; Flavell, 1976; Maturana & Varela, 1998; Metclafe & Shimamura, 1996; Resnick & Klopfer, 1989; Yussen, 1985). These developments also provide substantial opportunities for linking with other constructs and approaches, including situated cognition and problem-based learning (Greeno, 1989; Kuhn, 1999; Stepien, Gallagher & Workman, 1993). Given the heavy use of language and semantics within the framework and tools of CPS there will be important linkages with the areas of cognition and language (Chomsky, 1998; Frawley, 1997). These two meta-cognitive stages are now combined to form the fourth component of CPS; called Planning your Approach and it is supported by the need to take a more mindful approach to the creative process (Langer, 1989).

FUTURE IMPLICATIONS

The current practical approach to the CPS framework (version 5.3) is deliberately linked to a program of research (Isaksen & Puccio, 1992; Isaksen, Puccio & Treffinger, 1993). This unique opportunity will allow more continuous development of the skillbase and technology of CPS.

Whenever we learn something from pursuing our ecological program of research, it will readily be applied to the practice of CPS. As a result of direct observation from experience and of CPS, we can develop testable questions and development priorities. The potential synergy for future development and learning has been greatly increased. I believe that these conditions offer unprecedented potential for the future of the field. Not only will the level and quality of generative research and practice improve, it will be easier to pursue a transdisciplinary approach for future creativity research (Isaksen & Murdock, 1993). Many questions and developments will require the disciplines of anthropology, business, economics, engineering, social psychology, sociology, and others. This will involve necessarily interdisciplinary assistance and collaboration (beyond the traditional reliance on psychology) for the emerging field of creativity studies (Magyari-Beck, 1993).

In responding to papers presented as a part of a conference on problem solving and education, Reif (1980) pointed out a major gap. He claimed that there were two very different groups with very different perceptions about their common interests in problem solving. The cognitive scientists were described as thinking analytically in formulating explicit theoretical models. Their methodology usually mirrored that of the natural sciences or engineering by carrying out detailed experimental tests in order to validate their theoretical models. He stated:

> ...*cognitive scientists are usually not concerned with questions of direct educational interest. Thus, in pursuing their quest for basic understanding, cognitive psychologists may justifiably investigate puzzles, games, or other academic problems only remotely relevant to practical education. Similarly, although workers in artificial intelligence may have practical applied interests, their concern is usually primarily with computer implementation rather than with human subjects. (p. 42)*

The educators are on the other side of the problem-solving gap. They were described as more concerned with realistic teaching and instructional endeavors involving real human students. They often approach their tasks in more intuitive ways than the cognitive scientists. They often prefer using "rules of thumb" rather than analytic methods. Their instructional designs and programs are infrequently based on specific or explicit theoretical models. The criteria they use for educational success are often fuzzy and ill-defined; which also limits their productive use of many assessment approaches.

Reif (1980) asserted that the gap between educators and cognitive scientists was both enduring and wide. Although the differences in approaches are understandable for historical and sociological reasons, he believed that the persistence of the gap is detrimental to future progress. He indicated:

> *Thus work in education and problem solving could profit substantially if this gap were bridged, if people interested in practical education would build upon the insights and methods of the cognitive scientists, and if educators were to adopt modes of analytic thinking and quality standards of the kind prevalent in other sciences. (p. 43)*

Utilizing CPS could offer a bridge for both educators (and other practitioners) and cognitive scientists to continue to narrow the gap. As Weisberg (1988) noted, cognitive psychologists have, for the most part, devoted their efforts to the study of various laboratory problems and have simply assumed that creative thinking would be illuminated. Traditional tasks utilized by cognitive researchers could be broadened to include those of more interest to educators and trainers concerned with providing programs with impact. Future developments in designing or developing practical CPS methods and techniques could be based on an appropriate level of prescription (Scriven, 1980). CPS might even be developed to serve as an option for human cognitive engineering (Reif, 1980).

Conclusions

Philosophers were asking questions about the distinctiveness of human minds, the characterization of mental states, the relationship between mind and body and how minds learn about the physical world well before the disciplines of cognitive science, cognitive psychology, theoretical linguistics, artificial intelligence, cognitive neuroscience and anthropology arose (Bechtel, 1988). Our technology has currently evolved to a point where we can almost pinpoint the specific neural processes responsible for mental actions. Raichle (1994) has indicated that this ability:

> ...stems from developments in imaging technology that the past few years have seen, most notably positron-emission tomography and magnetic resonance imaging. Coupled with powerful computers, these techniques can now capture, in real time, images of the physiology associated with thought processes. They show how specific regions of the brain "light up" when activities such as reading are performed and how neurons and their elaborate cast of supporting cells organize and coordinate their tasks. (p.58)

Just as current scientific technology can shed significant light on questions that are centuries old, so working to understand, recognize, nurture and develop creativity can expand thinking and knowledge within the domain of problem solving and help move cognitive science forward.

Deliberate consideration of CPS, especially for tasks requiring novel solutions and approaches, can assist those interested in problem solving and creativity from both a scientific or theoretical and a practical or applied perspective. Gaps and tension currently exist. Gaps change based on current aspirations and location in relation to the vision. CPS involves continuous consideration and adjustment based on new knowledge and feedback. The pursuit of this line of inquiry and practice can enlighten future generations in ways we can only imagine. "To think is constantly to choose in view of the end to be pursued (Binet & Simon, 1916, p. 140)."

References

Amabile, T. M. (1990). Within you, without you: The social psychology of creativity and beyond. In M. A. Runco & R. S. Albert (Eds.). *Theories of creativity* (61-91). Newbury Park, CA: Sage Publications.

Anderson, H. H. (Ed.). (1959a). *Creativity and its cultivation: Addresses presented at the interdisciplinary symposia on creativity at Michigan State University.* New York: Harper and Row.

Anderson, H. H. (1959b). Creativity in perspective. In H. H. Anderson (Ed.), *Creativity and its cultivation: Addresses presented at the interdisciplinary symposia on creativity at Michigan State University* (pp. 269-280). New York: Harper and Row.

Arieti, S. (1976). *Creativity: The magic synthesis.* New York: Basic Books.

Baer, J. (1991). Generality of creativity across performance domains. *Creativity Research Journal, 4,* 23-39.

Barron, F. (1990). *Creativity and psychological health: Origins of personal vitality and creative freedom.* Buffalo, NY: CEF Press.

Basadur, M. S., Graen, G. B. & Green, S. G. (1982). Training in creative problem solving: Effects on ideation and problem finding in an industrial research organization. *Organizational Behavior and Human Performance, 30,* 41-70.

Bechtel, W. (1988). *Philosophy of mind: An overview for cognitive science.* Hillsdale, NJ: Erlbaum.

Besemer, S. P. (1998). Creative product analysis matrix: Testing the model structure and a comparison among products – three novel chairs. *Creativity Research Journal, 11,* 333-346.

Besemer, S. P. & O'Quin, K. (1993). Assessing creative products: Progress and potentials. In S. G. Isaksen, M. C. Murdock, R. L. Firestien, & D. J. Treffinger (Eds.), *Nurturing and developing creativity: The emergence of a discipline* (pp. 331-349). Norwood, NJ: Ablex.

Binet, A. & Simon, T. (1916). *The development of intelligence in children (Translated by E. S. Kite).* Baltimore: Williams & Wilkins.

Blattberg, R. C. & Hoch, S. J. (1990). Database models and managerial intuition: 50% model + 50% manager. *Management Science, 36,* 887-899.

Boden, M. A. (1991). *The creative mind: Myths and mechanisms.* New York: Basic Books.

Boden, M. A. (Ed.). (1994). *Dimensions of creativity.* Cambridge, MA: MIT Press.

Brooks, J. G. & Brooks, M. G. (1993). *In search of understanding: The case for constructivists classrooms.* Alexandria, VA: Association for Supervision and Curriculum Development.

Buijs, J. & Nauta, K. (1991). Creativity training at the Delft school of industrial design engineering. In T. Rickards, P. Colemont, P. Grøholt, M. Parker & H. Smeekes (Eds.), *Creativity and innovation: Learning from practice* (pp. 249-252). Delft, The Netherlands: Innovation Consulting Group - TNO.

Burnside, R. M., Amabile, T. M. & Gryskiewicz, S. S. (1988). Assessing organizational climates for creativity and innovation: Methodological review of large company audits. In Y. Ijiri & R. L. Kuhn (Eds.). *New directions in creative and innovative management: Bridging theory and practice* (pp. 169-185). Cambridge, MA: Ballinger.

Chomsky, N. (1998). *On language: Chomsky's classic works in one volume.* New York: The New Press.

Covington, M. V. (1987). Instruction in problem solving and planning. In S. L. Friedman, E. K. Scholnick, & R. R. Cocking (Eds.). *Blueprints for thinking: The role of planning in cognitive development* (pp. 469-511). London: Cambridge University Press.

Cramond, B., Martin, C. E. & Shaw, E. L. (1990). Generalizability of creative problem solving procedures to real-life problems. *Journal for the Education of the Gifted, 13,* 141-155.

De Schryver, L. (1992). The need for training impact. In T. Rickards, S. Moger, P. Colemont & M. Tassoul (Eds.). *Creativity and innovation: Quality breakthroughs* (pp. 131-134). Delft, The Netherlands: Innovation Consulting Group - TNO.

Dewey, J. (1910). *How we think.* Lexington, MA: D. C. Heath and Company.

Duell, O. K. (1986). Metacognitive skills. In G. D. Phye & T. Andre (Eds.), *Cognitive classroom learning: Understanding, thinking and problem solving* (pp. 205-242). Orlando, FL: Academic Press, Inc.

Duncker, K. (1945). On problem solving. *Psychological monographs, 58,* Whole No. 270.

Ekvall, G. (1987). The climate metaphor in organizational theory. In B. M. Bass & P. J. D. Drenth (Eds.), *Advances in organizational psychology: An international review* (pp. 177-190). Newbury Park, CA: Sage.

Ekvall, G. (1996). Organizational climate for creativity and innovation. *European Journal of Work and Organizational Psychology, 5,* 105-123.

Eyring, H. (1959). Scientific creativity. In H. H. Anderson (Ed.), *Creativity and its cultivation: Addresses presented at the interdisciplinary symposia on creativity at Michigan State University* (pp. 1-11). New York: Harper and Row.

Eysenck, H. J. (1993). Creativity and personality: Suggestions for a theory. *Psychological Inquiry, 4,* 147-178.

Firestien, R. L. (1993). The power of product. In S. G. Isaksen, M. C. Murdock, R. L. Firestien, & D. J. Treffinger (Eds.), *Nurturing and developing creativity: The emergence of a discipline* (pp. 261-277). Norwood, NJ: Ablex.

Flavell, J. H. (1976). Metacognitive aspects of problem solving. In L. B. Resnick (Ed), *The nature of intelligence* (pp. 231-235). Hillsdale, NJ: Erlbaum.

Frawley, W. (1997). *Vygotsky and cognitive science: Language and the unification of the social and computational mind.* Cambridge, MA: Harvard University Press.

Gardner, H. (1985). *The mind's new science: A history of the cognitive revolution.* New York: Basic Books.

Gardner, H. & Nemirovsky, R. (1991). From private intuitions to public symbol systems: An examination of the creative process in George Cantor and Sigmund Freud. *Creativity Research Journal, 4,* 1-21.

Geschka, H. (1993). The development and assessment of creative thinking techniques: A German perspective. In S. G. Isaksen, M. C. Murdock, R. L. Firestien & D. J. Treffinger (Eds.), *Nurturing and developing creativity: The emergence of a discipline* (pp. 215-236). Norwood, NJ: Ablex.

Getzels, J. W. (1964). Creative thinking, problem solving, and instruction. In E. R. Hilgard (Ed.), *Theories of Learning and Instruction: The sixty-third yearbook of the*

National Society for the Study of Education (pp. 240-267). Chicago, IL: University of Chicago Press.

Getzels, J. W. & Csikszentmihalyi, M. (1976*). The creative vision: A longitudinal study of problem finding in art.* New York: Wiley & Sons.

Getzels, J. W. & Jackson, P. (1962). *Creativity and intelligence.* New York: Wiley.

Glover, J. A., Ronning, R. R. & Reynolds, C. R. (Eds.). (1989). *Handbook of creativity.* New York: Plenum Press.

Gowan, J. C. (1972). *The development of the creative individual.* San Diego, CA: R. Knapp.

Greeno, J. G. (1980). Trends in the theory of knowledge for problem solving. In D. T. Tuma & F. Reif (Eds.), *Problem solving and education: Issues in teaching and research* (pp. 9-23). Hillsdale, NJ: Erlbaum.

Greeno, J. G. (1989). A perspective on thinking. *American Psychologist, 44,* 134-141.

Grønhaug, K. & Kaufmann, G. (Eds.). (1988). *Innovation: A cross-disciplinary perspective.* Oslo, Norway: Norwegian University Press.

Guilford, J. P. (1950). Creativity. *American Psychologist, 5,* 444-454.

Guilford, J. P. (1977). *Way beyond the IQ: Guide to improving intelligence and creativity.* Buffalo, NY: Bearly Limited.

Hallman, R. J. (1981). The necessary and sufficient conditions of creativity. In J. C. Gowan, J. Khatena, & E. P. Torrance (Eds.), *Creativity: Its educational implications* (pp. 19-30). Dubuque, IA: Kendall-Hunt.

Harrington, D. M. (1990). The ecology of creativity: A psychological perspective. In M. A. Runco & R. S. Albert (Eds.), *Theories of creativity* (pp. 143-169). Beverly Hills, CA: Sage.

Hilgard, E. R. (1959). Creativity and problem solving. In H. H. Anderson (Ed.), *Creativity and its cultivation: Addresses presented at the interdisciplinary symposia on creativity* (pp. 162-180). New York: Harper and Row.

Isaksen, S. G. (1984). *Organizational and industrial innovation: Using critical and creative thinking.* A paper presented to the Conference on Critical Thinking: An Interdisciplinary Appraisal sponsored by Kingsborough Community College, New York.

Isaksen, S. G. (Ed.). (1987). *Frontiers of creativity research: Beyond the basics.* Buffalo, NY: Bearly Limited.

Isaksen, S. G. (1989). *Creative problem solving: A process for creativity.* Buffalo, NY: Center for Studies in Creativity.

Isaksen, S. G. (1996). Task appraisal and process planning: Managing change methods. *International Creativity Network Newsletter, 6,* 4-6.

Isaksen, S. G. (In press). The Center for Studies in Creativity: A quarter century of progress. In M. K. Raina (Ed.), *International perspectives in creativity research.* New Delhi, India: National Council of Educational Research and Training.

Isaksen, S. G. & Dorval, K. B. (1993a). Changing views of CPS: Over 40 years of continuous improvement. *International Creativity Network, 3*, 1-5.

Isaksen, S. G. & Dorval, K. B. (1993b). Toward an improved understanding of creativity within people: The level-style distinction. In S. G. Isaksen, M. C. Murdock, R. L. Firestien, & D. J. Treffinger, (Eds.), *Understanding and recognizing creativity: The emergence of a discipline* (pp. 299-330). Norwood, NJ: Ablex.

Isaksen, S. G., Dorval, K. B., Noller, R. B. & Firestien, R. L. (1993). The dynamic nature of creative problem solving. In S. S. Gryskiewicz (Ed.), *Discovering creativity: Proceedings of the 1992 International Creativity and Networking Conference* (pp. 155-162). Greensboro, NC: Center for Creative Leadership.

Isaksen, S. G., Dorval, K. B. & Treffinger, D. J. (1994). *Creative approaches to problem solving.* Dubuque, IA: Kendall/Hunt.

Isaksen, S. G., Dorval, K. B. & Treffinger, D. J. (2000). *Creative approaches to problem solving* (Revised 2nd ed.). Dubuque, IA: Kendall/Hunt.

Isaksen, S. G., Dorval, K. B., & Treffinger, D. J. (1998). *Toolbox for Creative Problem Solving: Basic tools and resources.* Buffalo, NY: Creative Problem Solving Group - Buffalo.

Isaksen, S. G. & Murdock, M. C. (1993). The emergence of a discipline: Issues and approaches to the study of creativity. In S. G. Isaksen, M. C. Murdock, R. L. Firestien, & D. J. Treffinger (Eds.), *Understanding and recognizing creativity: The emergence of a discipline* (pp. 13-47). Norwood, NJ: Ablex.

Isaksen, S. G., Murdock, M. C., Firestien, R. L. & Treffinger, D. J. (Eds.). (1993a). *Understanding and recognizing creativity: The emergence of a discipline.* Norwood, NJ: Ablex.

Isaksen, S. G., Murdock, M. C., Firestien, R. L. & Treffinger, D. J. (Eds.). (1993b). *Nurturing and developing creativity: Emergence of a discipline.* Norwood, NJ: Ablex.

Isaksen, S. G. & Pershyn, G. (1994). Understanding natural creative process using the KAI. *KAI International, 3*, 5.

Isaksen, S. G. & Puccio, G. J. (1992). Profiling creativity: A position paper. In L. Novelli (Ed.), *Collected research papers: 1992 International Creativity and Innovation Networking Conference - Discovering creativity* (pp. 70-80). Greensboro, NC: Center for Creative Leadership.

Isaksen, S. G., Puccio, G. J. & Treffinger, D. J. (1993). An ecological approach to creativity research: Profiling for creative problem solving. *Journal of Creative Behavior, 23*, 149-170.

Isaksen, S. G. & Treffinger, D. J. (1985). *Creative problem solving: The basic course.* Buffalo, NY: Bearly Limited.

Isaksen, S. G. & Treffinger, D. J. (1987). *Creative problem solving: Three components and six specific stages.* Instructional handout. Buffalo, NY: Center for Studies in Creativity.

Isaksen, S. G. & Treffinger, D. J. (1991). Creative learning and problem solving. In A. L. Costa (Ed.), *Developing minds: Programs for teaching thinking* (Volume 2, pp. 89-93). Alexandria, VA: Association for Supervision and Curriculum Development.

Isaksen, S. G., Treffinger, D. J., & Dorval, K. B. (1997). *The creative problem solving framework: An historical perspective.* Sarasota, FL: Center for Creative Learning.

Johnson, D. M. (1972). *A systematic introduction to the psychology of thinking.* New York: Harper & Row.

Johnson-Laird, P. N. (1988). Freedom and constraint in creativity. In R. J. Sternberg (Ed.), *The nature of creativity: Contemporary psychological perspectives* (pp. 202-219). New York: Cambridge University Press.

Kaufmann, G. (1988). Problem solving and creativity. In K.. Grønhaug & G. Kaufmann (Eds.), *Innovation: A cross-disciplinary perspective* (pp. 87-137). Oslo, Norway: Norwegian University Press.

Kaufmann, G. (1993). The content and logical structure of creativity concepts: An inquiry into the conceptual foundations of creativity research. In S. G. Isaksen, M. C. Murdock, R. L. Firestien, & D. J. Treffinger (Eds.), *Understanding and recognizing creativity: The emergence of a discipline* (pp. 141-157). Norwood, NJ: Ablex.

Kaufmann, G. (1995). In G. Kaufmann, T. Helstrup, & K. H. Teigen (Eds.), *Problem solving and cognitive processes: A festschrift in honour of Kjell Raaheim* (pp. 45-76). Bergen, Norway: Fagbokforlaget.

Kaufmann, G. & Raaheim, K. (1973). Effect of inducing activity upon performance in an unfamiliar task. *Psychological Reports, 32,* 303-306.

Kirton, M. J. (1987). Adaptors and innovators: Cognitive style and personality. In S. G. Isaksen (Ed.), *Frontiers of creativity research: Beyond the basics* (pp. 282-304). Buffalo, NY: Bearly Limited.

Kneller, G. (1965). *The art and science of creativity.* New York: Holt, Rinehart & Winston.

Koestler, A. (1964). *The act of creation.* New York: MacMillan.

Kohler, W. (1947). *Gestalt psychology.* New York: Liveright.

Kuhn, D. (1999). A developmental model of critical thinking. *Educational Researcher, 28,* 16-25.

Kuhn, R. L. (Ed.). (1985). *Frontiers in creative and innovative management.* Cambridge, MA: Ballinger Publishing.

Lakoff, G., & Johnson, M. (1999). *Philosophy in the flesh: The embodied minds and its challenge to Western thought.* New York: Basic Books.

Langer, E. J. (1989). *Mindfulness.* Reading, MA: Addison-Wesley.

MacKinnon, D. W. (1970). Creativity: A multi-faceted phenomenon. In J. D. Roslansky (Ed.), *Creativity: A discussion at the Nobel conference* (pp. 17-32). Amsterdam: North-Holland.

MacKinnon, D. W. (1975). IPAR's contribution to the conceptualization and study of creativity. In I. A. Taylor & J. W. Getzels (Eds.), *Perspectives in creativity* (pp. 60-89). Chicago, IL: Aldine.

MacKinnon, D. W. (1978). *In search of human effectiveness: Identifying and developing creativity.* Buffalo, NY: Bearly Limited.

Magyari-Beck, I. (1993). Creatology: A potential paradigm for an emerging discipline. In S. G. Isaksen, M. C. Murdock, R. L. Firestien, & D. J. Treffinger, (Eds.), *Understanding and recognizing creativity: The emergence of a discipline* (pp. 48-82). Norwood, NJ: Ablex.

Maier, N. R. F. (1940). The behavior mechanisms concerned with problem solving. *Psychological Review, 47,* 43-58.

Maltzman, I. (1955). Thinking: From a behavioristic point of view. *Psychological Review, 62,* 275-286.

Maltzman, I. (1960). On the training of originality. *Psychological Review, 67,* 229-242.

Martinez, M. E. (1998). What is problem solving? *Phi Delta Kappan, 79,* 605-609.

Maslow, A. H. (1976). Creativity in self-actualizing people. In A. Rothenberg & C. R. Hausman (Eds.), *The creativity question* (pp. 86-92). Durham, NC: Duke University Press

Matlin, M. W. (1989). *Cognition* (2nd ed.). San Francisco: Holt, Rinehart and Winston.

Maturana, H. R., & Varela, F. J. (1998). *The tree of knowledge: The biological roots of human understanding* (Revised edition). Boston: Shambala.

Mayer, R. E. (1983). *Thinking, problem solving, cognition.* New York: W. H. Freeman and Company.

Meadow, A. & Parnes, S. J. (1959). Evaluation of training in creative problem solving. *Journal of Applied Psychology, 43,* 189-194.

Meadow, A., Parnes, S. J. & Reese, H. (1959). Influences of brainstorming instructions and problem sequence on a creative problem solving test. *Journal of Applied Psychology, 43,* 413-416.

Metcalfe, J. & Shimamura, A. P. (Eds.). (1996). *Metacognition: Knowing about knowing.* Cambridge, MA: MIT Press.

Miller, J. R., Polson, P. G., & Kintsch, W. (1984). Problems of methodology in cognitive science. In W. Kintsch, J. R. Miller, & P. G. Polson (Eds.), *Methods and tactics in cognitive science* (pp. 1-18). Hillsdale, NJ: Erlbaum.

Mitchell, T. R. & Beach, L. R. (1990). "...Do I love thee? Let me count..." toward an understanding of intuitive and automatic decision making. *Organizational and Human Decision Processes, 46,* 1-20.

Mooney, R. L. (1963). A conceptual model for integrating four approaches to the identification of creative talent. In C. W. Taylor & F. Barron (Eds.), *Scientific creativity: Its recognition and development* (pp. 331-340). New York: Wiley.

Moore, M. T. & Murdock, M. C. (1991). On problems in problem finding research. *Creativity Research Journal, 4,* 292-293.

Newell, A. Shaw, J. C. & Simon, H. A. (1958). Elements of a theory of human problem solving. *Psychological Review, 65,* 151-169.

Newell, A. Shaw, J. C., & Simon, H. A. (1962). The process of creative thinking. In H. E. Gruber, G. Terrell, & M. Wertheimer (Eds.), *Contemporary approaches to creative thinking* (pp. 63-119). New York: Atherton.

Noller, R. B. & Parnes, S. J. (1972). Applied creativity: The creative studies project, Part III - The curriculum. *Journal of Creative Behavior, 6,* 275-294.

Noller, R. B., Parnes, S. J. & Biondi, A. M. (1976). *Creative actionbook.* New York: Scribners.

Osborn, A. F. (1952). *Wake up your mind: 101 ways to develop creativeness.* New York: Charles Scribner's Sons.

Osborn, A. F. (1953, 1957, 1963, 1967). *Applied imagination: Principles and procedures of creative thinking.* New York: Charles Scribner's Sons.

Parkhurst, H. B. (1999). Confusion, lack of consensus, and the definition of creativity as a construct. *Journal of Creative Behavior, 33,* 1-21.

Parnes, S. J. (1961). Effects of extended effort in creative problem solving. *Journal of Educational Psychology, 52,* 117-122.

Parnes, S. J. (1963). The deferment-of-judgment principle: A clarification of the literature. *Psychological Reports, 12,* 521-522.

Parnes, S. J. (1966). *Manual for institutes and programs.* Buffalo, NY: Creative Education Foundation.

Parnes, S. J. (1967a). *Creative behavior guidebook.* New York: Scribners.

Parnes, S. J. (1967b). *Creative behavior workbook.* New York: Scribners.

Parnes, S. J. (1987). The creative studies project. In S. G. Isaksen (Ed.), *Frontiers of creativity research: Beyond the basics* (pp. 156-188). Buffalo, NY: Bearly Limited.

Parnes, S. J. (1988). *Visionizing.* Buffalo, NY: DOK Publishers.

Parnes, S. J. (Ed). (1992). *Source book for creative problem solving.* Buffalo, NY: The Creative Education Foundation Press.

Parnes, S. J., & Meadow, A. (1959). Effects of brainstorming instruction on creative problem solving by trained and untrained subjects. *Journal of Educational Psychology, 50,* 171-176.

Parnes, S. J. & Meadow, A. (1960). Evaluation of persistence of effects produced by a creative problem solving course. *Psychological Reports, 7,* 357-361.

Parnes, S. J. & Noller, R. B. (1972a). Applied creativity: The creative studies project, Part I - The development. *Journal of Creative Behavior, 6,* 1-22.

Parnes, S. J. & Noller, R. B. (1972b). Applied creativity: The creative studies project, Part II - Results of the two-year program. *Journal of Creative Behavior, 6,* 164-186.

Parnes, S. J. & Noller, R. B. (1973). Applied creativity: The creative studies project: Part IV—Personality findings and conclusions. *Journal of Creative Behavior, 7,* 15-36.

Parnes, S. J., Noller, R. B. & Biondi, A. M. (1977). *Guide to creative action.* New York: Scribners.

Pershyn, G. (1992). *An investigation into the graphic depictions of natural creative problem solving processes.* Unpublished Masters Thesis. State University College at Buffalo: Center for Studies in Creativity.

Piaget, J. (1954). *The construction of reality in the child.* New York: Basic Books.

Polanyi, M. (1981). The creative imagination. In D. Dutton & D. F. T. Rodier (Eds.), *The concept of creativity in science and art* (pp. 91-107). The Hague: Martins Nijhoff Publishers.

Raaheim, K. (1976). The paradoxes of productive thinking. *International Review of Applied Psychology, 24,* 117-121.

Raaheim, K. (1984). *Why intelligence is not enough.* Bergen, Norway: Sigma Forlag A. S.

Raaheim, K. & Kaufmann, G. (1972). Level of activity and success in solving an unfamiliar task. *Psychological Reports, 30,* 271-274.

Raaheim, K., Kaufmann, G., & Bengtsson, G. (1980). Attempts to predict intelligent behavior II: A study of problem solving. *Scandinavian Journal of Psychology, 21,* 119-121.

Raaheim, K., Kaufmann, G., & Kaufmann A. (1979). Attempts to predict intelligent behavior I: The categorizing test. *Scandinavian Journal of Psychology, 20,* 77-80.

Raichle, M. E. (1994). Visualizing the mind. *Scientific American, 270,* 58-64.

Reese, H. W., Treffinger, D. J., Parnes, S. J. & Kaltsounis, G. (1976). Effects of a creative studies program on structure of intellect factors. *Journal of Educational Psychology, 68,* 401-410.

Reif, F. (1980). Theoretical and educational concerns with problem solving: Bridging the gaps with human cognitive engineering. In D. T. Tuma & F. Reif, (Eds.). *Problem solving and education: Issues in teaching and research* (pp. 39-50). Hillsdale, NJ: Erlbaum.

Renzulli, J. S. (1982). What makes a problem real: Stalking the illusive meaning of qualitative differences in gifted education. *Gifted Child Quarterly, 26,* 147-156.

Resnick, L. B. & Klopfer, L. E. (1989). Toward the thinking curriculum: An overview. In L. B. Resnick & L. E. Klopfer (Eds.), *Toward the thinking curriculum: Current cognitive research* (pp. 1-18). Alexandria, VA: Association for Supervision and Curriculum Development.

Rhodes, M. (1961). An analysis of creativity. *Phi Delta Kappan, 42,* 305-310.

Rose, L. H. & Lin, H. (1984). A meta-analysis of long-term creativity training programs. *Journal of Creative Behavior, 11,* 124-130.

Rothenberg, A. (1971). The process of Janusian thinking in creativity. *Archives of General Psychiatry, 24,* 195-205.

Runco, M. A. (1994). *Problem finding, problem solving, and creativity.* Norwood, NJ: Ablex.

Runco, M. A. & Albert, R. S. (1990). *Theories of creativity.* Newbury Park: CA: SAGE.

Rugg, H. (1963). *Imagination: An inquiry into the sources and conditions that stimulate creativity.* New York: Harper & Row.

Russ, S. W. (1993). *Affect and creativity: The role of affect and play in the creative process.* Hillsdale, NJ: Lawrence Erlbaum.

Russell, D. (1956). *Childrens' thinking.* New York: Ginn and Company.

Scriven, M. (1980). Prescriptive and descriptive approaches to problem solving. In D. T. Tuma & F. Reif, (Eds.), *Problem solving and education: Issues in teaching and research* (pp. 127-139). Hillsdale, NJ: Erlbaum.

Selye, H. (1988). Creativity in basic research. In F. Flach (Ed.). *The creative mind* (pp. 243-268). Buffalo, NY: Bearly Limited.

Selz, O. (1922). *Zur psychologie des productiven Denkens.* Bonn: Cohen.

Schank, R. C. & Childers, P. (1988). *The creative attitude: Learning to ask and answer the right questions.* New York: MacMillan.

Shack, G. D. (1993). Effects of a creative problem solving curriculum on students of varying ability levels. *Gifted Child Quarterly, 37,* 32-38.

Simon, H. A. (1980). Problem solving and education. In D. T. Tuma & F. Reif (Eds.), *Problem solving and education: Issues in teaching and research* (pp. 79-88). Hillsdale, NJ: Erlbaum.

Simonton, D. K. (1991). Personality correlates of exceptional personal influence: A note on Thorndike's (1950) creators and leaders. *Creativity Research Journal, 4,* 67-78.

Smith, J. A. (1966). *Setting conditions for creative teaching in the elementary school.* Boston: Allyn and Bacon.

Stein, M. I. (1974). *Stimulating creativity.* New York: Academic Press.

Stein, M. I. (1987) Creativity at the crossroads: A 1985 perspective. In S. G. Isaksen (Ed.), *Frontiers of creativity research: Beyond the basics* (pp. 417-427). Buffalo, NY: Bearly Limited.

Stepien, W. J., Gallagher, S. A. & Workman, D. (1993). Problem-based learning for traditional and interdisciplinary classrooms. *Journal for the Education of the Gifted, 16,* 338-357.

Sternberg, R. J. (Ed.). (1988). *The nature of creativity: Contemporary psychological perspectives.* Cambridge, MA: Cambridge University Press.

Sternberg, R. J. (Ed.). (1994). *Thinking and problem solving: The handbook of perception and cognition* (Second edition). New York: Academic Press.

Sternberg, R. J. (Ed.). (1999). *Handbook of creativity.* New York: Cambridge University Press.

Taggart, W. & Valenzi, E. (1990). Assessing rational and intuitive styles: A human information processing metaphor. *Journal of Management Studies, 27,* 149-172.

Taylor, I. A. (1959). The nature of the creative process. In P. Smith (Ed.), *Creativity: An examination of the creative process* (pp. 51-82). New York: Hastings House.

Taylor, I. A. & Getzels, J. W. (Eds.). (1975). *Perspectives on creativity.* Chicago: Aldine.

Torrance, E. P. (1972). Can we teach children to think creatively? *Journal of Creative Behavior, 6,* 236-262.

Torrance, E. P. (1986). Teaching creative and gifted learners. In M. C. Wittrock (Ed.), *Handbook of Research on Teaching* (pp. 630-647). New York: MacMillan.

Torrance, E. P. (1987). Teaching for creativity. In S. G. Isaksen (Ed.), *Frontiers in creativity research: Beyond the basics* (pp. 189-215). Buffalo, NY: Bearly Limited.

Torrance, E. P. (1993). Experiences in developing technology for creative education. In S. G. Isaksen, M. C. Murdock, R. L. Firestein, & D. J. Treffinger (Eds.), *Understanding and recognizing creativity: The emergence of a discipline* (pp. 158-201). Norwood, NJ: Ablex Publishing.

Torrance, E. P. & Torrance, P. (1973). *Is creativity teachable?* Bloomington, IN: Phi Delta Kappa.

Treffinger, D. J. & Isaksen, S. G. (1992). *Creative problem solving: An introduction.* Sarasota, FL: Center for Creative Learning.

Treffinger, D. J., Isaksen, S. G., & Dorval, K. B. (1994). Creative problem solving: An overview. In M. A. Runco (Ed.), (1994). *Problem finding, problem solving, and creativity* (pp. 223-236). Norwood, NJ: Ablex.

Treffinger, D. J., Isaksen, S. G., & Dorval, K. B. (2000). *Introduction to Creative Problem Solving* (3rd ed.). Waco, TX: Prufrock.

Treffinger, D. J., Isaksen, S. G. & Firestien, R. L. (1982). *Handbook for creative learning.* Sarasota, FL: Center for Creative Learning.

Treffinger, D. J., Isaksen, S. G. & Firestien, R. L. (1983). Theoretical perspectives on creative learning and its facilitation: An overview. *Journal of Creative Behavior, 17,* 9-17.

Tuerck, D. G. (Ed.). (1987). *Creativity and liberal learning: Problems and possibilities in American education.* Norwood, NJ: Ablex.

Tuma, D. T. & Reif, F. (Eds.). (1980). *Problem solving and education: Issues in teaching and research.* Hillsdale, NJ: Erlbaum.

VanGundy, A. G. (1984). How to establish a creative climate in the work group. *Management Review, 73,* 24-38.

VanGundy, A. G. (1988). *Techniques of structured problem solving (Second edition).* New York: Van Nostrand Reinhold Company.

Vinacke, W. E. (1952). *The psychology of thinking.* New York: McGraw-Hill.

Voss, J. F. (1989). Problem solving and the educational process. In A. Lesgold & R. Glaser (Eds.), *Foundations for a psychology of education* (pp. 251-294). Hillsdale, NJ: Erlbaum.

Wallas, G. (1926). *The art of thought.* New York: Harcourt Brace.

Ward, T. B., Smith, S. M., Vaid, J. (Eds.). (1997). *Creative thought: An investigation of conceptual structures and processes.* Washington, DC: American Psychological Association.

Weisberg, R. W. (1988). Problem solving and creativity. In R. J. Sternberg (Ed.), *The nature of creativity: Contemporary psychological perspectives* (pp. 148-176). New York: Cambridge University Press.

Welsch, P. K. (1980). *The nurturance of creative behavior in educational environments: A comprehensive curriculum approach.* Unpublished doctoral dissertation, University of Michigan.

Welsh, G. S. (1973). Perspectives in the study of creativity. *Journal of Creative Behavior, 7,* 231-246.

Welsh, G. S. (1975). *Creativity and intelligence: A personality approach.* University of North Carolina at Chapel Hill: Institute for Research in Social Science.

Wertheimer, M. (1959). *Productive thinking.* New York: Harper & Row.

Woodman, R. W., & Schoenfeldt, L. F. (1999). An interactionist model of creative behavior. In G. J. Puccio & M. C. Murdock (Eds.), *Creativity assessment: Readings and resources* (pp. 467-477). Buffalo, NY: Creative Education Foundation.

Yussen, S. R. (1985). The role of metacognition in contemporary theories of cognitive development. In D. L. Forrest-Pressley, G. E. MacKinnon & T. G. Waller (Eds.), *Metacognition, cognition, and human performance* (pp. 253-183). Orlando, FL: Academic Press.

CHAPTER TWO

Understanding the History of CPS

Donald J. Treffinger
Center for Creative Learning
Sarasota, Florida

"The more things change, the more they stay the same."
Voltaire

Introduction

For more than fifty years many researchers and developers proposed a variety of models for problem solving by individuals or groups. Those models have been developed, studied, and applied in many settings: colleges and universities, public elementary and secondary schools, small and large businesses, and a variety of consulting organizations. Taken together, those applications and studies comprise the foundation for the premise of this book: that across many places, organizational settings, and people, the Creative Problem Solving framework provides tools that make a difference to individuals, to groups, and to the quality of life. Making a difference in any of these ways requires a framework that has stood the tests and scrutiny of inquiry over an extended period of time. It also requires that the framework we

This chapter is based, in part, on an earlier monograph entitled *The Creative Problem Solving Framework: An historical perspective* written by S. G. Isaksen, D. J. Treffinger, and K. B. Dorval and published in 1997 by the Center for Creative Learning.

use does not remain rigid and static, but continues to be enhanced and extended or informed by research evidence and the lessons of exemplary practice.

In order to understand the present, and to begin to chart the course for the future, we need an awareness and appreciation of our history. The history of the CPS approach is in itself one of the strongest distinctions between our framework and the ever-increasing proliferation of methods and models in the popular literature (and especially in education, training, and organizational development). Efforts to lead and manage change—to "make a difference"—should be based on approaches that are research-based and supported, not just the currently fashionable buzzwords, fads, or "gurus" of the day. The number of new (but not-really-so-new) process models seems to increase each year; the developers, and all their clients (ever eager to ride the newest wave), too often seem unconcerned with issues of long-term research and development. Understanding history might seem pedantic or unnecessary to some, but in the long run (and perhaps even for more immediate success), those who understand the richness of tradition will best be able to apply today's methods and to develop the methods they will need for the future.

Therefore, this chapter surveys the gradual, systematic development of the Creative Problem Solving (CPS) framework. CPS emerged through several decades of work by a number of writers, developers, researchers, and trainers (including, in alphabetical order, K. Brian Dorval, Roger L. Firestien, Scott G. Isaksen, Ruth B. Noller, Alex F. Osborn, Sidney J. Parnes, and Donald J. Treffinger). These scholars shared, for varying periods of time and with varying degrees of overlap, common institutional and geographical linkages. The CPS framework continues to evolve through a variety of research, development and dissemination efforts, even though many of the contributors are now operating from more diverse and varied contexts and settings. This chapter focuses primarily on the historical antecedents of our contemporary "independent components" approach to CPS (e.g., Isaksen, Dorval, & Treffinger, 1994; Treffinger, Isaksen, & Dorval, 1994a, 2000).

Many other developers, writers, and consultants have also accessed the same literature that we drew upon, of course, and developed their own approaches independently (e.g., Basadur, Graen, & Green, 1982; VanGundy, 1988). Yet other approaches have excerpted particular elements of the CPS orientation in their work (e.g., emphasis on deferred judgment or use of a specific tool, such as brainstorming). In the interest of brevity, those efforts are not incorporated into this review. Similarly, this chapter will not attempt to catalog educational or training programs or materials that have applied all or part the CPS framework in a specific context or setting (e.g., Chislett, 1994; Cramond, Martin & Shaw, 1990; Isaksen, 1998; Schack, 1993; Todd & Larson, 1992). Training issues have also been reviewed elsewhere (e.g., Isaksen, 1987; Isaksen, Murdock, Firestien, & Treffinger, 1993a, 1993b; Parnes, 1992; Stein, 1975; Treffinger, 1995; Treffinger, Cross, Feldhusen, Isaksen, Remle, & Sortore, 1993; Treffinger, Sortore, & Cross, 1993).

The major goal of this chapter, then, is to summarize the origins and evolutionary progress on which the contemporary, componential CPS framework builds (including its description and graphic representation), in order to establish a foundation for understanding the many and varied ways in which CPS makes a difference to individuals and organizations. Isaksen, Treffinger, and Dorval (1997) presented a more detailed historical survey of the CPS framework, upon which this chapter draws extensively.

In the current, componential version of CPS we sought to make the CPS process *natural, descriptive,* and *flexible* (Isaksen, Dorval, & Treffinger, 1994; Treffinger, Isaksen, & Dorval, 1994a). On the way to our current approach, however, CPS has undergone fundamental, structural changes and continuous updating or refinement within each of its historical forms (Isaksen & Dorval, 1993a; Isaksen, Dorval, Noller, & Firestien 1993; Treffinger, Isaksen & Dorval, 1994b). This chapter traces the versions of CPS in a broad chronological sequence.

THE ORIGINS OF CPS: MAKING THE CREATIVE PROCESS EXPLICIT AND DELIBERATE

Efforts to make productive thinking processes more visible, explicit and deliberate have been among the most formidable challenges for researchers for many years, from early efforts to study the creative process (e.g., Wallas, 1926) to the present day.

Alex Osborn, a founding partner of the Batten, Barton, Durstine and Osborn advertising agency and founder of the Creative Education Foundation, developed the original description of CPS. In his book, *Wake up your mind* (1952), Osborn presented a comprehensive description of a seven-stage CPS process. The stages were: *orientation* (pointing up the problem), *preparation* (gathering the pertinent data), *analysis* (breaking down the relevant material), *hypothesis* (creating alternative ideas), *incubation* (letting up to invite illumination), *synthesis* (putting the pieces together), and *verification* (judging the results). This process description was based on his work in the advertising field. Osborn's subsequent book, *Applied Imagination* (1953, 1957), popularized his description of CPS and the term brainstorming— now arguably the most widely known and used term associated with the concept of creativity—and all too frequently, the most misused term (see, Treffinger, Isaksen, & Young, 1998).

Osborn continued to read extensively about creativity and apply his process strategies and techniques in his work and teaching. In the 1963 revised edition of *Applied Imagination*, and its 1967 reprinting, Osborn modified his conception of CPS by condensing the seven-stage process into three more comprehensive stages: *fact-finding* (emphasizing problem definition and preparation), *idea-finding* (idea production and development), and *solution-finding* (evaluating and adopting a final solution).

Osborn (1965) was strongly committed to the mission of promoting a more creative trend in American education. As a result, he began to focus more directly on applying his view of CPS in the educational arena. In doing so, he began to work with his new colleague, Sidney Parnes. Together their goal was to enhance students' ability to understand and apply their personal creativity in all aspects of their lives. Parnes continued to work with the CPS process after Osborn's death in 1966. Parnes and his colleagues developed and tested experimentally a modification of Osborn's approach (Parnes, 1967a, b). This five-stage revision of Osborn's original framework was comprised of *fact-finding, problem-finding, idea-finding, solution-finding,* and *acceptance-finding.* This version of CPS was tested experimentally in programmed instructional format with secondary school students, through a grant project on "Programming Creative Behavior" (Parnes, 1966).

This version of CPS was also tested in an extensive, two year experimental program called the Creative Studies Project at Buffalo State College. The Creative Studies Project built on Osborn's earlier work as well as his collaboration with Parnes and others, and established an important academic instructional program. The project began with a pilot program at Buffalo State College in 1969, and included a four semester series of creative studies courses for the experimental group. This two-year experimental project provided empirical support for the courses' effectiveness and led the college to approve them for regular credit-bearing elective status in 1972 (Noller & Parnes, 1972; Parnes & Noller, 1972 a, b; Parnes & Noller, 1973a, 1973b, 1974; Parnes, 1987; Reese, Treffinger, Parnes & Kaltsounis, 1976).

The instructional program came to be known as the Osborn-Parnes approach to creative problem solving. The approach is well-established, and has been the focus of research and reviews by many other scholars (e.g., Basadur, Graen & Green, 1982; Rose & Lin, 1984; Torrance, 1972, 1986 & 1987). The materials used for the Creative Studies Project included Parnes' (1967a, b) books, *Creative Behavior Guidebook* and *Creative Behavior Workbook* which were drawn from earlier development efforts. The framework was eclectic in its evolution and development, drawing tools and methods from several other creativity and problem solving models and methods. Most of the initial descriptions of CPS consisted primarily or entirely of prose or text descriptions of processes and techniques. One of the first visual or graphic depictions of CPS appeared in Parnes' (1967b) workbook as a printed insert. The image in Figure 1 became the first in a series of graphic illustrations of CPS and provided an initial departure from the more common prose descriptions of CPS.

Ruth Noller worked with Parnes and others in subsequent extensions, revisions, and applications of the early five-step model (e.g., Noller, 1979; Noller, Heintz, & Blaeuer, 1978; Noller, Parnes, & Biondi, 1976; Noller, Treffinger, & Houseman, 1979; Parnes, Noller, & Biondi, 1977). These efforts resulted in the alternative graphic illustration of the five-step CPS model presented in Figure 2.

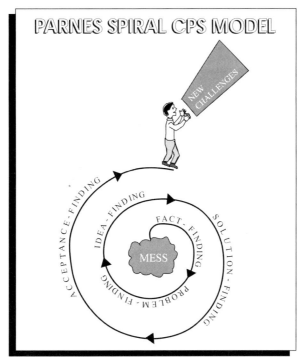

Figure 1: Parnes Spiral Graphic (1967b)

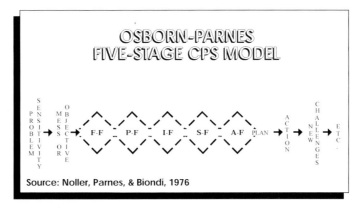

Figure 2: Osborn/Parnes Five Stage CPS Model

This new graphic depiction of CPS illustrated for the first time the alternation of divergent and convergent thinking in the CPS process. However, the graphic also conveyed an image of the creative process as a strictly linear and sequential series of stages. It suggested that CPS always begins at the same starting point (a "mess"), and then involves working through all of the five stages in order, ending with an action plan and being ready for new challenges. Although this is one possible pathway through the creative process, it is limiting in its depiction of people's natural creative problem-solving behavior. During this time period specific definitions of CPS also began to be proposed. Parnes, Noller & Biondi (1977) equated CPS to creative decision making and described it by suggesting:

> ...we first speculate on what "might be".... we sense and anticipate all conceivable consequences or repercussions... and we choose and develop our best alternative in full awareness. (p. 14)

Noller (1979) defined Creative Problem Solving by focusing on each of the three main words: creative, problem, and solving.

> By creative we mean: having an element of newness and being relevant at least to you, the one who creates the solution. By problem we mean: any situation which presents a challenge, offers an opportunity, or is a concern to you. By solving we mean: devising ways to answer or to meet or satisfy the problem, adapting yourself to the situation or adapting the situation to yourself. Creative Problem Solving or CPS is a process, a method, a system for approaching a problem in an imaginative way resulting in effective action. (pp. 4-5)

Treffinger, Isaksen, and Firestien (1982) recognized the importance of insuring that the CPS framework provided for deliberate balance between *divergent* and *convergent* thinking tools. At the time, most of the tools in the CPS framework (as well as the instructional emphasis) were divergent in focus. As a result, Treffinger, Isaksen, and Firestien undertook a number of efforts to provide deliberate tools for converging, and to translate the goal of "dynamic balance" between creative thinking and critical thinking (or "imagination and judgment," as often described in the programs of the time) into more concrete reality in practice. From their experiences with business and educational groups, Firestien and Treffinger (1983) also began to explore the importance of a clear understanding of the identity of the client or "problem owner" when using CPS. At this time we described CPS with a graphic depiction in which the stages remained the same, but the visual representation shifted from a horizontal to a vertical layout.

The Osborn-Parnes CPS approach provided a rich historical foundation for research. Some of the earliest studies conducted by Parnes and his associates evaluated the effects of creative problem solving programs and methods (Meadow & Parnes, 1959; Meadow, Parnes & Reese, 1959; Parnes, 1961 & 1963; Parnes & Meadow, 1959 & 1960). This approach continued to be widely diffused in the 1970's and 1980's in the academic programs at Buffalo State College and through a variety of workshops, institutes and seminars throughout the world.

Parnes (1981) continued to popularize this approach to CPS as well as integrate its use with concepts such as imagery and visualization (e.g., Parnes, 1988). He also continued to provide resource materials for those interested in facilitating CPS, and he wrote a fifty-year summary of the literature surrounding the deliberate development of creativity (Parnes, 1992).

Moving Beyond "Osborn-Parnes CPS"

The Osborn-Parnes tradition was founded and developed for many years through the productive involvement of both researchers and practitioners. Many important and significant contributions to the development, understanding, and use of CPS took place with the Osborn-Parnes tradition of CPS. These included developing a deliberate process for nurturing creative behavior, documenting the effectiveness of CPS training, establishing an academically-based CPS instructional program, developing an extensive network of informed CPS professionals, and disseminating a variety of support materials and resources.

However, a number of important challenges also faced the Osborn-Parnes tradition. The entire approach was widely perceived as involving only divergence, and sometimes equated entirely with brainstorming. Some enthusiasts viewed CPS as a kind of creativity cure-all: it would be good for any "ailment" or task. Referred to as "the process," CPS was revered by some proponents with a zeal that approached religious fervor. The umbrella of CPS sometimes seemed to expand, and expand, and expand—bringing under it a wide and diverse array of theories, tools, and techniques, in which anything attached to the term "creative" might somehow also be incorporated into creative problem solving.

Some practitioners or facilitators were naturally better than others in applying the methods effectively, but skilled CPS performance was generally a matter of intuition, common wisdom, and good faith "trying hard," rather than a challenge for carefully-planned and implemented development in relation to a well-defined, research-based set of competencies.

Despite informal admonitions to the contrary, CPS was commonly treated as a process "run through," in which any session consisted of a complete, linear, sequential application of all five stages. Given such a prescriptive, regimented view of the process, there was often more emphasis on using every step than on the intended outcomes or the appropriate process steps to help attain them. As a result, it was not uncommon to have marathon sessions lasting for many long hours until fatigue set in for everyone. Not surprisingly, then, many CPS users voiced serious concerns, especially about the possibility of "overkill" or ineffectiveness stemming from process sessions that often seemed endless.

On the other hand, the same users also reported that they could, and did, use a few stages or techniques more effectively by being selective. By far the most significant challenge facing the tradition was the need to improve our understanding of what methods worked for whom, and under what circumstances (Isaksen, 1987).

Linking Task, Person, and Situation with Process

Despite major advancements in research and development, the CPS process remained fundamentally unchanged in conceptual design and approach from 1967 through the early 1980's. Isaksen & Treffinger (1985) began to modify the Osborn-Parnes approach to CPS and also employed a new graphic representation and new text; that version of CPS is presented in Figure 3.

Isaksen and Treffinger began by adding a deliberate Mess-Finding stage at the "front end" of CPS. This stage included the personal *orientation* of the problem solver, the setting in which the work takes place (or situational *outlook),* and several important aspects of the task on which people would be working. Mess-Finding also highlighted the importance of recognizing important *outcomes* and *obstacles* that would influence the use and impact of CPS in any group or setting, and clarified the nature and importance of *ownership* in applying CPS (including influence, interest, and imagination).

As the next development, the authors renamed the Fact-Finding stage: it became Data-Finding. Effective problem solving requires people to consider more than facts as important influences when they are defining and solving problems. They recognized, for example, that feelings, impressions, observations, and questions were also important. The creative opportunity or challenge in a task often pertains as much or more to what might be unknown, uncertain, or unclear than to the indisputable "facts" of the situation.

This version of CPS also emphasized an on going and dynamic balance between creative and critical thinking. Creative thinking involves making and expressing meaningful new connections, perceiving gaps, challenges or concerns, thinking of many varied or unusual possibilities, and elaborating and extending alternatives. Critical thinking involves analyzing, evaluating, refining, organizing, or developing options.

To emphasize the flexible application of CPS, Isaksen and Treffinger (1985) also introduced the analogy of "buckets" to describe the six CPS stages. Each stage might be viewed as a container filled with ideas, methods, and tools that could be used to assist people with their problem-solving efforts. If a particular tool or method did not work, the problem solver could reach back into the bucket and try a different one. The analogy suggested that the six stages might be rearranged, excluded or included as necessary, based upon the problem-solver's needs.

Although Isaksen and Treffinger emphasized the flexible nature of CPS in this version, they eventually realized that its graphic representation continued to present

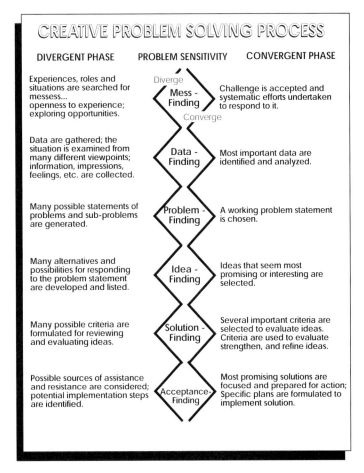

Figure 3: CPS as Presented by Isaksen & Treffinger (1985)

some challenges for us, and for others who worked with the model. The 1985 view of process seemed to suggest an image of CPS as a one-way "gravity feed" process in which problems were dropped in at the top and creative solutions emerged at the bottom. It became apparent that tension was building between the researchers' *intent* of describing CPS as a flexible framework, identifying stages of creative and critical thinking, and the *reality* of the graphic illustration, apparently continuing to present CPS as a framework prescribing a pre-set series of steps and stages. The graphic presentation of the framework, which became for some people an icon for the process, was not consistent with the flexibility of behavior that we knew was important for effective application of CPS.

Isaksen and Treffinger (1987) concluded that the new process modifications (adding more explicit emphasis on the front-end of CPS, with the clarification of three social roles of facilitator, client and resource group) made it nearly impossible to "run through" the entire process in one setting. This finding was also confirmed by examining how people actually applied CPS in real problem-solving situations. Isaksen and Treffinger noticed that people did not generally apply all six stages together at one time. Instead, they often used any of the six stages independently, based on their personal assessment of how the stages might naturally help them to deal with a certain task or challenge. As a result, it appeared that people used CPS to clarify their understanding of problems, generate ideas, and/or plan for taking action. One of the results of this separate use of "pieces" of the process was that people often failed to recognize that they were still using CPS. A common reaction was, "Oh, I don't really *do* CPS... I just use some parts of it."

Therefore, Isaksen and Treffinger concluded that the six stages of CPS could in fact be clustered and divided into three main components of problem-solving activity. As a result, they changed their description of the CPS framework to make it more workable and to reflect more accurately how it was actually being used by practitioners (Isaksen & Treffinger, 1987). The new description organized the six stages into three main components of activity based on how they were used naturally. Those three components were *Understanding the Problem* (which included Mess-Finding, Data-Finding and Problem-Finding), *Generating Ideas* (Idea-Finding) and *Planning for Action* (Solution and Acceptance-Finding). The component titles were added to clarify the view that the framework could be used flexibly as components, and the CPS graphic was modified to distinguish the components from one another more carefully; this version is illustrated in Figure 4.

The three components provided a convenient organizer for many kinds of CPS applications. The changes were reported in several articles, chapters, and course manuals (e.g., Isaksen, 1989; Isaksen & Treffinger, 1991; Treffinger & Isaksen, 1992). Although the new depiction of CPS had a componential focus, the process graphic continued to emphasize a linear series of stages. This approach, and a resultant instructional manual (Isaksen, 1989), were used as the basis for academic and public programs, seminars and workshops, and in our consulting, facilitation and training work with a variety of clients in our private practices. Isaksen and Treffinger focused on maintaining and disseminating a current understanding of CPS and its application, with on going refinement and continuous improvement (e.g., Isaksen & Treffinger, 1991; Treffinger & Isaksen, 1992).

The presentation of CPS as three components marked a transition away from a linear, six-step approach toward a more flexible componential approach. It is interesting to note, of course, that this direction was consistent with the view of CPS held by Osborn in 1967; in some ways, it is still true that, "the more things change, the more they stay the same."

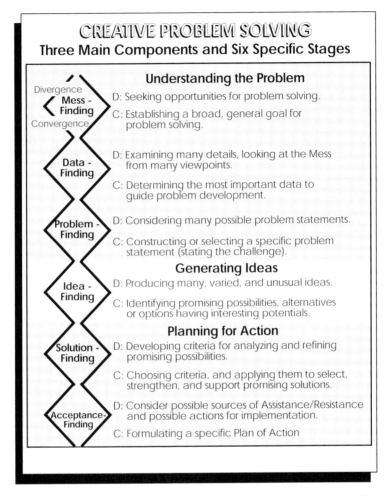

Figure 4: A Linear View of Six Stages and Three Components (Isaksen & Treffinger, 1987)

A Shifting Paradigm: Expanding a Descriptive Approach to CPS

By 1989, research had begun to examine deliberately the challenges associated with the graphic depiction of CPS and the impact of the presentation of the process on people's understanding of the nature and dynamics of effective CPS applications. Pershyn (1992) conducted a study in which he examined how people described their natural approach to solving problems. Subjects whose creativity style preference would be described as innovators (Kirton, 1987) more frequently described their process as non-linear, more complex, random and contiguous than those of subjects whose style preference was adaptive. Adaptors were more likely to draw processes that were linear, orderly and targeted. They also tended to include fewer stages as well as fewer end points. There were many similarities between the historical views of CPS described in this Chapter and the processes characterized in Pershyn's research as linear and sequential. Pershyn's findings suggested that effective, natural problem solving took a variety of forms and that the process graphic used to describe CPS would be more powerful and effective if it took these differences into account.

As a result, the graphic depiction of CPS was altered substantially by Isaksen & Dorval (1993a). The change initially envisioned in 1985 through the "buckets" analogy was amplified and extended in 1989 with a three component view, and then, as represented in Figure 5, the framework was broken apart completely in 1993, with a total shift in graphic depiction.

Research on the graphic depiction of natural approaches to problem solving validated the need to take a different approach to representing CPS. Given the dynamic nature of natural problem solving, it was important that the depiction of CPS be more representative of a wider array of problem-solving approaches. From experiences with the teaching and learning of CPS, researchers and developers found that identifying a common set of graphic depictions and language that was useful for sharing and discussing creative problem solving might be more appropriate than trying to identify THE one creative process. Therefore, Isaksen and Dorval's (1993a) representation of CPS, presented in Figure 5, provided separate symbols for each of the three main components (Understanding the Problem, Generating Ideas and Planning for

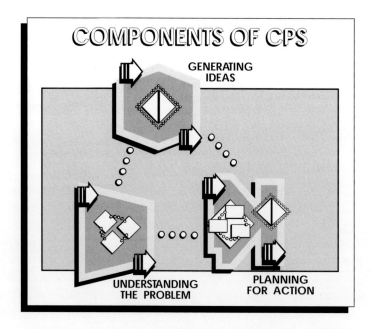

Figure 5: Components of CPS (Isaksen & Dorval, 1993a)

Action). The graphics were intended to portray the dynamic relationship between and among the CPS components and stages. Each component involved *inputs, processing,* and *outputs,* to help understand when and how the component might be used most appropriately. Although this representation of CPS was gleaned in many ways from powerful elements of the Osborn-Parnes tradition, its view no longer employed that framework. It represented a significant new pathway for research and practice, and although it stemmed from the rich heritage of prior versions, it represented a journey in very new directions.

A Contemporary Approach to Creative Problem Solving

Isaksen and Dorval (1993b) began to outline new ways and directions for framing and documenting a descriptive, and less prescriptive, understanding of CPS. 'Descriptive' means an approach to process that provides a flexible framework in which problem solvers have many choices and make them on the basis of observation, experience, context, and deliberate analysis of the task (or metacognition). By contrast, 'prescriptive' means an approach in which people learn and apply a predetermined or fixed set of steps or stages, for which there are specified approaches and outcomes that have been determined by custom, tradition, or reliance on expertise.

Viewing CPS as a descriptive framework implied that the components, stages, and phases of CPS might be used in a variety of different orders or sequences. Sometimes problem solvers might not need all the steps, and there might be tasks for which other methods might be just as effective as CPS, or perhaps even better choices! This approach did not view CPS as a panacea that should be applied to every task, nor as a magic formula or a religious dogma that must be accepted and applied in the same way, without departing from prescribed procedures, each time it is used. None of its developers or researchers received the CPS stages carved on stone tablets!

These issues led researchers and practitioners in new directions. As a result of several years of continuing work, Isaksen, Dorval and Treffinger presented a contemporary, natural, flexible, and descriptive version of CPS. They added a new refinement: the metacomponents of Task Appraisal and Process Planning (Isaksen, Dorval, & Treffinger, 1994; Treffinger, Isaksen, & Dorval, 1994a). This representation of CPS is depicted in Figure 6.

Metacomponents involve continuing to plan, monitor, manage, and modify behavior during CPS. Task Appraisal concerns determining whether or not CPS is appropriate for a given task, and whether modifications of one's approach might be necessary. During Task Appraisal individuals or groups consider the key people, the desired outcome, the characteristics of the situation, and the possible methods for handling the task. Task Appraisal enables them to assess the extent to which CPS might be appropriate—their method of choice, as it were—for addressing a given task or for managing change in appropriate ways (Isaksen, 1996).

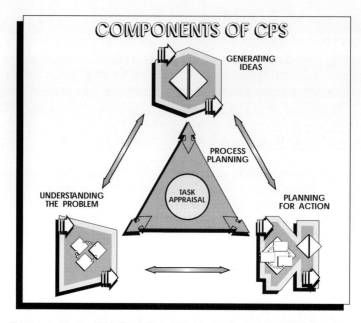

Figure 6:   Components of CPS Including Task Appraisal and Process Planning (Isaksen, Dorval, & Treffinger, 1994a)

If the person or group determines that CPS does offer relevant and helpful tools for working on a task, they then turn to Process Planning to plan their entry point into the framework, our pathway through the framework, and our appropriate exit from the framework. Since the approach is natural, descriptive and flexible, rather than fixed or prescriptive, Process Planning helps them to manage a number of important choices and decisions up front.

The contemporary view (Isaksen, Dorval & Treffinger, 1994, Treffinger, Isaksen, & Dorval, 1994a, 1994b, 2000) presents CPS as a broadly applicable framework that provides an organizing system for specific tools to help design and develop new and useful outcomes. Through this system productive thinking tools can be applied to understanding problems and opportunities, generating many varied and unusual ideas, and evaluating, developing and implementing potential solutions. CPS functions to transform tasks, needs and inputs into meaningful and valuable outcomes. CPS enables individuals and groups to recognize and act on opportunities, respond to challenges and overcome concerns.

The Understanding the Problem component includes a systematic effort to define, construct, or focus problem-solving efforts. It includes the three stages of Mess-Finding, Data-Finding and Problem-Finding. The Generating Ideas component includes coming up with many varied or unusual options in order to address or respond to a problem. This component has only one stage called Idea-Finding. The Planning for

Action component of CPS is used to make decisions about, develop or strengthen promising alternatives and plan for their successful implementation. The two stages included in the component are called Solution-Finding and Acceptance-Finding. The task and setting are continuously monitored in order to guide choices or decisions regarding the selection of appropriate components, specific stages, or specific tools for any stage.

Conclusion: CPS Yesterday, Today, and Tomorrow

Although theories, models, and prescriptions for creative problem solving abound in the literature of the social and behavioral sciences, few approaches can demonstrate the sustained heritage of theory, research, development, and application that characterize CPS. The richness and power of any process arise from sustained scholarship and implementation by many people, across many contexts, and over sustained periods of time. While the heritage provides strong "roots" for the process, the history of CPS is also a tale of both adaptive growth (a story of gradual and incremental but continuous refinement and improvement) and innovative development (breaking new ground and opening new directions and perspectives). Recent advances helped to "customize" the process and its applications, enabling individuals or groups to avoid wasting energy and efforts on "steps," activities, or tools they do not really need, and contributing to making CPS a flexible, user-friendly, and powerful process for individuals and groups of all ages.

Even though CPS has helped individuals and groups to make a creative difference for more than four decades, many important challenges remain for imaginative but disciplined research and development. Continuing research, development, and evaluation of all CPS components, stages, tools, and metacognitive elements will be needed to assure that the framework continues to be a powerful and productive set of tools that will continue to help make important differences for decades to come. Some of these needed developments are already unfolding and will be described in future publications.

References

Basadur, M. S., Graen, G. B. & Green, S. G. (1982). Training in creative problem solving: Effects on ideation and problem finding in an industrial research organization. *Organizational Behavior and Human Performance, 30*, 41-70.

Chislett, L. M. (1994). Integrating the creative problem solving and schoolwide enrichment models to enhance creative productivity. *Roeper Review, 17* (1), 4-7.

Cramond, B., Martin, C. E., & Shaw, E. L. (1990). Generalizability of creative problem solving procedures to real-life problems. *Journal for the Education of the Gifted, 12* (2), 141-155.

Firestien, R. & Treffinger, D. (1983). Ownership and converging: Essential ingredients of creative problem solving. *Journal of Creative Behavior, 17* (1), 32-38.

Isaksen, S. G. (Ed.). (1987). *Frontiers of creativity research: Beyond the basics.* Buffalo, NY: Bearly Limited.

Isaksen, S. G. (1989). *Creative problem solving: A process for creativity.* Buffalo, NY: Center for Studies in Creativity.

Isaksen, S. G. (1996). Task appraisal and process planning: Managing change methods. *International Creativity Network Newsletter, 6* (1), 4-11.

Isaksen, S. G. (1998). Transforming dreams into reality: The power of creative problem solving. In: D. J. Treffinger & K. W. McCluskey (Eds.), *Teaching for talent development: Current and expanding perspectives.* (pp. 35-44). Sarasota, FL: Center for Creative Learning.

Isaksen, S. G. & Dorval, K. B. (1993a). Changing views of CPS: Over 40 years of continuous improvement. *International Creativity Network, 3,* 1-5.

Isaksen, S. G. & Dorval, K. B. (1993b). Toward an improved understanding of creativity within people: The level-style distinction. In S. G. Isaksen, M. C. Murdock, R. L. Firestien, & D. J. Treffinger, (Eds.), *Understanding and recognizing creativity: The emergence of a discipline* (pp. 299-330). Norwood, NJ: Ablex.

Isaksen, S. G., Dorval, K. B., Noller, R. B. & Firestien, R. L. (1993). The dynamic nature of creative problem solving. In S. S. Gryskiewicz (Ed.), *Discovering creativity: Proceedings of the 1992 International Creativity and Networking Conference* (pp. 155-162). Greensboro, NC: Center for Creative Leadership.

Isaksen, S. G., Dorval, K. B. & Treffinger, D. J. (1994). *Creative approaches to problem solving.* Dubuque, IA: Kendall/Hunt.

Isaksen, S. G., Murdock, M. C., Firestien, R. L. & Treffinger, D. J. (Eds.). (1993a). *Understanding and recognizing creativity: The emergence of a discipline.* Norwood, NJ: Ablex.

Isaksen, S. G., Murdock, M. C., Firestien, R. L. & Treffinger, D. J. (Eds.). (1993b). *Nurturing and developing creativity: Emergence of a discipline.* Norwood, NJ: Ablex.

Isaksen, S. G. & Treffinger, D. J. (1985). *Creative problem solving: The basic course.* Buffalo, NY: Bearly Limited.

Isaksen, S. G. & Treffinger, D. J. (1987). *Creative problem solving: Three components and six specific stages.* Instructional handout. Buffalo, NY: Center for Studies in Creativity.

Isaksen, S. G. & Treffinger, D. J. (1991). Creative learning and problem solving. In A. L. Costa (Ed.). *Developing minds: Programs for teaching thinking* (Volume 2, pp. 89-93). Alexandria, VA: Association for Supervision and Curriculum Development.

Isaksen, S. G., Treffinger, D. J., & Dorval, K. B. (1997). *The Creative Problem Solving framework: An historical perspective.* Sarasota, FL: Center for Creative Learning.

Kirton, M. J. (1987). Adaptors and innovators: Cognitive style and personality. In S. Isaksen (Ed.), *Frontiers of creativity research: Beyond the basics* (pp. 282-304). Buffalo, NY: Bearly Limited.

Meadow, A. & Parnes, S. J. (1959). Evaluation of training in creative problem solving. *Journal of Applied Psychology, 43,* 189-194.

Meadow, A., Parnes, S. J. & Reese, H. (1959). Influences of brainstorming instructions and problem sequence on a creative problem solving test. *Journal of Applied Psychology, 43,* 413-416.

Noller, R. B. (1979). *Scratching the surface of creative problem solving: A bird's eye view of CPS.* Buffalo, NY: DOK.

Noller, R. B., Heintz, R., & Blaeuer, D. (1978). *Creative problem solving in mathematics.* Buffalo, NY: DOK.

Noller, R. B. & Parnes, S. J. (1972). Applied creativity: The creative studies project, Part III - The curriculum. *Journal of Creative Behavior, 6,* 275-294.

Noller, R. B., Parnes, S. J. & Biondi, A. M. (1976). *Creative actionbook.* New York: Scribners.

Noller, R. B., Treffinger, D. J., & Houseman, E. D. (1979). *It's a gas to be gifted: CPS for the gifted and talented.* Buffalo, NY: DOK.

Osborn, A. F. (1952). *Wake up your mind: 101 ways to develop creativeness.* New York: Charles Scribner's Sons.

Osborn, A. F. (1953, 1957, 1963, 1967). *Applied imagination: Principles and procedures of creative thinking.* New York: Charles Scribner's Sons.

Osborn, A. F. (1965). *The creative trend in education.* Buffalo, NY: Creative Education Foundation.

Parnes, S. J. (1961). Effects of extended effort in creative problem-solving. *Journal of Educational Psychology, 52,* 117-122.

Parnes, S. J. (1963). The deferment-of-judgment principle: A clarification of the literature. *Psychological Reports, 12,* 521-522.

Parnes, S. J. (1966). *Programming creative behavior.* Buffalo, NY: State University of New York at Buffalo, Final Report of NDEA Title VII Project #5-0716, Grant #7-42-1630-213.

Parnes, S. J. (1967a). *Creative behavior guidebook.* New York: Scribners.

Parnes, S. J. (1967b). *Creative behavior workbook.* New York: Scribners.

Parnes, S. J. (1981). *The magic of your mind.* Buffalo, NY: Creative Education Foundation.

Parnes, S. J. (1987). The creative studies project. In S. Isaksen (Ed.), *Frontiers of creativity research: Beyond the basics* (pp. 156-188). Buffalo, NY: Bearly Limited.

Parnes, S. J. (1988). *Visionizing.* Buffalo, NY: DOK Publishers.

Parnes, S. J. (Ed). (1992). *Source book for creative problem solving.* Buffalo, NY: The Creative Education Foundation Press.

Parnes, S. J., & Meadow, A. (1959). Effects of brainstorming instruction on creative problem solving by trained and untrained subjects. *Journal of Educational Psychology, 50,* 171-176.

Parnes, S. J. & Meadow, A. (1960). Evaluation of persistence of effects produced by a creative problem solving course. *Psychological Reports, 7,* 357-361.

Parnes, S. J. & Noller, R. B. (1972a). Applied creativity: The creative studies project, Part I - The development. *Journal of Creative Behavior, 6,* 1-22.

Parnes, S. J. & Noller, R. B. (1972b). Applied creativity: The creative studies project, Part II - Results of the two-year program. *Journal of Creative Behavior, 6,* 164-186.

Parnes, S. J. & Noller, R. B. (1973a). Applied creativity: The creative studies project: Part IV—Personality findings and conclusions. *Journal of Creative Behavior, 7,* 15-36.

Parnes, S. J. & Noller, R. B. (1973b). *Toward supersanity: Channeled freedom.* Buffalo, NY: DOK.

Parnes, S. J. & Noller, R. B. (1974). *Toward supersanity: Channeled freedom. (Research Supplement).* Buffalo, NY: DOK.

Parnes, S. J., Noller, R. B. & Biondi, A. M. (1977). *Guide to creative action.* New York: Scribners.

Pershyn, G. (1992). *An investigation into the graphic depictions of natural creative problem solving processes.* Unpublished Masters Thesis. State University College at Buffalo: Center for Studies in Creativity.

Reese, H. W., Treffinger, D. J., Parnes, S. J. & Kaltsounis, G. (1976). Effects of a creative studies program on structure of intellect factors. *Journal of Educational Psychology, 68,* 401-410.

Rose, L. H., & Lin, H. (1984). A meta-analysis of long-term creativity training programs. *Journal of Creative Behavior, 11,* 124-130.

Schack, G. D. (1993). Effects of a creative problem solving curriculum on students of varying ability levels. *Gifted Child Quarterly, 37,* 32-38.

Stein, M. I. (1975). *Stimulating creativity. Volume II: Group procedures.* New York: Academic Press.

Todd, S. M., & Larson, A. (1992). In what ways might statewide advocates for gifted and talented education coordinate and focus their efforts? *Gifted Child Quarterly, 36* (3), 160-164.

Torrance, E. P. (1972). Can we teach children to think creatively? *Journal of Creative Behavior, 6,* 236-262.

Torrance, E. P. (1986). Teaching creative and gifted learners. In M. C. Wittrock (Ed.). *Handbook of Research on Teaching* (pp. 630-647). New York: Macmillan.

Torrance, E. P. (1987). Teaching for creativity. In S. G. Isaksen (Ed.), *Frontiers in creativity research: Beyond the basics* (pp. 189-215). Buffalo, NY: Bearly Limited.

Treffinger, D. J. (1995). Creative problem solving: Overview and educational implications. *Educational Psychology Review, 7* (3), 301-312.

Treffinger, D. J., Cross, J. A., Feldhusen, J. F., Isaksen, S. G., Remle, R. C., & Sortore, M. (1993). *Handbook of productive thinking. Volume 1: Rationale, criteria, and reviews.* Sarasota, FL: Center for Creative Learning.

Treffinger, D. J. & Isaksen, S. G. (1992). *Creative problem solving: An introduction.* Sarasota, FL: Center for Creative Learning.

Treffinger, D. J., Isaksen, S. G., & Dorval, K. B. (1994a). *Creative problem solving: An introduction.* (Rev. ed.). Sarasota, FL: Center for Creative Learning.

Treffinger, D. J., Isaksen, S. G., & Dorval, K. B. (1994b). Creative problem solving: An overview. In M. A. Runco (Ed.), *Problem finding, problem solving, and creativity* (pp. 223-236). Norwood, NJ: Ablex.

Treffinger, D. J., Isaksen, S. G., & Dorval, K. B. (2000). *Creative problem solving: An introduction.* (3rd ed.). Waco, TX: Prufrock Press.

Treffinger, D. J., Isaksen, S. G. & Firestien, R. L. (1982). *Handbook for creative learning.* Sarasota, FL: Center for Creative Learning.

Treffinger, D. J., Isaksen, S. G., & Young, G. C. (1998). Brainstorming: Myths and realities. *National Inventive Thinking Association Newsletter, 9* (3), 1,4-5+7.

Treffinger, D. J., Sortore, M., & Cross, J. (1993). Programs and strategies for nurturing creativity. In: K. A. Heller, F. J. Mönks, & A. H. Passow (Eds.), *International handbook of research and development of giftedness and talent.* (pp. 555-567). Oxford: Pergamon.

VanGundy (1988). *Techniques of structured problem solving* (2nd ed.). New York: Van Nostrand Reinhold Company.

Wallas, G. (1926). *The art of thought.* New York: Harcourt Brace.

CHAPTER THREE

FACILITATING CREATIVE PROBLEM SOLVING

Scott G. Isaksen
and
K. Brian Dorval
Creative Problem Solving Group — Buffalo

> "If anyone desires to be first, the same shall be last of all,
> and servant of all."
> **Jesus the Christ,** *Mark 9:35*

INTRODUCTION

If you were asked to name the inventors of the telephone, airplane, or light bulb, you would probably experience little difficulty in recalling the names of Bell, the Wright brothers, or Edison. In contrast many people experience difficulty in naming the "inventor" of the 747 jumbo jet, the 800 inward watts number, or the silicon chip. Aside from the major differences in level of inventiveness and how much more current the latter three products are, a major difference between these two categories is that the more recent products have been the result of group creativity.

All types of organizations recognize the growing importance of group creativity (Freedman, 1988; Kuhn, 1988). The need for organizations to be competitive and to focus on increasing levels of complexity and change has forced managers, administrators, and others who are concerned with the future viability of our places of work to deal with innovation and creativity (Hamel & Prahalad, 1994). Although many think of creativity primarily as an individual affair, there is a need to examine the application of this personal power within the context of groups. Creativity in groups and in individuals is not an either/or affair. When you are concerned with facilitating group creativity you must simultaneously be able to address the issue of promoting individual creativity.

The purpose of this chapter is to examine the role of the facilitator as one who provides facilitative leadership when applying Creative Problem Solving (CPS) in groups. It will examine a model to help you understand and manage the different roles involved in the application of CPS. In particular, this chapter will examine seven key clusters of qualities associated with what a facilitator knows, does, and believes, when applying CPS. This CPS facilitator "skillbase" will be relevant when applying CPS at a personal level, as well as when applying CPS in a group or organizational setting.

THE FACILITATOR: PROCESS-ORIENTED INCLUSIVE LEADERSHIP

We believe the role of the facilitator is a leadership role — however not in the conventional or popular sense. The facilitator role is different from the view of the lone herioc leader at the top of the organization. Facilitation is process-oriented leadership that involves interactions among two or more people. It is an inclusive role that involves sharing leadership with others in ways that help them get their needs met. To understand what we mean by process-oriented inclusive leadership, let us examine each element and what it entails.

The Facilitator

There are a variety of popular conceptions and misconceptions about the word "facilitator." We often ask participants in our training courses what is meant by the word "facilitator" in their organization. We hear how facilitators are viewed as nothing more than meeting planners, logistics people, passive supporters who respond to emergent needs, or even flipchart secretaries who record the content of what is discussed during a meeting. In worst-case scenarios, facilitators are seen as simply cheerleaders to energize groups or as "scapegoats" to blame when a meeting is not productive (see Figure 1).

These perceptions reflect some of the key issues people face when taking on the role of facilitator. Perceptions like these can result in barriers to using facilitative leadership skills. The two greatest barriers we typically find are the lack of management support, and poor organizational climate or culture. Managers can create resistance or even refuse to let course participants use the skills they developed during training. Newly trained facilitators have heard comments like, *"You can facilitate, as long as you get your real work done."* It is unlikely that a facilitative approach to leadership will be effective in groups or organizations where this is the prevailing attitude.

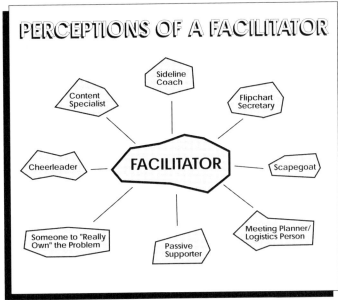

Figure 1:   Common Perceptions of a Facilitator

There are also some responses from participants where facilitators are said to have valuable roles, such as project managers. In some situations, organizations have dedicated facilitation teams that provide a variety of support services. However, we explore perceptions of facilitators with participants to help prepare them for how they might be received when re-entering their organization. We also use the results of these discussions to set up a dialogue about effective facilitation.

It is interesting to ask newly trained facilitators what someone in a facilitator role needs to know, do, and believe, in order to facilitate groups effectively. Usually, the reaction is surprise about the amount of things to which effective facilitators pay attention. When asked to explain further, they suggest facilitators need to know when and how to use a range of creativity methods, tools, and techniques. They need to know how to manage group dynamics and how to clarify and move a group toward the desired outcomes. They need to be able to intervene on unproductive behaviors and manage the process itself while establishing a climate for creativity. They also need to use their belief in the power of the process and the creative potential of the group to keep a group engaged during tough times.

Our hope when we use these activities during training is to help people develop a productive and comprehensive understanding and appreciation of the role and responsibilities of an effective facilitator. There are other characteristics to the role that are important to address as well. Facilitation is about process-oriented inclusive leadership.

Process-Oriented

"Process-Oriented" means that the focus of the facilitator role is on understanding, planning, and managing process. The process we refer to is the creative process, and more specifically, CPS. Therefore, when we use the word process, we mean much more than simply using "tools." Process means focusing on "how" things get done. This includes focusing on the overall change process in a group or organization and the specific details associated with planning specific meetings, workshops, etc.

Process orientation means paying attention to how people are involved in the change process and the way they interact with each other — both what they say and how they say it. It means focusing on the environment or situation in which people are thinking and working to ensure it is conducive to using creativity and making change. Process orientation also means ensuring people have a clear understanding of the purpose and desired outcome from the application of CPS. It also means identifying, preparing, and using methods, approaches and, yes, tools that enable people to do their best work in accomplishing the desired outcome.

CPS facilitators orient themselves toward these issues and let the content or topic of the work be driven by the client(s). They focus their expertise on understanding and managing the use of CPS. They use this knowledge to plan where to enter and exit the CPS framework, what language to use to encourage different forms of thinking, and what tools to use in order to focus a group on accomplishing particular outcomes. They also know when to say no to applying CPS and when to suggest alternative methods for effecting change.

Inclusive Leadership

Inclusive leadership is a concept that has emerged from a variety of research projects. One is the *Innovation Survey* conducted by PricewaterhouseCoopers (Davis, et. al, 1998). The research examined the gaps between the most innovative companies and the lowest performers among the Times 1000 organizations in the United Kingdom. The goal was to understand what "best practices" were used to drive organizational innovation. One of the findings was that three basic capabilities distinguished the top 20% of those organizations (who earned the highest percentage of turnover from new products and services) from the bottom 20% (see Figure 2). Those capabilities are: taking an inclusive approach to leadership, building a creative climate, and having deliberate processes for applying creativity. The top 5% of the Times 1000 organizations focused on these capabilities to an even greater extent.

One powerful message from this research is that those organizations that are most effective at driving innovation focus on *all three* areas at the same time, not just on one or two. Although all three are relevant to our thinking about CPS facilitators, inclusive leadership best characterizes what we mean by the role of facilitator. Organiza-

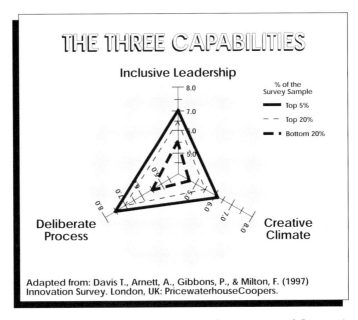

Figure 2: Three Capabilities for Driving Organizational Innovation

tions in the top 20 percent had the philosophy that leadership was everyone's business, and that the best ideas in the organization could come from anyone at any level, not just the top leadership group. If you walked into these organizations, you would have some difficulty determining who the formal "leader" was, because the lines between leaders and followers are muddled. Leadership and followership were balanced, in that each person could take a leadership or followership role, depending on the particular work being done. Leadership responsibility was shared with everyone in the organization.

Whether you talk about a professional setting in business, education, not-for-profit organizations, or the personal life of the family, we believe the facilitator role involves inclusive leadership in much the same way. It involves sharing leadership responsibilities with others. Facilitators take leadership responsibility for managing process, while others take leadership in guiding the direction of change efforts and the quality of thinking necessary to accomplish change. Still others take leadership responsibility to provide input, suggestions, and feedback to those leading change or guiding the process. These forms of leadership exist whether you are involved in setting a strategic vision for a global company, planning the curriculum for a local school district, or deciding on where to take the family for the holidays.

Facilitators use their leadership to serve the needs of others. The process they manage is subservient to the topic being addressed or the change being planned. In order to exert effective process-oriented leadership, facilitators must understand what the group needs in order for them, as facilitators, to make decisions about the process. This is most closely associated with Greenleaf's (1991) concept of servant leadership, as described in the introductory chapter, The Story Behind this Book.

Facilitators use their leadership to help others create extraordinary levels of accomplishment in much the same way as that described by Kouses and Posner in *The Leadership Challenge* (1995). CPS facilitators lead others in five important ways.

- ✦ *They challenge the process* by helping people who own tasks search for new and more valuable ways of thinking that change their current approaches to getting work done. They challenge how people view situations by clarifying ownership and sponsorship, as they identify and confirm people's needs for change.

- ✦ *They inspire shared vision* by helping task owners and groups create common and agreed upon images of a future state. This results in buy-in and commitment from all involved. They inspire shared vision by helping groups understand the challenges and opportunities associated with the future and reach consensus about direction and priorities.

- ✦ *They enable others to act* by helping leaders establish an environment that supports diverse perspectives and encourages cooperation, trust, and risk taking. They enable others to act by structuring a safe environment that uses flexible processes to encourage involvement and interaction as well as learning and growth.

- ✦ *They model the way* by helping groups be clear about what they see as important and using their time effectively to accomplish that which is pronounced as important. They model the way by using methods, language, and tools that remove barriers to group productivity and create powerful plans that transform the group's ideas into reality.

- ✦ *They encourage the heart* by helping leaders identify and reward accomplishments of the group in ways that increase people's performance and stimulate their desire to be involved in similar future work. They encourage the heart by providing opportunities to reflect on accomplishments, provide feedback to the group, and stimulate follow through on work conducted.

We have a very clear understanding of what we mean when we use the phrase CPS facilitator. CPS facilitators are leaders who take on the social role and responsibility to plan and manage process. They use their leadership to help others get their needs met. They believe that all people are creative, and that, given the right climate, they can help people unleash their creative potential through the power of CPS. They know how to use the CPS language, framework, and tools to increase the creative productivity of individuals and groups.

A MODEL FOR FACILITATING CPS

Whatever your approach to understanding leadership, one thing is clear: leadership is related to followership. Gardner (1990) indicated:

> *Leadership is such a gripping subject that once it is given center stage it draws attention away from everything else. But attention to leadership alone is sterile–and inappropriate. The larger topic of which leadership is a sub-topic is the accomplishment of group purpose, which is furthered not only by effective leaders, but also by innovators, entrepreneurs and thinkers; by the availability of resources; by questions of morale and social cohesion; and by much else...*

Clark and Clark (1994) indicated that taking a leadership role involves a conscious choice and commitment to lead. In describing this choice, the Clarks also outline a few of the tasks that come with the commitment:

> *In every case, leadership occurs only when one chooses to lead. To make that choice means that the leader mobilizes the talents and energies of the total group to address a problem, complete a task, or achieve a mission. The leader facilitates. The leader clarifies. The leader inspires. The leader resolves conflicts. The followers of such a leader comment that they exert more effort for the leader, that the leader clarifies the importance of each person's role and is concerned that each person will develop and grow as a result of the experience, and that the organization will improve and prosper. (page vii)*

As with other forms of leadership, the facilitator's role is a social role that involves interacting with others (e.g., business associates, students, family members). In one situation you might be the leader and in another the follower. Leaders can have this social role when talking with one other person or when addressing a room full of people. The same holds true for the role of facilitator. In one social setting you might be the person responsible for managing process (the facilitator) and in a different situation, you might be responsible for the task itself (e.g., the project manager or classroom teacher).

To help manage the social roles associated with CPS, Isaksen (1983) developed the model shown in Figure 3. The model for facilitating CPS identifies three social roles (and their primary responsibility) that come together during the application of CPS. The model is used to help people understand how they will contribute during a CPS application in ways that promote productive and novel outcomes.

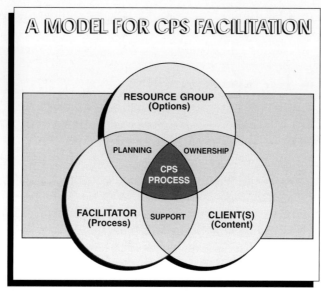

Figure 3: A Model for Facilitating CPS

As we mentioned, *facilitators* provide leadership by planning and managing the process. They make decisions about the methods and tools to be used, ensure a productive working environment, manage the dynamics of the people involved, and focus a group's energy on accomplishing desired outcomes.

Client(s) provide leadership to the group in relation to the topic or content on which CPS is being applied. Clients can be one or more people who own and are responsible for the content. Therefore, they are the primary decision-makers and use their knowledge, expertise, and influence to guide the content in the desired direction in order to create specific and meaningful outcome(s). (For more information about the client role, see Chapter 5, Managing Clients and Resource Groups.)

Resource-group members take part during a CPS application when clients need help dealing with a task. When they are involved, they take an active leadership role in using their diverse knowledge and varying perspectives to provide clients with many, varied, and unusual alternatives to consider. Resource groups can come in a variety of sizes and kinds (see Chapter 5, Managing Clients and Resource Groups). You do not have to use a resource group for all applications of CPS. Sometimes just having a productive interaction with a client can lead to significant breakthroughs.

Facilitators are responsible to ensure that people in these three roles understand the role and its related responsibilities. The key issue between the client and the resource-group is *ownership*. Facilitators need to ensure that primary ownership for the task remains with the client(s). Resource-group members can get excited about the task at hand and forget who has ultimate responsibility for making decisions guiding its direction.

Bringing a group together is one of the most popular and expensive things an organization can do. When using a resource-group, the primary issue for the facilitator to manage is *planning*. Planning involves such things as identifying who should be included in the group, ensuring they are ready to contribute, and planning for their involvement throughout the process. This often includes having group members conduct pre-work activities that will help them prepare for their work together. Facilitators need to manage this planning process carefully to ensure the client gets the best return from the investment in using a resource group.

The primary issue between the facilitator and the client is one of *support*. A critical responsibility of the facilitator is to clarify the level and kind of support the client needs to accomplish the task. In particular, the facilitator must help manage expectations by ensuring the client understands the process-orientation of the facilitator role. There may be times when you as a facilitator might be better able to contribute to the success of the client by being involved in the content. In this situation, it may be best to have someone else take the facilitator role while you provide content support in a resource-group member role.

Facilitating CPS in a group application (the center of the diagram in Figure 3) involves an interaction among all three roles. Planning, ownership, and support issues need to be considered throughout the preparation, implementation, and follow-up from any CPS application. This is why facilitating CPS in a group setting is one of the more complex ways to apply CPS. It is also why we identify the role of CPS facilitator as facilitative leadership.

Distinguishing and Managing Process and Content

One of the reasons we find the model for facilitating CPS valuable is that it helps us distinguish process from content and makes someone responsible for each. There are a number of reasons why distinguishing process and content is important. First, it *helps keep the ownership for the content clear.* Facilitators need to be able to "roam" around in the content in order to develop a productive understanding of the needs, the people, and the context, in order to make the best decisions about what approaches to take. However, a facilitator who "takes over" the content, runs the risk of steering content in a direction for which a client does not have ownership (interest, influence, or need for imagination). This can have a profoundly negative impact on the likelihood of a client implementing anything from the application.

Second, *the role of facilitator needs to be validated as a role unto itself.* The level and degree to which a facilitator can add value by designing and managing process is great. Absence of this kind of leadership can have a powerfully negative impact on individual or group productivity. The model helps us make the leadership role of facilitator more deliberate and explicit and identifies how people in this role interact and add value to the creative productivity of people.

The third reason why it is important is that doing so *helps maintain role clarity.* Distinguishing process and content, and making someone different be responsible for each, helps people better understand how they will contribute to the group. At the same time, this helps them take on a level of responsibility they can manage. The client and facilitator roles can both be very complex and demanding. Taking on both the client and facilitator roles equates to taking all the information, responsibility, and complexity associated with each role, and placing it in one person's head. From our experience, this is a tremendous task for any one person to manage at any one time. The consequence is often a general level of confusion that results in less effective process and lower quality outcomes. People in each role already have enough to think about without having to take on the responsibilities of the other.

Constant interactions between process and content can result in a lack of clarity or confusion about the roles. Clarifying roles gives people a "home base" from which to manage their contribution to the work and provide appropriate influence on the group. For example, from our perspective, clients have the expertise and social responsibility necessary to make the best decisions about the content. Facilitators have the expertise necessary to make the best decisions about how to design and manage the process, in order to get the best results for clients. Putting different people in charge of each helps avoid undo influence the facilitator can have on steering the content. It also helps clients focus their attention on directing the content. From our experience, when something becomes "everyone's job," it usually means that no one does it.

After people understand the amount of complexity involved in each role, most agree that taking on both at the same time is difficult and not generally suggested. This often creates tension for people, because their organizations frequently ask them to take on both roles at the same time. This may be for financial reasons, a lack of effective facilitation skills available, or even a general lack of understanding and appreciation for the responsibilities associated with facilitative leadership.

What happens in these situations is that people are forced to make trade-offs between focusing on process or on content. Often, the decision is almost always made in the direction of content. The implication is that no one is really needed to manage the process. The result is that meetings typically get packed with twice as many agenda items as is humanly possible to accomplish in the time provided. People get into wandering debates that often lead nowhere. Meetings go off track and end up taking twice or three times as long as planned — and often with less productivity then expected. When all the leadership focuses on the content, no one provides leadership on the process. And most of us know what happens when there is an absence of leadership for a task... nothing!

Characteristics of CPS Facilitators

The concept of a facilitator has special meaning for those of us concerned with the high-quality and professional facilitation of CPS. One of the best ways to describe the concept is to identify those important attributes or qualities of the facilitator. The following characteristics have been identified as key abilities and skills associated with an effective CPS facilitator.

While it is possible to identify these characteristics, it is important to remember that they describe facilitative leaders. Facilitative leadership is more than a set of competencies and behaviors. It is an attitude that involves the desire to share leadership responsibilities with others and to take on a process-oriented approach to serving their needs. The following seven sections identify the knowledge and skills associated with having this attitude.

The list of competencies is in no particular order of importance nor is it complete. It was not developed through empirical research, but derived from many years of extensive experience with an international group of over fifty skilled professionals from business, education, and government, who have demonstrated sustained high-level performance as facilitative leaders. The characteristics are not distinct from each other, but provide a dynamic and overlapping "profile" of qualities. Each characteristic needs to be present, however, not all necessarily to the same degree. If we focus on only one or two of the skill clusters, we lose a part of the system that makes facilitative leadership work.

The first major set of characteristics deals primarily with the "people side" of the role. These include: using a facilitative leadership approach, having people-management skills, and observing and managing group behavior. The next three characteristics deal primarily with the "process side" of the role. These include: appraising tasks, designing process, and conducting a productive application of CPS. The final cluster, encouraging productive implementation, places the role of the facilitator within the larger domain of change management.

The remainder of this chapter, then, gives an overview of how CPS facilitators provide their leadership.

Use a Facilitative Leadership Approach

Taking a facilitative approach to leadership means focusing more on service than control. A facilitator is more likely to be a "guide by the side" than a "sage on the stage." CPS facilitators are not necessarily consultants, counselors, or therapists. They may have those roles outside the context of a CPS application, but generally the kind of behavior associated with CPS facilitation will not include providing content expertise on the client's problem or challenge area, nor providing a clinical intervention.

CPS facilitators, as distinct from the common conception of leaders, usually do not have the authority or responsibility to implement the results of CPS application. Their focus is more on designing process approaches and less on actually having the ownership for the content or work process under consideration. They major in the how rather than the what. In fact, facilitators must often work to stay out of the content area so that they can focus on managing the working environment, process, and interactions of group members.

CPS facilitators have process awareness and expertise. The CPS facilitator possesses a clear and productive understanding of the CPS framework. This includes knowing not only the specialized CPS language and guidelines, but also the subtle differences among the concepts of the CPS framework, components, stages, phases, and tools. The facilitator needs to make decisions about the effective application of the many CPS tools.

Having the ability to use diverse tools provides the facilitator with an efficient means of meeting the needs of a client by more fully using the group's resources. Facilitators have a number of other process languages at their disposal. For example, it is very helpful to be able to make connections between CPS and models like Targeted Innovation (Gryskiewicz, 1981), Synectics (Prince, 1970), or Kepner-Tregoe (Kepner & Tregoe, 1981). Some group members may not have had direct training in CPS, but they may have had some experience with other process models.

Having a firm foundation of CPS language and structure for tools, roles, and guidelines does not mean the facilitator should baffle a group or spend an inordinate amount of time forcing people to learn a specialized language or jargon. The facilitator uses CPS transparently with groups. This means the facilitator has sufficient clarity and sophistication to use natural and simple language, which is also correct and meaningful, to guide creative behavior. This is particularly important when working with groups who are anxious to have a solution to a problem rather than to learn about a framework for problem solving.

While the group is preparing for and engaging in problem solving, the facilitator must be able to maintain an awareness of the group process and dynamics, as well as keep an eye on the time, energy level, and the client's needs. In short, the facilitator must be able to juggle many issues at once. One major expertise necessary for CPS facilitation is the ability to set an appropriate environment. This can be done by removing barriers that affect personal and group creativity, and by removing those that inhibit progress toward the desired outcome. Having an awareness of the CPS process helps remove these barriers and improve the environment for creativity.

CPS facilitators provide teaching, training, and coaching. Before CPS facilitators engage individuals or groups in CPS, they must be certain that they are as prepared as possible to help the people benefit from the use of the process. Facilitating CPS often requires people to think and act in new ways, and this requires learning. Therefore, one of the most important roles a facilitator can perform is that of educator. Establishing a learning environment is a critical factor in enabling people to share what they know and feel, as well as to take the risks necessary to grow.

Establishing a learning environment may not be enough, however, to ensure creative productivity. Groups will need to know the CPS language, guidelines, and tools in order to apply them effectively. This may mean providing opportunities for people to develop enough of an understanding about CPS to apply it productively. It might involve providing brief "warming-up" activities during the CPS application, or even providing wide-scale training workshops. In any case, facilitators ensure participants understand the method well enough to remove barriers to its effective application. Teaching others to use CPS also provides facilitators an opportunity to further develop and strengthen their own knowledge and skills. The best way to learn something is to teach it.

CPS facilitators leverage personal experience. The effective CPS facilitator can draw upon a wealth of personal experiences that illustrate key insights about the process. Some of the most teachable moments occur when a CPS facilitator shares specific examples of interactions and events from previous applications — anonymously as appropriate — to help others learn the value and most productive use of the CPS framework, language, and tools. Providing these examples can help build trust in the facilitator and the process itself by establishing a history of successful application. It also provides a way of building a relationship between the facilitator and the group by using appropriate personal disclosure.

CPS facilitators believe in the power of creative thinking. Effective CPS facilitators believe in the power of creativity. They believe that all people have creativity and that it can be used to create valued novelty for an individual, group, or organization. CPS facilitators trust in the power of CPS as an effective method for drawing out the potential of people to think creatively and thereby solve problems in new ways.

Have People-Management Skills

CPS facilitators interact with a variety of people and thus need a variety of interpersonal skills. Facilitators must inherently and genuinely enjoy working with others. They will need to build productive interpersonal relationships that may be both short and long-term. People with whom they work and interact will need to see the facilitator as a credible person.

CPS facilitators possess appropriate personal qualities. Effectively facilitating CPS takes a great deal of personal energy. We are certain that there is no one particular mold from which all excellent CPS facilitators are formed. There is a wide variety of specific personal qualities associated with effective CPS facilitators. However, there are some broad personal qualities that seem to be shared by many. For example, CPS facilitators are able to show enthusiasm and have a genuinely optimistic attitude: they have positive beliefs about creativity, and have enough belief-in-self to ask a group for help; they are self-confident enough to indicate how much they don't know! They also have a sense of humor and a high degree of personal integrity.

CPS facilitators fit their style to the situation. The facilitator must be able to manage the transition from showing people how to use the language and tools to actually using them. This requires that those involved know enough about matching the appropriate style to the situation in order to apply CPS. They know how to accomplish this by assessing the competence and commitment levels of all group members. CPS facilitators know when to direct, coach, and support group members, as well as when to delegate activities in order to help them be successful. One of the worst mistakes to make is to assume that because "everyone" knows how to brainstorm, they are ready for the effective application of CPS language and tools.

A situational approach to providing leadership is absolutely necessary. Moving individuals and groups from a learning mode to a doing mode, and then reflecting on what was done, takes a special level of expertise and lots of practice.

CPS facilitators use communication skills. The CPS facilitator must be a skillful communicator. The facilitator must be able to listen and comprehend well and fast enough to understand both content (what has been said) and process (how it has been said). The facilitator must be skilled at paraphrasing, speaking, presenting as well as listening, clarifying narrative comments, asking questions to guide thinking and acting, and respond to narrative succinctly. Skilled communication includes processing both the cognitive and emotional aspects of human interaction. The client and resource-group learns about the integrity of the facilitator through his or her verbal *and* non-verbal behavior. If the communication is skillful, the people interacting with the facilitator will be encouraged to think and feel creatively.

CPS facilitators balance content and process. It is important for the facilitator to be able to listen to a client and understand the context enough to comprehend the nature of the task at hand. CPS facilitators need to know enough about the content in order to make good decisions about the process. This means being a "quick study" for the main subject matter and key information within the domain of the task. It is quite helpful for the facilitator to have a broad background and a good general vocabulary to help acquire knowledge from a variety of contexts. More importantly, managing the balance between becoming an expert within the specific problem domain and offering appropriate process interventions is a major area of judgment for the CPS facilitator. Managing the content-process balance allows the facilitator to be more objective or neutral on the content during a CPS application.

Observe and Manage Group Behavior

The CPS facilitator must feel comfortable with a social role that involves a great deal of interaction with other people. Facilitators need to be able to deal effectively with group dynamics, interpersonal skills, and communication (see Chapter 4, Setting the Stage for CPS). Handling those sudden changes in course which groups often provide offers a constant source of challenge to those who choose to work with others. An effective facilitator knows how to observe and use the behavior, interest, and motivation of others, while helping them move and refocus their efforts toward productive outcomes.

CPS facilitators ensure role clarity. The facilitator has the responsibility to manage productive interactions with both the client(s) and the resource-group members. There is a sharp and clear difference between the three social roles of facilitator, client, and resource-group member. However, when groups are engaged in CPS, these roles become less clear and harder to manage. The role of the CPS facilitator encompasses teaching and leading, as well as managing the other social roles of client and resource group members.

The facilitator must function as a "participant-observer" within the group. When facilitating, the facilitator manages the process and observes the process at the same time. When needed, the facilitator provides the necessary intervention to drive the content forward, but must always have the clear awareness of the purpose and goal of the application work. They remain in their role as facilitator as long as the social setting requires it. They help the client solve the problem, as opposed to solving the problem for the client.

CPS facilitators manage client interaction. Process and content will be present whenever a group gets together. Therefore, the facilitator and client roles need to be managed if process is to serve content productively. The facilitator interacts with the client before, during, and after a CPS application to ensure productive preparation, intervention, and implementation. The results of this interaction will have a key impact on the likelihood of successful change. The CPS facilitator must be sure that the client understands the responsibilities and characteristics associated with the critical nature of the role (see Chapter 5, Managing Clients and Resource Groups).

CPS facilitators plan for resource-group interaction. Facilitators know how to help clients decide if a resource-group is necessary and they guide in the selection of group members, if a group is needed. The facilitator may interact with a resource group before, during and after a CPS application. They may be involved in inviting them to participate and providing them with some background information and preparation activities. The main interaction often occurs during the group application work itself. In planning to interact with the resource-group, facilitators consider group development. They understand the implications on process of the age of the group

— i.e. newly formed vs. existing team. Facilitators also ensure clients have some degree of contact following the working session to provide feedback to the members of the group (see Chapter 5, Managing Clients and Resource Groups).

CPS facilitators promote teamwork. Group application of CPS offers a unique opportunity for teamwork. Many general characteristics of productive teams are desired for these sessions — such as understanding individual differences, articulating a shared vision, dealing with group norms, etc. The CPS facilitator knows what these desired roles and characteristics are. They also know about some of the common barriers or "tripwires" to effective teamwork, and how to avoid them or address them when they emerge (see Chapter 6, Encouraging Teamwork in CPS Groups).

CPS facilitators observe group and team dynamics. Knowing what to look for during a group application of CPS is an important skill for facilitators. New facilitators are often so concerned about the tools they will use or the reaction of the client during a session that they can forget to look at a whole range of group dynamics. While facilitators manage tools and client interaction, they must also observe and manage a number of other issues such as the general level of energy in the group and other aspects of the interpersonal climate.

CPS facilitators intervene and deal with curves. There are a number of curves (counter-productive or dysfunctional dynamics or events) that may occur during the application of CPS. Knowing about them in advance can often prevent them from occurring. If they do occur, the facilitator needs to have a number of levels and kinds of interventions ready for use (see Chapter 9, Planning for the Unexpected).

Appraise Tasks

The CPS facilitator must be able to make effective decisions about the appropriateness of applying any particular method to help accomplish a desired outcome. The facilitator makes these decisions based on information derived from interactions with the client(s). This happens while appraising tasks (see Figure 4) before or during a specific application of CPS. During the Appraising Tasks component of CPS, facilitators draw on the four types of information below as they make their decisions.

CPS facilitators understand Personal Orientation. CPS facilitators work to understand the people involved in the task. They strive to learn as much as possible about issues of ownership, clientship, and sponsorship, as well as who might be potential members of the resource-group. This may include examining the "spirit" of the team, the commitment to solve the problem or take advantage of the opportunity, and how the client or sponsor sees the role of facilitator. They figure out the level of content or process expertise, as well as the general style preferences or personalities of the key people involved. They also strive for a general understanding of others who are involved in the challenge or change.

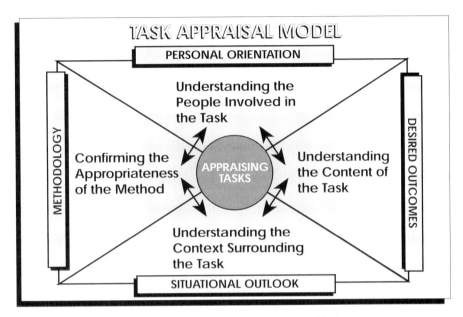

Figure 4: A Model for Appraising Tasks

Facilitators use this information to decide about using CPS or some other methods. If CPS is appropriate, facilitators use this information to design how people will be involved in the application of CPS.

CPS facilitators identify Desired Outcomes. CPS facilitators develop an understanding of the content surrounding the client(s)' need. They work with the client(s) to clarify the scope and size of the change as well as the "deliverables" from the overall desired outcomes. They also figure out how clear the image of the preferred future is and use this information to clarify potential perceptions of the desired change.

Facilitators use their understanding of the desired outcomes to help make decisions about the use of CPS. If appropriate, the information is used to plan the specific process intervention(s) necessary to accomplish the desired outcome.

CPS facilitators clarify the Situational Outlook. CPS facilitators are able to assess the readiness of the context for receiving the change desired. This includes developing an understanding of the present climate, the culture, the strategy, the availability of resources, and the sense of urgency, pressure, or immediacy surrounding the task. They use this information to decide how to approach the task. This includes the possibility of taking no action at all because the timing is not right for using CPS.

CPS facilitators determine the Method. One of the major reasons for learning about the client(s)' needs, the key people involved, and the readiness of the situation for change is to make a decision about the use of CPS. CPS facilitators know enough about CPS (and other methods) to make decisions about its use, given what is learned from the client(s). They understand the benefits and costs of using CPS and the likelihood of it being successful, given what is learned. They also know enough about other methods to make recommendations for applying methods beyond the use of CPS.

Design Process

When CPS is qualified for use, the facilitator must design an appropriate process approach. Designing the process approach requires a sufficiently high level of process expertise in order to make good choices about what methods and tools should be used to accomplish the desired outcome. Facilitators know how to develop large-scale plans for making change as well as specific plans for using CPS throughout a change process. They take into consideration information from Appraising Tasks to make productive decisions when designing the process.

CPS facilitators plan for involvement of ownership, clientship, and sponsorship. CPS facilitators confirm that the client has the necessary influence, interest, and need for newness. They also ensure that the client has the needed organizational support in the form of sponsorship to accomplish the larger desired outcome. If sponsorship is not present, facilitators understand the implications for Designing Process and the application of CPS.

CPS facilitators determine how the process will be applied. CPS facilitators use their understanding of the client(s)' needs to make decisions about how the process will be used. This includes planning how CPS will be integrated into the overall change process. It also includes making specific decisions about where to enter and exit the CPS framework when designing specific applications (i.e., during meetings, workshops, etc.) that take place throughout the change process.

It is possible that after listening to a client, the facilitator ends up with several possible pathways through the process. Facilitators know how to check with clients about the most desirable outputs by providing clear choices about the possible results or "end points" from each of the possible pathways. This helps ensure productive outcomes from the CPS application.

CPS facilitators plan resource-group involvement if necessary. CPS facilitators know how to use their understanding of the task to help make decisions about resource-group involvement along the entire process of applying CPS. Some parts of the overall plan for using CPS may best be done by the client alone, while other parts might require client and facilitator interaction. Still other parts might benefit from the involvement of a resource group. CPS facilitators know when to use them, how to select them, and how to get maximum benefit from their energy. They know the benefits and limitations to using groups, make them known to clients, and use this information to plan how and when they are involved.

Apply CPS Productively

Actually applying CPS in a group setting is at the heart of what many believe facilitation to be. Although there is a great deal of planning, preparation, and design involved, conducting the actual application is often the most visible aspect of the role of the CPS facilitator. CPS facilitators productively manage that specific application by meeting the following five requirements.

CPS facilitators use a task summary. CPS facilitators prepare groups for being productive by using Task Summaries. These are short summaries of the task being addressed that are used to help a group get started, stay on track, and know if they were successful in accomplishing what they set out to do. They usually contain a title for the meeting, key background information that the group needs in order to be productive, and some agreed-upon definition of the desired outcome. Facilitators also use these summaries to "educate" the group about the kind of thinking and the structure of the language they will subsequently use during the application work.

CPS facilitators select and prepare to use tools. With clarity about the outcomes to be accomplished, the CPS facilitator is in a position to plan and use specific creative-thinking and problem-solving tools. New facilitators may sometimes be tempted to apply their favorite tools rather than use those that are most appropriate for the task. CPS facilitators know how to select, prepare, and use tools based on the needs of the task rather than on their personal preferences. They know how to modify the tools using a variety of techniques in order to make them more effective for the group and the situation they face (see Isaksen, Dorval & Treffinger, 1998).

CPS facilitators develop and use agendas. People can usually benefit from having some form of flexible structure to guide their thinking and behavior. CPS facilitators use agendas to help orient and guide groups, as well as to keep groups on track when distractions occur. The classic agenda for a CPS group application working session includes: a welcome and overview of the purpose, a defining of roles and responsibilities, a clarifying the task at hand, a plan for generating and focusing options, and a time for determining next steps and making closing comments. Although the agenda may appear to be quite structured, the CPS facilitator knows how to set out the framework for action while simultaneously allowing for and encouraging spontaneity. A creative design of the agenda provides for some degree of surprise and chaos — preplanned flexibility.

CPS facilitators balance generating and focusing. A central dynamic to be managed when facilitating CPS is knowing how and when to generate and focus options. Facilitators know how to separate and manage the productive balance between generating and focusing. They manage the percentage of time spent doing each and know how to productively transition back and forth according to the needs of the client. CPS facilitators have a deep understanding of the guidelines for generating and focusing options to enable all this to happen. They know and educate others on the distinction between brainstorming as a CPS tool and the concept of generating options. They also understand the need for focus, follow-through, and implementation to ensure value from the generation activity.

CPS facilitators manage logistics. A major responsibility of the facilitator is to establish and manage a productive environment for thinking and learning. CPS facilitators are able to manage the planning of a wide range of details before, during, and after any application session. Some of the logistical issues addressed before application work include: having a variety of resources for applying whatever method and tools are needed, arranging the physical environment so people are comfortable and have adequate eye contact, and preparing people for their roles and responsibilities.

One key logistical issue that a CPS facilitator knows how to manage is the productive flow of information created during the application. This includes ensuring the group's thinking is captured and organized in a way that can be followed and used subsequently to promote productive thinking.

Dealing with logistics is often (and erroneously) minimized as an important quality of effective CPS facilitators. The larger issue is maintaining an appropriate balance between strategy and tactics. There have been sessions that have not worked as productively as they might have because of a lack of attention to details, such as making sure flipcharts, markers, and hanging tape were available, or scheduling an effective planning meeting prior to the session.

Encourage Productive Implementation

Although implementation of outcomes from a CPS application is the responsibility of the client(s), CPS facilitators use their knowledge, understanding, and experience with change management to help encourage successful and productive implementation. They help clients see change as a continuous process, not as a single event. In other words, the work is not done when the "session" is finished. There are numerous responsibilities to complete after any application of CPS.

CPS facilitators ensure outputs are documented. They make plans to document the output of the CPS application before the group work actually happens. This includes ensuring that roles and responsibilities are in place prior to the start of the session. During the application the information and insights created are recorded and used to create an accurate memory of what took place. After the application, the CPS facilitator ensures that the output gets summarized and preserved in such a way that the group members can use it to move forward on the overall change process.

CPS facilitators use feedback. Following through on a CPS application will typically include providing feedback to the people involved in the application work. The

CPS facilitator ensures that clients summarize and communicate the progress made and results accomplished when they implement what was created during the application of CPS. This helps those involved (i.e. resource-group members and the facilitator) understand the impact of their contribution. Facilitators also ensure that clients use feedback to keep people informed about possible future contributions in the change process.

CPS facilitators debrief and develop insights. Applying CPS in groups provides an opportunity for a client to engage people in accomplishing important tasks. It also provides an opportunity for facilitators to develop and strengthen their skills in using process to positively impact the creative productivity of groups. CPS facilitators are continuous learners in that they reflect on what occurred during each CPS application in order to learn and improve their capacity to facilitate (see Chapter 9, Guiding the Experiential Learning of CPS).

Whenever possible, CPS facilitators involve others (i.e., client and resource-group members) in this debriefing and developing activity. They use this feedback to also guide and tailor future work related to that particular application of CPS. Facilitators may also involve assistant facilitators to provide a "second pair of eyes" on their work and to increase their ability to learn.

CPS facilitators link to larger change initiatives. CPS facilitators know that facilitating CPS is more than "running a session." They are aware of the larger practice of change management and use this understanding to help groups follow up on their application of CPS. They ensure that clients think and act on change management issues throughout the process — this includes interactions ranging from the original Appraising Tasks meeting to delivering typed flipchart pages soon after a working session.

CONCLUSION

The goal of this chapter was to broaden the popular conception of a "facilitator" into one of facilitative leadership. At the base of facilitative leadership is an attitude to share leadership responsibility while serving the needs of others. What a facilitative leader needs to know, do, and believe in order to effectively apply this process-oriented approach to leadership was examined. A profile of core qualities and skills that facilitative leaders possess and use to help unleash the creative potential of groups was identified.

There are many issues to consider when planning to take on a facilitative leadership role. The next chapter attempts to identify some of the key issues to think about when "setting the stage" for a productive CPS application.

REFERENCES

Clark, K. E. & Clark, M. B. (1994). *Choosing to lead.* Greensboro, NC: Center for Creative Leadership.

Davis, T., Arnett, A., Gibbons, P., & Milton, F. (1998). *Innovation survey.* London: PricewaterhouseCoopers.

Freedman, G. (1988). *The pursuit of innovation: Managing the people and the processes that turn new ideas into profits.* New York: AMACOM.

Gardner, J. W. (1990). *On leadership.* New York: The Free Press.

Greenleaf, R. K. (1991). *Servant leadership: A journey into the nature of legitimate power and greatness.* New York: Paulist Press.

Gryskiewicz, S. S. (1981). Targeted innovation: A situational approach. In S. S. Gryskiewicz (Ed.), *Creativity Week III, 1980 Proceedings (pp. 77-103).* Greensboro, NC: Center for Creative Leadership.

Hamel, G. & Prahalad, C. K. (1994). Competing for the future. *Harvard Business Review, 72,* 122-128.

Isaksen, S. G. (1983). Toward a model for the facilitation of creative problem solving. *Journal of Creative Behavior, 17,* 18-31.

Isaksen, S. G., Dorval, K. B., & Treffinger, D. J. (1998). *Toolbox for Creative Problem Solving: Basic tools and resources.* Buffalo, NY: The Creative Problem Solving Group – Buffalo.

Kepner, C. H., & Tregoe, B. B. (1981). *The new rational manager.* Princeton, NJ: Princeton Research Press.

Kouses, J. M. & Posner, B. Z. (1995). *The leadership challenge.* San Diego, CA: Jossey-Bass Publishers.

Kuhn, R. L. (Ed.). (1988). *Handbook for creative and innovative managers.* New York: McGraw-Hill.

Prince, G. M. (1970). *The practice of creativity: A manual for dynamic group problem solving.* New York: Harper & Row.

CHAPTER FOUR

SETTING THE STAGE FOR CREATIVE PROBLEM SOLVING

Ken W. McCluskey

The University of Winnipeg, Canada

> "Tom had discovered a great law of human action,
> without knowing it — namely, that in order to make a
> man or a boy covet a thing, it is only necessary to make
> the thing difficult to attain."
> **Mark Twain, The Adventures of Tom Sawyer, c. 2**

INTRODUCTION

For many decades and in many situations Creative Problem Solving (CPS) has shown itself to be a highly efficient, effective process for developing and enhancing creative and critical thinking (cf. Isaksen, Dorval, & Treffinger, 1994, 1998; Treffinger, Isaksen, & Dorval, 1994). However, it does not take place in isolation. Each and every participant involved in applying CPS brings something unique to the table: there are individual styles, personal qualities and predispositions and idiosyncratic ingredients that make each of us what we are (and different from what others are). But there are also social, group-based variables at work. And; to further complicate matters, the internal and external elements intertwine, interact and, in effect, become inseparable. When one stops to consider the dynamic interplay among individual, social and other factors involved in virtually any application of CPS, there's a whole lot of stuff going on!

As a consequence, it behooves practitioners to be sensitive not only to the overt theory, strategies and tools of CPS, but also to a multiplicity of subtle impinging variables. It would be naive to attempt to address all of these in any one CPS planning, application or training session, for there are day-to-day realities to consider: time and task constraints, client needs and specific business-that-must-be-done issues. Still, in planning and stage setting for effective problem solving, it is necessary to be aware of the behind-the-scenes factors. Here, then, are some suggestions for identifying and responding to a few of the traits and tendencies, both individual and social, that are woven inextricably into the CPS process.

As we examine these variables, it will be important to remember that they can be considered during personal, one-on-one, small-group and organizational applications of CPS.

STYLES OF LEARNING AND CREATIVITY

Different people access, absorb, and interpret information in different ways. In their well-known learning styles research Rita and Ken Dunn (1978, 1992, 1993) emphasize that some individuals take primarily a visual approach to problem solving (seeing or envisioning), others attend more to the auditory dimension (listening), while still others rely heavily on hands-on kinesthetic/tactile cues (doing). Some folk prefer to work alone; others have a need to operate more collaboratively. Some take a piece-by-piece approach; others are more global. And "morning people" are at their best early in the day, while for those at the opposite end of the spectrum, Neil Diamond's "Thank the Lord for the night time" applies (McCluskey, 1999). In educational settings it is important to recognize and respond to individual differences and learning preferences by presenting information and measuring learning in a variety of ways (cf. Woolfolk, 1998).

Taking a different tack, Michael Kirton (1976, 1989) has identified two very distinct styles of creativity. Those with a more adaptive orientation tend to work primarily within the existing structures or organizational framework. They are typically seen as thorough, reliable, goal-oriented individuals who attempt to reach their objectives through proven, traditional means. On the other end of the continuum are those with a more innovative preference who are more apt to push existing boundaries and challenge "the way it has always been done." They enjoy seeking new combinations and totally redefining existing paradigms.

Depending on the time and place, there are strengths and weaknesses that come with each style. For example, under certain unfortunate conditions, adaptors may become boring, by-the-book, progress-blocking "bean counters" for whom the means become the ends. On the upside, however, adaptors can provide comforting stability and, by doing their homework and moving ideas expeditiously through the proper channels, they do make things happen. Innovators, for their part, can at times be undisciplined dreamers who generate irreverent, impractical, off-the-wall ideas ad infinitum. But, in the right situation, they can also breathe new life into the organizational structure by coming up with ingenious, energizing ideas. Both adaptors and innovators, then, deliver something unique and potentially valuable to the party. Innovators, by their very nature, are likely to develop novel, system-stretching approaches. And, make no mistake about it, adaptors can also contribute their own form of originality. Are not highly creative accountants much in demand?

Opportunities for successful problem solving are maximized by helping people become more aware of their learning and creative preferences, and by fostering communication and understanding among those with dissimilar strengths and viewpoints. To this end, if circumstances and time permit, it can be helpful to have participants work through the Learning Styles Inventory (LSI) (Dunn, Dunn, & Price, 1978) and the Kirton Adaption-Innovation (KAI) Inventory (Kirton, 1976). If one goes this route, however, either-or interpretations are to be avoided — most of us do not fall solely into the visual learner category, for instance, or register as "terminally innovative," or whatever.

Instruments of this sort give only a general sense for a person's possible location on a continuum; they should not be used for rigid labeling, pigeon-holing or "dichotomizing." Nonetheless, although not magical or definitive by any means (cf. Eggen & Kauchak, 1999; Woolfolk, 1998), such inventories do serve to highlight the immutable fact that people encode, decode, and interpret "data" and "facts" quite differently. Once this sensitivity for individual differences is placed on the front burner, so to speak, the business of solving problems can proceed more efficiently. More specifically, with increased awareness about their own styles and the styles of others, participants are better positioned to adjust their behavior flexibly, to remain respectful of other points of view, and to interact more productively overall.

If left to our own devices, most of us will gravitate toward others who share our worldview — the birds-of-a-feather-flock-together rule often guides group formation. However, once information is gathered concerning participants' learning and creative styles, it becomes possible to mix and match for more effective problem solving. To illustrate: while a group made up solely of adaptors, for example, might tend to take a cookie-cutter approach to attacking problems, one composed of adaptors, innovators, and middle-of-the-road folk probably would not. Having participants work, at least for part of the time, with others who digest and process information differently from themselves introduces a system of healthy checks and balances, broadens the scope, and builds strength through diversity.

PERSONAL CHARACTERISTICS

A sensitive observer can often identify various "personalities" during a visit to an office or school staff room. There are the law-and-order types ("You must have organization, maintain firm discipline, and — for fairness' sake — treat everyone precisely the same!"), the touchy-feely, lovey-dovey contingent ("We must meet the emotional needs!"), the relaxed, lump-like lounge lizards ("Let's not get too excited or move too quickly..."), and the go-getters ("Time's a wastin'; let's get in gear!") who are always on the move (to the point of striding purposefully through the hallway at day's end, car keys in hand, even though the parking lot is still distant and out of view). There are countless variations on these and other personae. And indeed, the interpersonal disputes and annoyances notwithstanding, it's as it should be. Although people with markedly disparate personality characteristics frequently run afoul of one another, it would be terribly boring and limiting if we were all alike.

It is clearly not the intent to make this a Psychology of Personality 201 paper, but, to my mind, it is worth going just a little further down the individual differences road at this point. In the natural order of things, there will be a blend or mixture of people in any office, institution, or CPS group: those who are willing to share, and others (perhaps with insightful contributions to make) who are more reluctant or reticent; the comfortable and the threatened; the assertive and the passive; the questioning and the accepting; the positive and the less so; and all those in between. Unseen, dispositional forces, including personal needs and agendas, will come into play.

In problem-solving sessions one must be mindful of the factions that can develop, restrict the range of thinking, and inhibit the flow of creative juices. At times professionals and university-types — accustomed as they are to the analytic scenario — may unintentionally dominate their groups. Other participants with less confidence and lower perceived status might then, metaphorically speaking, retire to the backbenches. Hunt (1987) has admonished those in ivory towers to control their "little professor" impulses, and has urged them to shift from the idea that "in the beginning there was a blackboard" to the more global view that "in the beginning there was an experience." Everyone in a CPS group should be made to feel secure that their experiences — their background, thoughts, and observations — are important. The more varied the points of view, the more ideas that can be generated.

Once again, rather than allow any negativity to take hold, diversity should be seen as an opportunity. A first step in savoring and building upon individual differences and strengths can be to run participants through the Myers-Briggs Type Indicator (Myers & McCaulley, 1985), or similar instruments (Keirsey & Bates, 1984). Of course, assessment is, at the best of times, fraught with danger. This is particularly true in the ethereal realm of personality, where — with all of the confounding variables at work — it is nigh on impossible to identify and measure traits accurately. However, for the purposes at hand, perfect precision is not an absolute requirement. Respect for individual differences and viewpoints is an essential ingredient in meaningful problem solving, and the goal in using Myers-Briggs or similar indicators is simply to assist participants to become more aware, appreciative, and tolerant of idiosyncratic foibles and personal characteristics.

On the one hand, of course, it is decidedly inappropriate to employ a force-fit procedure to squeeze people into uncomfortable, prefabricated moulds or roles. Twain's poignant observation comes to mind: "Don't try to teach a pig to sing. It won't work, and besides you'll annoy the pig!" On the other, people benefit if they can put themselves in the place of the other and see the world through new, unfamiliar lenses. Acknowledging, accepting, and understanding personal differences can help lay a positive foundation for problem solving.

Self-Serving Bias

An oft-neglected, but powerful effect is what is termed the self-serving bias — the tendency most of us have to perceive ourselves in a positive light (cf. Myers, 1987). This I-am-moral-and-right tendency is one of the most subtle biases affecting behavior in groups, but, for all its subtlety, it is extremely pervasive and powerful. In sports, for example, players accept credit for their wins, but usually blame losses on the weather, the officials, the artificial turf, or bad bounces. Adjustors dealing with car accident claims must have a terrible time — no one is ever at fault in an accident. As noted in a July, 1977 issue of the Toronto News, drivers — in their accident reports — make statements such as "An invisible car came out of nowhere, struck my car and vanished;" or the ever-popular "A pedestrian hit me and went under my car." Myers outlines these and other examples, including self-serving bias in a Scrabble game. When people win, it's obviously due to their superior vocabulary, linguistic adroitness and verbal skill, but if they lose, there is an emergent refrain of "What rotten luck! It's just impossible to do anything with a Q and no U!"

As Myers (1987) highlights, many students show a self-serving bias. On the SAT's (Scholastic Aptitude Test), the College Entrance Examination Board sometimes asks high school students how they feel they compare with other young people their age. One year, when it came to "leadership ability," only 2% rated themselves as below average. And in "ability to get along with others," 0% rated themselves below average (60% felt they were in the top 10%, and 25% in the top 1%). Clearly, America is in good shape, with so many youth so far above the mean. Most professors understand that students who do poorly on tests tend to blame everything and everyone but themselves (Davis & Stephan, 1980), but profs show less awareness for the fact that they do very much the same when their articles are rejected by professional journals (Wiley, Crittenden, & Birg, 1979). Myers sums up his self-serving bias discussion by reminding us of Freud's old joke about the elderly fellow who informed his wife that, "If one of us should die, I think I would go live in Paris."

One must ask, can we all be so far above average, more ethical, less prejudiced, and generally better than others? Of course not, yet it seems that most of us have the ability to twist or adjust reality so as to perceive ourselves positively. With the best will in the world, biases still creep in. For example, we think of achievement, cognitive, or other tests as being standardized, objective, and fair, but who designs the tests? Psychologists (who, for good or ill, have a disproportionately larger number of democrats and atheists in their ranks than the general population) are not immune to the phenomenon. They are likely to feel they are doing something worthwhile and scientific, when perhaps they are not. Even with modern technology there are biases, for the computer cannot be considered androgynous: far more programmers are male than female. Individuals in groups, and thus groups themselves, may fall into the trap as well (where they see their efforts as correct and valuable, while perhaps un-dervaluing the work of others). Since forewarned is forearmed, participants in CPS sessions should be given some information about self-serving and other biases.

One quick and powerful way to do precisely that is to have group members, after they have worked together for awhile, complete a brief questionnaire. Adapting fairly directly from Bolt and Myers (1983), I've pulled together a SSB survey, offered here as Exercise 1. Ostensibly, the initials stand for Scale of Social Behavior, but naturally the true purpose is to get at the Self-Serving Bias per se. Not surprisingly, since 1, 3, and 5 are more or less neutral, the vast majority of groups average in the 50% range when responding to these items. To illustrate: in a typical group, people with doctoral degrees — since they obviously realize that they have more extensive formal educa-tion than most — are apt to respond with nearly 100% on the first item. In contrast, individuals who have completed only a few grades of public schooling will likely answer closer toward 0%. And those with a couple of years of university, knowing they fall somewhere in the middle, might say 50%. Keeping in mind the normal curve, it is probable that the individual responses will average out to somewhere near that 50% mark.

Everything being equal, answers to SSB items 2, 4, and 6 should also average around 50%. But not everything is equal, for these questions are much more emotionally-laden. In field testing to date, respondents have been far less accurate in reacting to these items: they tend to overestimate socially-desirable traits such as sense of hu-mor, altruism, and sensitivity — to the extent that answers here usually fall in the 70-80% range. Once people see how they have allowed their biases to operate, even after being urged to answer "as honestly as possible," they become more reflective and cautious in their interpretations.

Sociologists have long talked about the importance of being able to "take the point of view of the other." Actually, my wife and I have endeavored to emphasize this skill during real-life experiences with our two children. Many years ago we set off with our son and daughter (aged 10 and 9 at the time) to Mexico. We all hopped in the van and — since we wanted to see Carlsbad Caverns en route — ended up in New Mexico. At that juncture we had an idea. We would have done better to have had it sooner, for we had to backtrack halfway across Texas, but we eventually ended up at the Alamo in San Antonio. And that old mission is done up well, with commemora-

---

Exercise 1: SSB
(Scale of Social Behavior)

Please answer each of the following questions as quickly and as honestly as possible. For each question, give a percentage from 0 to 100. All responses are anonymous.

1. I'd guesstimate that I have more years of formal education than _____%
   of others in this group.
2. I'd guesstimate that I have a better sense of humor than _____% of others
   in this group.
3. I'd guesstimate that I am more physically fit than _____% of others in this
   group.
4. I'd guesstimate that I am more helpful toward others than _____% of
   others in this group.
5. I'd guesstimate that I have more years of work experience than _____% of
   others in this group.
6. I'd guesstimate that I am more sensitive than _____% of others in this
   group.

---

tive fountains, coonskin caps, Bowie knives, and Davey Crockett's rifle Old Betsy, which apparently remained beside him after he fell. During our visit, both Chris and Amber were, quite rightly, incredibly impressed by this glorious stand. These brave heroes could have escaped, but they remained to defend their country. Chris bought several books, and read them as we continued southward. A couple of days later we reached Mexico City and our first stop there — Chapultepec Castle. The Mexican guide explained during the tour how California, New Mexico, Texas, Florida, et cetera had all been Mexican territory at one time. He also talked about how the American hordes, in 1846 — 10 years after the Alamo — descended upon Chapultepec, then a military school for young cadets. Those boys, in their last stand, attempted to hold the fort against the much larger attacking force. The last lad left alive wrapped himself in the Mexican flag and — so it wouldn't fall into enemy hands — jumped off the cliff to his death. Christopher looked at us and said: "This isn't in any of my books. Did this happen?" We suggested that he ask the guide, who responded unequivocally and emotionally that: "They stole two thirds of our country." Here was firsthand experience with the other point of view! There were amazing acts of heroism, and terrible atrocities, on both sides — all too often we hear only one.

I have also had occasion to use a walk-a-mile-in-my-moccasins exercise on a Canadian reservation in the far north. At the time I was trying to explain the point-of-view-of-the-other concept to a small group of high-school students. Abruptly a striking Native youth rose to his feet and said confrontationally: "Okay, white man! ..." Being an educator of incredible perspicacity, I realized that I was about to have a problem. The angry fellow went on to state: "You've taken our land; our language. Why should I listen to you? I refuse to be part of this. You talk big about the other viewpoint, but you haven't lived what I have!" Taken aback, I was at a loss how to respond. I was partly sympathetic, but also felt anger swelling up — after all, I didn't think that I personally should bear sole responsibility for past injustices. Happily at that moment a young lady got up to answer with a powerful message of her own: "Okay, Indian macho. I'm Métis, and I've been bullied, beaten up, and frightened from the time I entered school — and you have been a part of that. Our families aren't even allowed to live in the community — you've got us stuck out in Back River. You talk about prejudice, but it's alive and well right here." The young man, to his everlasting credit, stopped dead and replied: "You're right, I have been a part of that; it will never happen again." Taking the other point of view can have this kind of impact. Naturally, things don't always work out so perfectly — but I see no reason to share any of my failures. However, it can frequently be extremely useful to calm down, step back, and look at things from a different perspective.

Individuals and groups can reach a point in their problem solving where they plateau, "run out of gas," or get "bogged down" in interpersonal conflict. At such times, taking the point of view of the other can help in getting "unstuck." To stress this point, we occasionally use a mini-debating technique outlined in Exercise 2.

RELATIONSHIP BUILDING AND GROUP DYNAMICS

"No man is an island unto himself": other people affect virtually all of what we say and do. To put things in perspective: would your behavior at a major league baseball game remain the same if you were the only person in the stands? Clearly, the presence of others makes a real difference. Even a seemingly private act, such as taking an examination, still has highly public overtones. For example, the presence of others in the room may affect behavior and — while no one knows what a student is writing during testing — his or her thoughts will be open to public inspection as soon as the professor gets a hold of the exam booklet. To put it another way, one is writing with another in mind, making it very much a social event. Private behavior, including solitary thinking, is also profoundly affected by parents, grandparents, siblings, teachers, and peers, whether they are physically present or not. Do we not remember and follow the advice of significant others, even when they are no longer living?

**Exercise 2: A Mini-Debate
(Getting "Unstuck" through Changing Perspective)**

Divide the group into pairs. Randomly select one partner in each group, and give him or her (in oral or written form) the following instructions:

"State your views on one of these controversial topics: corporal punishment in child rearing, capital punishment, abortion, or raising the legal age for drinking and/or driving."

After this task has been completed, continue as follows:

"Now, **arguing in favor of the opposite point of view**, briefly debate the issue with your partner."

While participants are still in dyads, you may choose to ask questions such as:

✦ "In dealing with complex issues, what is gained by looking at things differently"?

✦ "How might taking a different point of view help us get "unstuck" in our present situation?"

Reconvene and share thoughts with the total group.

In the social psychology realm, researchers dealing with the well-known error of attribution (Heider, 1980) have helped us to understand that all too often people make the mistake of attaching too much importance to internal dispositional factors ("Johnny is a bad kid"), and not enough to social variables ("Johnny behaves badly because he is abused at home, doesn't have enough to eat, and has only seen violent models throughout his young life"). Similarly, a leader who is successful in one setting because of a fortuitous fit between his personality and the situation, might well become singularly ineffective under altered conditions. His style may remain constant, but the circumstances, and therefore the results, can change (Peter & Hull, 1969). As conditions shift, then, in our problem-solving groups, it makes sense to encourage different individuals to take the initiative at different times.

Knapp (1984) has examined the face-to-face processes that are involved in interpersonal interactions. He observes that, as relationships form, people go through specific stages: from initiating to experimenting, to intensifying, to integrating, to bonding. Concomitantly, there are identifiable stages when relationships dissolve: differentiating, circumscribing, stagnating, avoiding, and terminating. There are also definite stages of small-group development, which some have christened "forming," "storming," "norming," and "performing" (cf. Tuckman & Jensen, 1977). These terms reflect the fact that, to become truly productive, groups (and the individuals therein) must have time to come together tentatively, go through an experimenting period of uncertainty, and establish organizational procedures and strategies (see *Chapter 5: Managing CPS Groups* for more information). Unfortunately, though, many groups are pressured to make quick decisions during their "forming" and "storming" stages, before they are ready. Is it a good idea to expect — as we often do — a newly-elected town council, with many first-time members, to deal immediately with urgent budget and staffing issues?

TIME

To repeat, interpersonal bonding and positive group development take time. Yet we are so often ruled and rushed by the clock. Time, essentially no more than an artificial human invention to help describe motion and change, has been made to seem so real that it governs the way we think in our society. Charleston (1989), an Aboriginal professor and theologian, speaks of the "tyranny of time," and of how it pervades our thinking: we spend, waste, borrow, and save time; we budget, invest, and manage it. We turn back its hands. We rationalize neglecting our children by saying that we provide them with "quality time." Even at rest we can't escape — that's "down time."

Although we must live in, adapt to, and use the language of today's world, we can at least give ourselves some time, peace, and breathing space. So, while slipping back into the vernacular of the day, let's not forget that acts of basic humanity — caring, generosity, helping — all take time. Research conducted at a theological seminary brings this point home in powerful fashion (Darley & Batson, 1973). In the study in question, several students of religious studies were asked to walk from one campus building to another, an adjacent recording studio, to give a short, off-the-cuff speech about the Good Samaritan (not an especially onerous task for seminarians). For individuals in the first group, everything went smoothly; they knew there was more than enough time to stroll leisurely to the session. On the way, though, they encountered a groaning "victim" — a confederate — collapsed in a doorway. Of these unhurried seminarians, approximately two-thirds stopped and offered assistance. Those in the second group, however, were put in a time squeeze — they were told they had to rush to make it to the studio on time. When these harassed, hurried students encountered the same victim, very few (only 10%) stopped to lend a hand. Many circled around; some stepped over him! As Myers (1987) points out, this is one of the most deliciously ironic moments ever captured in a study of human behavior:

theology students, mentally rehearsing a speech on the Good Samaritan parable, ignoring a victim lying in front of them! Extrapolating, it gives one pause to think about what happens when beleaguered educators are faced with impossibly large classes, or when nursing care is cut back in our hospitals, leaving overworked staff stretched to the limit.

Lonely people, desperate for a relationship, sometimes push too hard too fast and "turn off" potential partners by trying to "make time" before it is appropriate. It is often a serious error to force things and to move too quickly. In organizations, it can be unwise as well. It takes time for an employee to gain acceptance. All too frequently, newly-appointed, naive, save-the-world type managers set about to redefine paradigms the moment they walk in the door, without stopping to think that there may be people in place who have given decades of service to the company. If administrators truly want to be accepted and have a long-term impact, they should take the time to earn what Hollander (1958) calls "idiosyncrasy credits." These "brownie points', as it were, build up as new employees pay their dues. Once a reasonable supply of credits has been acquired, one can take more risks and deviate from procedure. After a foray of pushing the limits, it may be time to lie low for a bit, until another stock of figurative credits are accumulated. Basically, by learning, establishing rapport, and first giving staff what they want, skilled leaders may eventually earn the opportunity to give them what they need (McCluskey, 1976).

Likewise, it is a mistake to rush to create instant working groups artificially, or to expect immediate success once they have been formed. Time must be given to allow for things to evolve and coalesce. There is usually no need to force personal disclosures or deal with heavy-duty issues too early in the problem-solving process. There are always "safe supplies" — the weather or the local news — to talk about for a spell, and comfortable issues with which to start the proceedings. One cannot expect to bring a group together and move to the performing stage right off the bat. It is true there is a great deal of information to examine when applying or training CPS, but if the first few days are too intense, camaraderie, understanding and effectiveness may be sacrificed. Since more and better ideas are generated in safe, supportive environments, it is only logical to start off in a leisurely, nonthreatening manner. Once the group jells, it should be possible to pick up the pace with a vengeance.

CONFORMITY AND GROUPTHINK

In life, it is essential that there be a certain degree of predictability and conformity. For example, chaos would result if we didn't know to stop at red lights, line up at movie theaters, take our assigned seats on an airplane, or arrive at work on time. However, although we require order in our world, following routines without thinking can sometimes cause us to restrict observations, misinterpret events and miss opportunities. This can occur at both the individual and group levels.

Three separate studies undertaken by Sherif, Asch, and Milgram illustrate the potentially debilitating impact of overconformity. Sherif (1937), in one of the earliest attempts to examine the issue, seated experimental subjects alone in a darkened room. A pinpoint of light appeared 15 feet in front of each of them and, after a few moments, it began to waver erratically. When asked to guess how far the light moved, the subjects responded, on average, around 8 inches. In another condition, however, subjects were joined by two confederates, who repeatedly gave lower answers (1 or 2 inches). Gradually, several of the real subjects were influenced to adjust their guesses downward. That is, because of pressure created by others, many subjects changed their decisions. The irony of the entire situation was that Sherif's study also illustrated the autokinetic phenomenon (a perceptual illusion where in a stationary light — that never moves at all — appears to shift in the dark).

Several years later, Asch (1956) arranged for one legitimate subject to be joined by several actors or confederates. The real subject was deceived into thinking that the confederates were also participants in the study. All of the individuals sat in a classroom, and the experimenter placed two cards in front of the group. The card on the left had a single line on it, while the one on the right had three (one of which was precisely the same length as the line on the left). Basically, the task was straightforward: subjects were to identify the line on the right that matched the one on the left. The discriminations were not at all difficult. Everything started off in routine fashion — on the first two trials, all subjects agreed on the correct answers. On the third trial, however, each and every confederate confidently gave the wrong response before the true subject's turn came around. It was easy to see that the social pressure had an impact, for the legitimate participants typically appeared puzzled, anxious, and rather distraught. There were, of course, pronounced individual differences in ability to withstand the conformity pressure. Many people, despite their discomfiture, stayed the course and maintained their original judgments. Many others, however, did not: they changed their minds and chose obviously wrong alternatives. A control condition demonstrated the power of the social pressure. Alone, subjects made few mistakes — the error rate was only 7.4%. In the experimental, conformity condition, it rose to a startling 33.2%.

More disturbing yet were Milgram's (1965, 1974) studies on the effect of pressure from an authority figure. Responding to an advertisement, a true subject appeared at the psychology laboratory at Yale University, along with a solitary confederate. They were met by a formal, imposing experimenter who started out by stating that this was an experiment dealing with the effects of punishment on learning. The task put before the two was to learn word pair lists. One subject was to teach the other, and punish mistakes by administering electric shocks of increasing severity. Both drew their respective roles out of a hat. Naturally, however, the draw was "rigged" so that the real subject became the "teacher" while the confederate was cast in the "learner" role. That learner, a middle-aged man of gentle appearance, was ushered into an adjoining room and strapped into a seat: an electrode was attached to his wrist. The experimenter then led the teacher back into the main room and placed him in front of a "shock generator" apparatus, with switches supposedly designed to administer shocks of 15 though 450 volts (with 15-volt increments). The apparatus was clearly marked, from "slight shock" at the lower end, to "severe shock," to "XXX." Each time the learner feigned an error, the teacher was instructed to increase the severity of the shock by 15 volts. In the lower range, the actor playing the part of the learner would grunt as the shock was supposedly administered, and by 120 volts he was exhibiting clear discomfort. At 150 volts, he cried out that he refused to continue. By 270 volts, he was emitting screams of agony. And as the real subjects threw the switch to 300 volts, the learner screamed out another refusal; at 330 volts he fell completely silent. Throughout, the experimenter was not allowed to intervene, other than to give some simple verbal prods such as "Please go on," "It's essential that you continue," and the like. Amazingly, despite the learner's intensely agonized screams and requests to be removed from the experiment, well over 60% of the teachers went all the way to 450 volts.

This study has been replicated with similar results. In fact, in one variation, the confederate complained about a heart condition. Still, the teachers persisted. Importantly, it was not that they enjoyed the experience; many were trembling, groaning, and under obvious stress. Although they didn't like it, however, they complied— which illustrates the point that even good people can abandon their moral standards and do bad things under certain circumstances. When debriefing occurred, many subjects explained their obedience to the fact that they were simply "following orders" — the self-same defense of Eichmann, Lieutenant Calley, and Oliver North.

Upping the ante still further, Janis (1971, 1982a, 1982b) used the term "groupthink" to describe a phenomenon where critical and creative thinking are virtually obliterated in groups that became too cohesive and unidimensional. In most cases, of course, group mind is more expansive than individual mind (or to put it more colloquially, "Two heads are better than one!"). However, with groupthink, the group dynamics often cause things to go very wrong.

Janis identified eight specific characteristics of groupthink: (1) Illusion of Invulnerability (where group members, looking at the situation from only one perspective, feel that they cannot fail); (2) Rationalization (where people in the group justify or rationalize their actions, ignoring any evidence which is incompatible with their chosen path); (3) Inherent Morality (where the players believe passionately that their actions are justified — some horrible atrocities are committed by those who are absolutely convinced they are "doing the right thing"); (4) Stereotypes (where individuals caught up in the process tend to dismiss, belittle, and minimize the worth of others who hold different points of view — such simplistic stereotyping is often seen during war time); (5) Conformity Pressure (where pressure is applied, often by authority figures who manipulate the agenda for their own purposes); (6) Self-censorship (where many group members, because of the circumstances of the situation, end up censoring their own thoughts — they fail to voice doubts or concerns); (7) Mindguards (individuals who blindly uphold the leader, to the point of suppressing information, reproaching dissenters, and restricting discussion — in business, we call such people assistant managers; in schools, vice-principals); (8) Illusion of Unanimity (when few criticisms are raised, most people become doubly reluctant to express their own doubts and, hearing none from others, they assume that everyone is in agreement).

There is no shortage of examples. Janis (1971) illustrated his original groupthink argument by using the 1961 Bay of Pigs fiasco, where President Kennedy and his advisors (including Robert Kennedy, Arthur Slessinger, and Robert McNamara) decided to launch a patently inane attack on Cuba. It was doomed to failure from the beginning, but — in the face of information readily available to Kennedy and his advisors — the group forged ahead anyway. There have been many other illustrations of groupthink, including escalating the conflict in Vietnam and the Watergate cover-up (Janis, 1982b), as well as the Challenger space shuttle disaster and the Iran-Contra affair (Whyte, 1989). At a personal level, most of us can surely think of some situation — in business, education, or elsewhere — where things went sadly awry because, bowing to conformity pressure, we kept silent instead of speaking out.

Obviously, overly similar, cohesive groups — where everyone agrees and thinks alike — are particularly vulnerable to groupthink. Some insecure administrators, obsessed with hiring nonthreatening personnel, end up with an office full of clones in an at-risk climate. In contrast, a strong leader possesses the confidence and wherewithal to seek out diversity and those who may challenge prevailing views.

Janis (1982a) has also outlined several methods for guarding against groupthink, and most can be used directly in problem-solving training. Some of these suggestions, in adapted or extended form, are presented below (see Figure 1):

1. Make a point of sharing concrete information about the groupthink phenomenon. When individuals and groups are wary and mindful of the dangers, they are less likely to fall into traps. It's better to prevent than to lament — and awareness is the key to prevention. By regularly discussing the dynamics of groupthink with colleagues, staff, and other groups, potential problems can be nipped in the bud.

2. Form subgroups. Since it is much easier to voice doubts in a small, intimate setting than in a large forum, subgroups should be created periodically — especially when weighty decisions are to be taken. The members of each mini-group can bounce around ideas and issues in "emotional comfort," and then that unit can report back to the main body. In the close, more personal setting, it is much more likely that doubts, objections and concerns will be expressed and considered.

MANAGING GROUPTHINK

- Make a point of sharing concrete information about the groupthink phenomenon.

- Form Subgroups.

- Use inside "experts."

- Use outside "experts."

- Assign a devil's advocate.

- Mix and Match participants for some of the time.

- Gently prod trainers and facilitators to accept criticism and encourage doubts to be expressed.

- Help group members frame doubts and objections positively rather than confrontationally.

- Hold second chance meetings.

- Provide participants with a repertoire or "toolbox" of problem-solving skills.

Figure 1: Suggestions for Guarding against Groupthink

3. Use inside "experts." There is a tendency to look far afield for input and advice, while ignoring talent close at hand (the never-a-prophet-in-your-own-land syndrome). Yet sometimes, perceptive individuals from within may notice things that the leaders and other organizational members have overlooked. Talented insiders should be identified, acknowledged, and encouraged to voice their ideas and suggestions — and, if need be, to challenge the direction of the group as a whole.

4. Use outside "experts." It is also true that the people within an organization do not always have entirely accurate, unbiased perceptions — they may be just too close to the situation. It's akin to having a long-lost friend, one you haven't seen in years, suddenly appear and immediately observe, "Look how big the kids have gotten!" You may be somewhat taken aback to find — having been so close to the youngsters day after day — that their development has quietly "snuck up" on you. Similarly, consultants or other outsiders can sometimes notice things about an operation that insiders miss. Every now and again, therefore, such people should be invited in — formally or informally depending on the context — to "evaluate" the goings-on.

5. Assign a devil's advocate. In business and education, it is not always necessary to search for a devil's advocate: there are often very visible ones close at hand. To prevent any one person from becoming the proverbial "whiner," however, it is a good plan to ask various staff members to rotate in and out of the naysayer role. Those cast in the part should be encouraged to make others think by looking for the flaws, gaps, or possible objections to ideas or policy.

6. "Mix and match" participants for some of the time. Obviously, a diverse group composed of members with different styles, viewpoints, and ideas, is less likely to march blindly onward in one narrow, inflexible direction.

7. Gently prod trainers and facilitators to accept criticism and encourage doubts to be expressed. It isn't easy, but secure leaders solicit and genuinely welcome dissent and divergent viewpoints, rather than sweep criticism under the table.

8. Help group members frame doubts and objections positively rather than confrontationally. Adversarial attacks are counterproductive for the most part, but positive questioning fosters meaningful problem solving. The point is, as Lincoln so lucidly put it, that "He has a right to criticize who has the heart to help."

9. Hold second chance meetings. While some decisions have to be made immediately, most don't. The world won't come to an end if we defer action for a brief spell; in fact, many bad decisions are made precisely because people rush forward too impetuously. It is easy to hop on bandwagons with alacrity, but more difficult to get off: we would usually be better served if more time were spent carefully considering alternatives. A good tool for slowing things down a bit, without impeding progress, is to have second or last chance meetings. After the group decides on a policy or direction, the leader should allow some time for ideas to "perk" — a pressure-free period when people can talk things over with members of their units, their families, or significant others. In other words, give people "some breathing space" and a chance to "sleep on it." In a week or two, the issues will still be there; and people will have had time to think things out thoroughly before final implementation gets underway.

10. Provide participants with a repertoire or "toolbox" of problem-solving skills (Isaksen, Dorval, & Treffinger, 1994, 1998; Treffinger, Isaksen, & Dorval, 1994). This procedure is the very essence of CPS and will allow individuals and groups to redefine, recast, and work through issues, and to some extent liberate themselves from ever-present biases and social pressures.

Nonverbal Signals

Although most of us, at first consideration, would probably think of communication as primarily verbal, man does not live by word alone. In interpersonal interaction, for example, people can stop talking, but — because of nonverbal signals — they can never stop communicating. No one would disagree that even a corpse sends out a strong message! There has been a great deal of pioneering research in the nonverbal realm in general (cf. Adler & Towne, 1993; Alcock, Carment, & Sadava, 1998; Argyle, 1969; Gazda, Asbury, Balzer, Childers, Phelps, & Walters, 1999; Hall, 1969; Mehrabian, 1971, 1972), and on specific dimensions such as facial expression (Ekman & Friesen, 1971), gestures (Birdwhistle, 1970), personal space (Hall, 1963; Sommer, 1969), tone of voice (McCluskey & Albas, 1981), and cultural differences (McCluskey & Albas, 1978). For illustrative purposes here, rather than attempt to probe any one area in depth, an effort will be made to highlight the ubiquitous power of "nonverbals" by discussing briefly three compelling concepts from the literature in the field.

First, let's consider "personal space" or "proxemics." While the paving-the-way investigator here was E. T. Hall (1963), others, most notably Sommer (1969), went on to note that human behavior reflects the fact that there is a personal space zone or "invisible bubble" around each of us. Many sociologists and social psychologists have noted that, in our culture, standard interactional space between communicators tends to be approximately 18 to 20 inches. If someone comes too close, invades our territory, and figuratively "bursts our bubble," most of us feel uncomfortable. For example, on a crowded bus, individuals who are forced to stand may defend their immediate territory by raising their arms, shopping bags, or purses; and in a university library or study hall, if actual dividers are not used to create separate "containers," students tend to state nonverbally that "This is my territory!" by leaving markers, such as jackets on the chairbacks, or pens, books, and papers scattered on the table.

As others have noted, you can test the personal space notion in real-life settings. Take, for instance, an intimate dinner-for-two scenario. To elicit behaviors associated with territorial defense, all you have to do is unobtrusively push a few of your eating utensils across to the other half of the table: most often, your "date" will then begin to feel a trifle uneasy and, at the earliest opportunity, shove the items in question back into "your" territory.

Perhaps the classic example of proxemics at work is in an elevator. As people enter, they typically try to maximize the available distance among them. Thus, the first few passengers take up positions with their backs to the wall: corners are usually occupied first, more central space next. As others come in, positions are rearranged to divide the available territory equitably. Because of the ongoing invasion of space in such close quarters, the ride can become rather tense as an elevator grows more crowded, and people are packed together in canned sardine fashion. Actions show that most of us understand implicitly the nonverbal rules, for how many times — in the midst of an engaging conversation in the hall with a friend — do we abruptly fall silent upon entering the elevator, and remain so until stepping out? (At which point we pick up the broken-off conversation, as if there had been no interruption.)

Moving on, the second behavior for discussion is "civil inattention," which — according to Goffman (1963) — is a ritualized means of acknowledging a stranger's dignity. The "civil" part of the term refers to the fact that typically we recognize another's humanity by a brief glance; immediately after, though, we move to the "inattention" or avoidance-of-eye-contact phase. Goffman describes the situation where two people approach one another on a sidewalk. At a distance, they take a quick look, but as they come closer, both will avert their gaze. Similarly, in the crowded elevator situation, the problem of what to do with the eyes is usually solved by staring fixedly at something innocuous, such as the ground or the lights indicating the floor numbers. And in a doctor's packed waiting room, we grab a safe magazine to page through: it doesn't even matter if the only periodical left is the Manitoba Surgical Review!

Consider the subtlety. Even though many of us can't recall having been formally taught to avert our eyes in particular social situations, we have nonetheless learned the hidden rule of civil inattention. The proof is in the pudding: people who catch one another looking too closely on the sidewalk, in an elevator, or in a waiting room, appear guilty and quickly focus their gaze elsewhere.

The third concept is "body gloss." Another term coined by Goffman (1972), it refers to a whole range of gestures that people will often use in public situations to make their behavior comprehensible to bystanders — especially when their actions are open to misinterpretation. Occasionally, examples occur in public parking lots, when individuals mistakenly attempt to unlock the wrong car — one that is the same model as theirs. Those caught in such a compromising position (for it may appear to onlookers that theft is the motive) will stop, look around, put on weak smiles, shake their bowed heads, and orient themselves toward their own vehicle — anything to communicate that they have simply made a mistake, not embarked upon a life of crime. With body gloss, we're sending nonverbal messages about ourselves that are under our conscious control. Athletes wear their sports crests, tough guys black leather, business managers custom-made suits, and some intellectuals their long hair. By engaging in impression management we can arrange nonverbal cues to make a positive impact on others. In interviews, for example, there is reason to dress appropriately, maintain eye contact, "lose" the gum or cigarette, and send out alert, respectful messages.

Physical "props" can also be arranged purposefully. Anyone who has been intimidated in a business executive or principal's office will know the feeling: it can be demeaning to be placed in an immobile chair (without arm rests), and left to stare across a gigantic desk at a person who is obviously much more important than you.

The wall-to-wall carpeting, rows of books (likely unread) on the shelves, and the general officious tone send a forceful message. Some authoritarian types go further, by taking a high-status pose (e.g., reclining in their chairs and — with hands clasped behind the head — making elephant ears). In contrast, many counselors structure furniture for nonverbal warmth, by placing their desks against the wall, supplying round tables and armed chairs so guests can be received as equals, hanging pleasant pictures or posters on the wall, and displaying family pictures prominently (to communicate what caring human beings they are).

Since nonverbal communication is so all-encompassing, CPS facilitators, and those who are guiding change, should give a great deal of thought to establishing a secure, positive atmosphere for the sessions: through the nonverbal arrangement itself it is possible to foster productivity. It's always nice if there is comfortable furniture, good lighting, acres of wall space for hanging flipchart paper, and plenty of room: sterile facilities are not stimulating, and cluttered surroundings breed cluttered thinking.

Verbally, part of Creative Problem Solving training involves deferring judgment at times, and on other occasions framing questions and statements positively and supportively. It is important, however, that participants learn to defer judgment nonverbally as well. What is the use of withholding negative comments, only to scowl, slouch, or otherwise communicate displeasure or boredom? Exercise 3 has been designed to help participants understand the need to set a positive nonverbal tone, and to encourage them to be more attentive toward others on the hidden-message channel.

Attitudes, Expectations, and Positive Tone

Research speaks to the fact that we should do our best to view our co-workers, our students, and situations in general in a positive light. In their time-honored work on self-fulfilling prophecy, for example, Rosenthal and Jacobson (1968) assessed elementary school children and "identified" a number of "late bloomers" who — although they had shown no special talent to that point — were supposedly soon about to blossom. To be more precise, teachers were told that cognitive testing had revealed that a few of the youngsters possessed latent potential that was about to burst forth. Of course, Rosenthal had practiced a deception: the students in question had simply been chosen by chance, not on the basis of any test results. Somehow, though, during reassessment, it was found that the IQ's of these randomly selected "late bloomers" had in fact gone up. Self-fulfilling prophecy had been at work, in that the teachers got precisely what they expected.

Exercise 3: NB/NA
(Speaking without Words)

The Scenario

It is suggested that there be two facilitators for this exercise. Begin by stating that we will warm up with an ice-breaking, getting-to-know-you activity. Ask two volunteers to give a 3-minute "speech" to the group on "My Favorite Activity." (It is expected that the more extroverted types will self-select and volunteer.) The speakers will present individually. One facilitator will leave the room with the two speakers and help them prepare for this "event." At the same time, the other facilitator will work to prepare the group. There will be two conditions:

NB — For Speaker One, the audience will act "Nonverbally Bored." That is, the scene will be staged so that group members appear to be uninterested. Some will avoid eye contact; others will slouch back in their chairs, arms folded across their chests; some will stare, with pursed lips, in unsmiling fashion; and all will assume an unenthusiastic mien. Further, one member will stretch out and make "elephant ears" (with hands locked behind the head), one will "unobtrusively" read a magazine, and another will quietly walk out of the room during the presentation. There will be no note-taking.

NA — For Speaker Two, the audience will be "Nonverbally Alert." This time around, group members will react in a more motivated fashion, leaning forward intently, maintaining eye contact, smiling, taking notes, and nodding encouragingly every now and again.

Observations

Group members will be asked to watch the reactions of Speaker One and Speaker Two. After each presentation, they will be given a minute or two to write down some of their observations.

Debriefing and Discussion

During this phase of the exercise, speakers will describe their reactions to the nonverbal feedback they received. Also, group members will be asked:

- ◆ How did you feel in each situation?
- ◆ Did you sense that you could communicate your emotional intent nonverbally?
- ◆ Even though staged, were the emotional reactions contagious?
- ◆ Is there a lesson to be learned here about being positive group members?

To some degree, Rosenthal may have been a victim of his own expectations, for the self-fulfilling prophecy effect has been shown to be less powerful than he first suggested (Elashoff & Snow, 1971; McCormick & Pressley, 1997). Be that as it may, many other studies have verified that our attitudes do matter and that our expectations definitely do affect outcomes. Teachers certainly can send I-think-you're-bright-and-I-expect-you-to-do-well messages by speaking encouragingly to their young charges. Not surprisingly in light of the foregoing discussion, however, positive expectations can also be conveyed nonverbally, by supportive hugs, reinforcing looks, and attentive listening. All students need to receive such messages.

In CPS groups too, the more we search for, appreciate, and communicate the positive, the more likely we are to get it. To help participants internalize nurturing attitudes in problem-solving sessions (and beyond), it is almost obligatory that facilitators plan for success, set an upbeat, optimistic tone, and walk the walk by modeling appropriate behavior.

Ekvall (1983) has identified 10 characteristics that make for creative working environments, including risk-taking, idea time, humor, freedom from conflict, and idea support. There are lessons to be learned from his observations. To function as creatively as possible, participants must feel secure enough to take risks (for making mistakes is a major part of the learning process). It is necessary to respect each individual's space and comfort level.

Although Ekvall's suggestions for setting a creative climate have been dealt with in depth elsewhere (Isaksen, Dorval, & Treffinger, 1994), the notion of "idea time" is worth further elaboration. In some organizations, managers deem it efficient to schedule or fill in each and every employee's time for each and every minute of the day. But is that efficiency? If every minute is booked, when do you casually share and discuss ideas with colleagues? When do you have the "down time" perks that bring fun and joy to the workplace? When do you think? No, over-scheduling is not a sign of efficiency — quite the opposite.

In today's world, it is easy to get too hung up on the corporate agenda and forget about the "therapeutic value of kindness" (Long, 1997; McCluskey & Treffinger, 1998). Exercise 4, Why the Impact?, tries to illustrate this point by asking participants to list the major characteristics of a teacher who had a major impact on their lives. For the most part, they respond by listing "personal" qualities rather than "professional" ones. When lists are coded and clustered, "people words" such as "kind," "compas-

Exercise 4: Why the Impact?

Too many of us seem to forget what it was like to be a child. Some of the best "teachers" are those who remember their childhoods vividly: the joys, the fears, the highpoints, the embarrassments, the achievements, and the disappointments.

Thinking back to your school years, identify — in your own mind — a teacher who had a truly positive impact on your life. List 5 traits that you feel best characterize that particular educator.

1. _____

2. _____

3. _____

4. _____

5. _____

Now, as a group, let's share some of our responses. Would anyone care to share his or her list? We'll identify and record common words or themes.

sionate," "enthusiastic," "caring," "giving," "humorous," "down-to-earth," "sensitive," "empathic," "encouraging," "motivating," and "positive" far outnumber "business words" such as "organized," "efficient," "reliable," "thorough," and so on. It seems that people who have created a positive tone are the ones who have had a lasting impact on most of us; we should all try to do the same!

CONCLUSION

It goes without saying that, in any CPS session, there is a great deal of content to get through: theories, tools, strategies, practice, and real-world issues. However, it is critical for all of us involved in problem solving to remember that, while the task-oriented business is being done, there are a plethora of individual and social events taking place in "a parallel universe" of sorts. The overt goals may monopolize the agenda and intrude more heavily on our consciousness, but unobtrusive factors are having a major influence as well. Devoting some time to these personal, social, and value-laden variables will, at the end of the day, broaden the scope of the problem-solving experience and strengthen its effectiveness.

REFERENCES

Adler, R. B., & Towne, N. (1993). *Looking out/looking in* (7th ed.). Fort Worth, TX: Harcourt Brace & Company.

Alcock, J. E., Carment, D. W., & Sadava, S. W. (1998). *A textbook of social psychology* (4th ed.). Scarborough, ON: Prentice-Hall Allyn and Bacon Canada.

Argyle, M. (1969). *Social Interaction*. New York: Aldine-Atherton.

Asch, S. E. (1956). Studies of independence and conformity: A minority of one against a unanimous majority. *Psychological Monographs, 70* (9, Whole No. 416).

Birdwhistle, R. (1970). *Kinesics and context: Essays on body motion communication*. Philadelphia, PA: University of Pennsylvania Press.

Bolt, M., & Myers, D. G. (1983). *Teacher's resource and test manual to accompany social psychology*. New York: McGraw-Hill.

Charleston, S. (1989). The tyranny of time. *Lutheran Woman Today, 2* (7), 27-32.

Darley, J. M., & Batson, C. D. (1973). From Jerusalem to Jericho: A study of situational and dispositional variables in helping behavior. *Journal of Personality and Social Psychology, 27,* 100-108.

Davis, M. H., & Stephan, W. G. (1980). Attributions for exam performance. *Journal of Applied Social Psychology, 10,* 235-248.

Dunn, R., & Dunn, K. (1978). *Teaching students through their individual learning styles: A practical approach*. Reston, VI: Reston Publishing.

Dunn, R., & Dunn, K. (1992). *Teaching elementary students through their individual learning styles*. Boston, MA: Allyn & Bacon.

Dunn, R., & Dunn, K. (1993). *Teaching secondary students through their individual learning styles*. Boston, MA: Allyn & Bacon.

Dunn, R., Dunn, K., & Price, G. (1978). *Learning Styles Inventory*. Lawrence, KS: Price Learning Systems.

Eggen, P., & Kauchak, D. (1999). *Educational psychology: Windows on classrooms* (4th ed.). Upper Saddle River, NJ: Merrill.

Ekman, P. & Friesen, W. (1971). Constants across cultures in the face and emotion. *Journal of Personality and Social Psychology, 17,* 124-129.

Ekvall, G. (1983). Climate, structure and innovativeness of organizations: A theoretical framework and an experiment. Stockholm, Sweden: The Swedish Council for Management and Organizational Behaviour.

Elashoff, J., & Snow, R. E. (1971). *Pygmalion reconsidered*. Worthington, OH: Charles A. Jones.

Gazda, G. M., Asbury, F. R., Balzer, F. J., Childers, W. C., Phelps, R. E., & Walters, R. P. (1999). *Human relations development: A manual for educators* (6th ed.). Boston, MA: Allyn and Bacon.

Goffman, E. (1963). *Behavior in public places: Notes on the social organization of gatherings.* New York: The Free Press of Glencoe.

Goffman, E. (1972). *Relations in public.* New York: Harper and Row.

Hall, E. T. (1963). A system for the notation of proxemic behavior. *American Anthropologist, 65,* 1003-1026.

Hall, E. T. (1969). *The hidden dimension.* New York: Doubleday.

Heider, F. (1980). *The psychology of interpersonal relations.* New York: Wiley.

Hollander, E. P. (1958). Conformity, status, and idiosyncrasy credit. *Psychological Review, 65,* 117-127.

Hunt, D. E. (1987). *Beginning with ourselves in practice, theory, and human affairs.* Cambridge, MA: Brookline Books.

Isaksen, S. G., Dorval, K. B., & Treffinger, D. J. (1994). *Creative approaches to problem solving.* Dubuque, IA: Kendall-Hunt.

Isaksen, S. G., Dorval, K. B., & Treffinger, D. J. (1998). *Toolbox for creative problem solving: Basic tools and resources.* Buffalo, NY: Creative Problem Solving Group - Buffalo

Janis, I. L. (1971, November). Groupthink. *Psychology Today,* pp.43-46.

Janis, I. L. (1982a). Counteracting the adverse effects of concurrence-seeking in policy-planning groups: Theory and research perspectives. In H. Brandstatter, J. H. Davis, & G. Stocker-Kreichgauer (Eds.), *Group decision making.* (pp. 477-501). New York: Academic Press.

Janis, I. L. (1982b). *Groupthink* (2nd ed.). Boston, MA: Houghton Mifflin.

Keirsey, D., & Bates, M. (1984). *Please understand me: Character and temperament types.* Del Mar, CA: Prometheus Nemesis.

Kirton, M. J. (1976). Adaptors and innovators: A description and measure. *Journal of Applied Psychology, 61* (5), 622-629.

Kirton, M. J. (1989). *Adaptors and innovators: Styles of creativity and problem-solving.* New York: Routledge.

Knapp, M. L. (1984), *Interpersonal communication and human relationships.* Boston, MA: Allyn and Bacon.

Long, N. J. (1997). The therapeutic power of kindness. *Reclaiming Children and Youth: Journal of Emotional and Behavioral Problems, 5* (4), 242-246.

McCluskey, K. W. (1976). Problems of the educational psychologist. *Education Canada, 16* (2), 12-17.

McCluskey, K. W. (1999). At-risk: A catch-all term for a diverse population. *Think, 9* (3), 18-20.

McCluskey, K. W., & Albas, D. C. (1978). Differential sensitivity to contradictory communication as a function of age and culture. *Journal of Cross-Cultural Psychology, 9* (2), 167-178.

McCluskey, K. W., & Albas, D. C. (1981). Perception of the emotional content of speech by Canadian and Mexican children, adolescents, and adults. *International Journal of Psychology*, *16*, 119-132.

McCluskey, K. W., & Treffinger, D. J. (1998). Nurturing talented but troubled children and youth. *Reclaiming Children and Youth: Journal of Emotional and Behavioral Problems*, *6* (4), 215-219, 226.

McCormick, C., & Pressley, M. (1997). *Educational psychology: Learning, instruction, assessment*. New York: Longman.

Mehrabian, A. (1971). *Silent messages*. Belmont, CA: Wadsworth.

Mehrabian, A. (1972). *Nonverbal communication*. Chicago: Aldine-Atherton.

Milgram, S. (1965). Some conditions of obedience and disobedience to authority. *Human Relations*, *18*, 57-76.

Milgram, S. (1974). *Obedience to authority*. New York: Harper and Row.

Myers, D. G. (1987). *Social psychology* (2nd ed.). New York: McGraw-Hill.

Myers, I. B., & McCaulley, M. (1985). *Manual for the Myers-Briggs Type Indicator*. Palo Alto, CA: Consulting Psychologists Press.

Peter, L. J., & Hull, R. (1969). *The Peter Principle*. New York: William Morrow & Co., Inc.

Rosenthal, R., & Jacobson, L. (1968). *Pygmalion in the classroom*. New York: Holt, Rinehart and Winston.

Sherif, M. (1937). An experimental approach to the study of attitudes. *Sociometry, 1*, 90-98.

Sommer, R. (1969). *Personal space: The behavioral basis for design*. Englewood Cliffs, NJ: Prentice-Hall.

Treffinger, D. J., Isaksen, S. G., & Dorval, K. B. (1994). *Creative problem solving: An introduction* (2nd ed.). Sarasota, FL: Center for Creative Learning.

Tuckman, B., & Jensen, M. (1977). Stages of small group development revisited. *Group and Organizations*, *2*, 419-427.

Whyte, G. (1989). Group-think reconsidered. *Academy of Management Review*, *14*, 40-56.

Wiley, M. G., Crittenden, K. S., & Birg, L. D. (1979). Why a rejection? Causal attribution of a career achievement event. *Social Psychology Quarterly*, *42*, 214-222.

Woolfolk, A. E. (1998). *Educational psychology* (7th ed.). Boston, MA: Allyn and Bacon.

CHAPTER FIVE

MANAGING CLIENTS AND RESOURCE GROUPS

Scott G. Isaksen
Creativity Research Unit
Creative Problem Solving Group — Buffalo

> "Nothing is more interesting for humans than human activity — and the most characteristically human activity is solving problems; thinking for a purpose, devising a means to some desired end."
>
> George Polya

INTRODUCTION

Up to now you have been reading about the method of Creative Problem Solving, its foundation and developmental history, and the role and factors for its effective facilitation. The two other roles included in our Model for CPS Facilitation include the client and the resource group. These are social roles in that they each have a unique function when CPS is being applied. This chapter will describe the desired characteristics within each role as well as a model for how groups develop and grow.

The CPS Client

It is important for group members to know that their efforts have some meaning and relevance. This can be achieved only if someone within the group has a sincere interest in implementing the solutions the group generates. Thus the facilitator must interact with a client. This is the individual who has decision-making authority, responsibility for implementation or ownership over a particular situation or challenge. The role of client in CPS groups supplies content-related expertise. The client provides focus and guides decision making during the group's session. The client helps to keep the group on track by clarifying the situation, choosing directions and approaches, and actually participating in the group's session. In the final analysis, it's the client who needs to have a problem solved or an opportunity reached. Therefore, the role of client is an important one in determining the effectiveness and productivity of the group's effort. (For more information on the client's role see: Firestien & Treffinger, 1983; Jay, 1977.)

Clients need guidance from the facilitator for making choices and judging at appropriate times, and they need to have support for permitting, encouraging and participating in the generating activities of the group. Clients must demonstrate sincere interest in working with the group and process to bring about change. For clientship to be present, there must be room for a new approach or fresh idea which the client is willing and able to implement. The client must also have enough clear influence to implement the outcomes of the CPS process. This type of ownership builds commitment to the group process and helps in the development of effective groups.

The role of client helps to provide the group access to a clear definition of the task at hand. The client shares the most important background data and provides other information the group needs to know before proceeding. Elements of the client's task must be specified and have clear connection to his or her responsibilities. In short, the client provides much of the domain-relevant expertise necessary for productive problem solving.

Many times it is possible to identify just one clear client. At other times the ownership is distributed among a group. More broadly, there are some challenges and opportunities that have widely distributed ownership. For example, all of us are currently concerned (to varying degrees) about global warming or the threat of nuclear destruction. Managing group clientship provides the facilitator with an even more complicated challenge. Usually group clientship requires special attention be given to the focusing aspects of CPS. It may be necessary to modify the process technology, the time-frame within which the group will work, and other factors when working with more than one client. In particular, the time and energy necessary for effectively working through Appraising Tasks, Designing Process, and Session Planning, as well as session time for focusing activities, will expand substantially as the number of clients increases.

The client for a CPS session can be a sponsor (or a sustaining sponsor) of an organizational change. In the best case there is a clear connection between the client of the session and the sponsor of the change (Connor, 1993). A sponsor is someone who has the clear and legitimate authority to initiate an organizational change. Often a sponsor can involve someone else in the change initiative who can take on the role of a sustaining sponsor. This is someone who has a direct relationship with the sponsor and who can also take legitimate authority to implement the change. As a CPS facilitator, it will be important to know who the sponsor is and to confirm the clientship for the session. This may involve having the sponsor or sustaining sponsor serve in the role of client before, during and after the session. This can also involve the sponsor in kicking off a session for which the sponsor has delegated clientship to someone else. You will need to be involved in making the delegation agreement clear to the resource group in order to ensure a productive session. This also ensures that the results of the session will add value to the overall change initiative.

Identifying Characteristics of Effective Clients

First, a distinction must be drawn between client and clientship. A client is a person who has a particular social role before, during and after a CPS session. Clientship is synonymous with ownership. Ownership implies that there is sufficient motivation or interest to work on the problem or challenge; there is appropriate authority, responsibility or influence to take action, and there is a need to consider novel approaches which require the use of imagination. In addition to ownership, there are a number of other characteristics held by many of the most effective clients with whom we have worked. A few of the more important of these characteristics are described below.

Genuinely Interested in Taking Action

Effective clients are interested and motivated to deal with the problem situation. They actively seek involvement and contribution from others. They display a positive attitude and commitment by attending and actively participating in planning meetings and group sessions, as well as by taking action on the outcomes of meetings.

Assumes Authority and Responsibility for Problem Situation

Effective clients have the authority and responsibility to take action on the problem situation. They are able to engage in CPS, see value in its use and take action on its outcomes. It is possible for a client to be a "sole proprietor" as well as a "stakeholder." Ownership may be closely held or widely distributed. In either case, the actual level of responsibility and breadth of accountability for implementation must be clearly identified. Clients are able to effectively answer the question: "Why is this your challenge?"

Willing to Change or Modify Paradigms

You know you have a good client when they show you that they can tolerate ambiguity or question some of their assumptions. The whole notion of putting a great deal of time and energy into planning your approach may be an entirely new way of working for many clients. Effective clients are willing to change or modify existing ways of doing tasks. They consciously seek novel and imaginative outcomes. They promote the involvement of "outsiders" as resources to assist in providing a diversity of novel perspectives.

Committed to the Use of CPS

Effective clients understand the value of CPS and are willing to provide the time, energy and planning necessary for productive outcomes. They see value in all three CPS roles (client, facilitator and resource group) and take the responsibilities associated with their role seriously. They actively collaborate with facilitators to plan, deliver and debrief the CPS session or application. They provide feedback to facilitators and resource group members when they have implemented change.

Trusts CPS Process

Clients often become involved in CPS activities with which they may not be familiar. Effective clients trust the process in that they follow the guidelines and principles necessary to provide the desired outcome or result. They remain open to the generation of novel and unusual perspectives and tolerate the ambiguity which might accompany the use of certain CPS principles and tools.

Flexible in Thinking and Perceptions

It is often necessary to "shift gears" and pursue new avenues or directions. Effective clients remain open to the changes in direction. They listen and accept different approaches taken during various stages and phases of CPS. They stay open to the fact that they might "change their mind."

Has Good People Skills

Effective clients have the ability to make others feel at home and supported. They "read" the facilitator and resource group members and know when and how to respond. They maintain an appropriate level of eye contact with others and listen carefully to options; their non-verbal behavior matches the purpose of the session, as well as their verbal comments, and they provide an appropriate level of encouragement without smothering or controlling the session.

Has Integrity

Effective clients have a strong set of beliefs in the value of diversity and the importance of unleashing human creativity. They see value in working with people to identify and solve problems. They see people as part of the solution, not the problem. They are honest in dealing with others and themselves. If the possibility of a "hidden agenda" emerges, they are able to identify it openly and find productive alternative approaches.

Has Expertise in the Problem Area

Productive CPS outcomes can often be influenced by the knowledge level and experience of the client. Effective clients are knowledgeable in the problem area to the point that they can communicate the nature of the situation in a simple, clear and understandable manner. In effect, they know their area so well that they could describe it to an eight-year-old child. The client's knowledge and expertise is often necessary for making some sense out of the novel perspectives generated during CPS. There may be special applications of CPS with groups of experts within a particular content domain. Generally, however, if there must be an expert in most CPS sessions or applications, it should be the client.

Is Process Aware

Effective clients are willing to learn and understand the CPS process. They have a general level of awareness of the roles of a CPS session or event, how the tools will operate, and can effectively communicate with the facilitator and the resource group using CPS language. After applying the process, they often engage in a post-session meeting designed to provide feedback about the general level of productivity. This meeting will also help identify the outcomes which were most useful or intriguing, and how the tools generated the variety of outcomes. The purpose of the meeting is to be able to identify if and how the application of the CPS process added value.

Effective clients often take the responsibility for communicating these learnings to the facilitator and the resource-group participants. They see the entire affair through a systems approach. They actively seek out productive learning from the investment everyone has made in the CPS session or application.

THE RESOURCE GROUP

The other members of a CPS group are called participants and they function collectively as the resource group. These resource-group members suggest options and provide a wide range of alternatives during a CPS session or event. Effective resource-group members show an interest in the client's content, but do not make decisions for the client. They support the decisions the client makes and provide a divergent range of possibilities from which the client can choose. In short, they practice effective listening strategies and find ways to make productive contributions to the problem-solving session.

Resource-group members provide energy, diversity of experience, and a variety of viewpoints. The facilitator's challenge is to capitalize on the group's assets and limit their liabilities by providing the necessary balance of creative and critical thinking processes in meeting the needs or goals of the client. Effective use of CPS requires a dynamic balance between deferring judgment when generating options and using affirmative judgment to focus, analyze and develop options.

Another major challenge to the CPS facilitator is to effectively balance and reinforce the roles of facilitator, client, and resource group. Part of this responsibility includes making these roles explicit for all group members so that everyone knows what is expected of them. Although it is beyond the scope of this chapter to thoroughly examine the functional roles and responsibilities of group members (see Benne and Sheats, 1948; Isaksen, 1983 & 1992), these three roles provide the basic interpersonal framework for facilitating CPS in groups.

Deciding to Use a Group

Many people who have attempted to use groups for developing novel and useful alternatives find out that using groups is not always easy, pleasurable or effective. Using groups has both positive and negative aspects. Much of the work done within organizations must be done with groups, but the benefits of participation and involvement have corresponding costs. Anyone who has worked with a large and diverse group to obtain consensus can attest to the fact that it takes a great deal of time and effort.

In considering whether or not to use a group for obtaining a better understanding of the situation, generating options, or making a decision the facilitator needs to pay attention to a number of key factors. These factors include: aspects of group development; the skills and styles of leadership; the roles of client and resource group; group orientation, composition and size; process technology; and the structure of the environment. In addition, the facilitator may need to consider the required quality of the outcome as well as the level of acceptance needed from group members.

Table 1, describing assets and liabilities of using groups, has been developed by weaving together the work of Maier (1970), Vroom (1974), Van Gundy (1984) and Vroom & Jago (1988).

When considering the use of small groups for CPS the facilitator needs to evaluate the existence of the liabilities and assets. The goal is to maximize the positive aspects of group involvement while minimizing the liabilities. As the facilitator can increase the productive use of diversity the likelihood of individual dominance should decrease. In general, if there is a need to provide for participation to increase accep-

ASSETS & LIABILITIES OF USING GROUPS FOR CPS

Potential Assets	Potential Liabilities
Provides greater availability of knowledge and information.	Limits contributions and increases conformity due to social pressures.
Increases the likelihood of building and improving upon ideas of others.	Encourages convergence on options with greatest agreement, regardless of quality.
Provides a wider range of experiences and perspectives.	Provides dominant individuals undue influence and impact on outcomes.
Increases understanding, acceptance, commitment and ownership.	Reduces accountability, allowing for riskier decisions.
Provides opportunities for communication, teaming, and group development.	Causes unproductive levels of competition from conflicting opinions.

Table 1: Potential Assets and Liabilities of Using a Group

tance, if the information is widely held, if there is a need to build on and synthesize the diverse range of experiences and perspectives or if it is important to develop and strengthen the group's ability to learn, you may choose to involve a group in CPS.

SELECTING RESOURCE GROUP MEMBERS

Once you've decided that a group will be beneficial, you will work with the client(s) to select, invite and prepare the members of the resource group. There are a number of key considerations for selecting potential participants for this role. Generally, you want resource-group members who have energy and interest in the task for the session. You also want to be sure that those who participate in CPS sessions have a beneficial perspective to bring to bear on the task. This can include having particular content expertise or experience, or can focus on having a representative voice for a target group of people who will be affected by or will influence the resulting changes.

One major criterion we often consider is the degree of diversity that is required for a particular task. Sometimes we have found it useful to invite people who have absolutely no background with the task to offer a fresh perspective. For other tasks, we need some novel perspectives but also a high degree of expertise with the problem because of its specific technical nature. In one case, we found a retired research chemist who had a great deal of technical experience and background, but felt free to offer a large quantity of varied and original perspectives.

We have found the following considerations helpful when thinking about who should be invited to take on a resource-group role for a CPS application. Will the resource group member:

- ✦ Provide novel perspectives on the task?
- ✦ Be involved in the implementation of the task?
- ✦ Have domain-relevant knowledge of the task?
- ✦ Be at the same organizational level as other resource-group members?
- ✦ Commit to taking on the role and responsibilities of a resource-group member?
- ✦ Be able to work effectively with other resource-group members?
- ✦ Be able to take the needed time for the meeting, session or other form of application?
- ✦ Have the willingness, ability and opportunity to bring something to the application of CPS that the client may find both novel and useful?

Once selected, participants should be briefed about the session's purpose. In the best case, a memo is sent to each invited participant well in advance of the session. This allows for plenty of incubation and individual ideation. The reason for the invitation and other information about the session can also be provided.

CONSIDERING GROUP DEVELOPMENT

Once the group leader has decided that the resources of a group should be convened, there are a number of dynamics to consider. One of the first of these is the notion that groups go through certain phases of development (Bales & Strodtbeck, 1951; Lacoursiere, 1980; Tuckman, 1965; Tuckman & Jensen, 1977). Groups are not static. Like individuals, they are unique, dynamic, complex, living systems capable of learning and development. Figure 1 depicts a model for group development. According to this model, the stages a group goes through while moving toward some desired goal are relatively predictable and controllable. In reality, it is quite clear that in practice these stages are not necessarily linear and sequential. Some groups seem to skip stages, others will approach them in reverse order. Still others will reach a level and need to begin all over again because a new member has joined the group. One of the classic leadership dilemmas is getting the work done, while at the same time maintaining positive human relations. It is this essential tension which is nicely displayed within the context of group development (see Figure 1).

Understanding where groups are and where you want them to be can be helpful in planning for maximum effectiveness and productivity. The two dimensions of the model are personal relations and task functions. In other models these dimensions go by other names, but a number of people involved in group development have identified these two dimensions as being central to the process. Some balance is sought between concern for people and concern for task (Blake & Mouton, 1964).

The personal relations dimension refers to the development of the "human side" of the activity that occurs in the group. Whether it is a task group or a growth group, people progress in development from individuals to group members. They move to become people who feel some attachment to each other and, finally, to people who

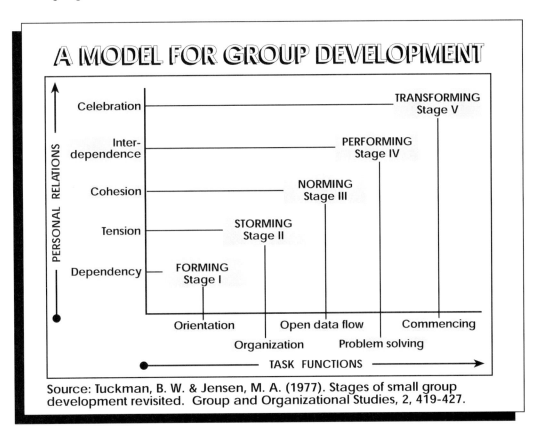

Figure 1: A Model for Group Development

are able to link up in creative kinds of ways. Personal relations involve how people feel about each other, how people expect each other to behave, the commitments that people develop with each other, the kinds of assumptions that people make about each other, and the kinds of problems people have in joining forces with each other in order to get work done. The assumption is that the kinds of groups that are referred to here are all organized for the purpose of achieving goals, tasks, production, etc. and that personal relations refers to the human component in the accomplishing of these purposes.

The other dimension is task functions. Characteristic behaviors can also be identified in the different stages of group development with regard to tasks. A group comes together, learns what the task is, mobilizes to accomplish the task, and does the work. So, the two dimensions, personal relations and task functions, form a matrix in which there is an interaction between characteristic human relations and task-oriented behaviors at the various stages of group development. No two-dimensional model can completely subsume all the data of group interaction without a loss of some precision. The purpose of looking at group development in this relatively simplistic way is to underline the importance, not only of the two dimensions — personal and task — but also to provide a common language whereby group members can explore the emerging characteristics and parameters of the group.

Stage One: Forming

In the initial stage, called forming, personal relations are characterized by dependency, and the major task functions concern orientation. In the beginning of the group's life, the individual members must resolve a number of dependency problems and characteristic behaviors on the personal relations dimension. They tend to depend on the leader to provide all the structure: the group members depend on the facilitator, chairman, or manager to set the ground rules, establish the agenda, and to do all the "leading." The parallel stage in the task function to be accomplished is the orientation of group members to the work that they are being asked to do. The issues have to be specified. The nature of the work itself has to be explored so there is a common understanding of what the group has been organized to do. Common behavior at this point is questioning: why are we here, what are we supposed to do, how are we going to get it done, and what are our goals?

There are clear implications for the CPS facilitator when the group is at this stage of group development. This is the stage where the skills associated with training and teaching are critical. The CPS facilitator must take charge long enough to provide a basic orientation for the group and establish basic ground-rules and norms for operating together. This is accomplished by sharing the results of task appraisal, the session agenda, the task summary and coaching the client to provide a clear introduction to the task. It is during this stage of group development that the facilitator helps set expectations for the roles and responsibilities when working together.

Stage Two: Storming

Stage two is characterized by tension in the personal relations dimension and organization in the task functions dimension. It is referred to as "storming" because interpersonal conflict inevitably ensues as a part of small-group interaction. It may be that the interpersonal tension remains hidden, but it is there. We bring to small group activity a lot of our own unresolved issues with regard to authority, dependency, rules, and agenda. We also experience interpersonal tension as we organize to get work done. As groups move beyond forming, individuals share different points of view and some anxiety is created regarding which way to go and which options to choose. Who is going to be responsible for what? What are the rules? What are going to be the limits? What is going to be the reward system? What are the criteria? The variety of organizational concerns that emerge reflect interpersonal tension over leadership structure, power, and authority.

When learning and applying CPS, members of groups will often have different perspectives on the use of tools, guidelines and language. Some members will be done with storming at different times. Often questions are put forward regarding the value or appropriateness of CPS. On the one hand, it is important for this type of disagreement or questioning to occur. On the other hand, it must be met with effective answers, explanations and modeling. The CPS facilitator must be able to respond effectively to this kind of storming by keeping the purpose of the process transparently clear.

Identifying the three roles, having a good understanding of the needs of the client and selecting the group members carefully can often pay dividends during this stage of group development. Managing interpersonal tension regarding options or ideas is critical at this stage. Keeping this kind of tension separate from personal tension, where individuals might attach the person to the idea, is also important. This is the essential difference between conflict and debate.

We use the word conflict to describe the existence of personal tension. Debate describes the situation where there is idea tension. Debate occurs when there is a diversity of viewpoints and the tension that results is focused on the options or alternatives. When this tension turns into conflict, it has become focused on the person. Conflict means that people will be threatened, and having a different point of view is confused with having the wrong or inferior perspective.

The CPS facilitator must help encourage the diversity of viewpoints, while keeping the personal tension to a minimum. Groups must often be helped through this stage or they will not form into a more cohesive unit capable of high-level performance. This is the stage at which effective application of situational leadership practices are needed.

Stage Three: Norming

In stage three, the personal relations area is marked by cohesion, and the major task function is data-flow. It is during this "norming" stage of development, assuming the group gets this far, that the people begin to experience a sense of "groupness" and a feeling of clarity at having resolved interpersonal conflict. They begin sharing ideas, feelings, giving feedback to each other, soliciting feedback, exploring actions related to the task, and sharing information related to the task. This becomes a period during which people feel good about what is going on; they feel good about being a part of a group, and there is an emerging openness with regard to task. Sometimes during stage three there is a brief abandonment of the task and a period of play that is an enjoyment of the cohesion that is being experienced.

When CPS groups reach this stage, it will be important for the facilitator to provide some recognition and celebration of the group's success. It would be analogous to the feast following the hunt or the song after successfully navigating a raft through the white water. A major challenge for the facilitator is to channel this positive energy onto the client's task. It is often at this stage that facilitators begin to feel the energy and weight of the group, whereas at earlier stages the goal structures were more individualistic and competitive. Now the group may want to cooperate on every task and get hung up when they can't be "...all for one and one for all." Maintaining the focus on the CPS process while encouraging the meeting of the client's need is the major task for the facilitator. The challenge is to let the celebration of consensus last long enough to recharge and refocus the group, but not too long so as to invest unnecessary energy in managing the group for the group's own sake. CPS groups are not formed necessarily or solely as social support systems. Usually the purpose is to move the needed outcomes forward.

Stage Four: Performing

The fourth stage is called "performing" and is marked by interdependence on the personal relations dimension and problem solving on the task functions dimension. Interdependence means that members can work singly, in any sub-grouping, or as a total unit. They are both highly task-oriented and highly person-oriented. The activities are marked by both collaboration and functional competition. The group's tasks are well defined, there is high commitment to common activity, and there is support for experimentation and risk-taking. Stage four is rarely achieved by most groups in general.

This is the stage at which the CPS facilitator can "push the boundaries" on applying the process. If the dynamics have been managed well, the use of the CPS framework should help more groups get to this stage of development. The performing stage is what really describes the effective group application of CPS. This is the stage where the facilitator's challenge will be more focused on selecting the appropriate tools to "ride the wave." Observing the energy of the group and keeping them focused on the task while understanding the reactions of the client become significant challenges for the facilitator.

It is during the performing stage where individual members are both empowered and aligned. They have a shared vision for why they are together and how they are operating. It is at this point where it is appropriate to use the label "team." It is important to remember that groups will not stay at this stage forever (nor should they). During the norming process, the group has very probably formed around an implicit set of assumptions. Occasionally, the facilitator will need to test the boundaries or even question their existence.

Stage Five: Transforming

Stage five is a more recent addition to previous models for group development (see Tuckman & Jensen, 1977). Stage five is called transforming and reflects commencing on the task dimension and celebration on the personal relations dimension. This is the stage within which the group realizes that it has accomplished its purpose and is ready for a transition. Following the completion of the task and purpose the group celebrates its accomplishment and takes the time to honor its members for their contributions. Decisions are taken regarding new purposes or tasks the group may take on or address. Some groups may simply need to focus on starting new work elsewhere and the individual members will leave the group and join others. Some refer to this as terminating. Other groups may need to change membership based on a redefined task or purpose. Still other groups may need to stay together, but address an entirely new task. These conditions are often referred to as adjourning.

When groups reach this stage, the CPS facilitator usually needs to help the group close down and determine its next steps. Much like what happened during the norming stage, the facilitator needs to be ready to help the group recognize its accomplishments and celebrate meeting its purpose. This celebration may take the form of applauding the entire group or observing and congratulating a few of the unique contributions of individuals within the group. To help the group commence, the facilitator may need to help manage the recording of the output of a session and identifying the next steps that need to be taken. Finally, it is helpful to engage in some reflection regarding the learning from what the group did and how it worked together during the transforming stage. This stage represents an excellent opportunity for the facilitator to engage in experiential learning (see Chapter 9 entitled Guiding the Experiential Learning of CPS).

Applying the Model of Group Development

When applying the model it is important to remember that this is not a static description of how groups develop. In other words, it is highly unlikely that a particular group would work their way through this process in a systematic manner. Groups will continually develop. Each time a new member joins or a new task is introduced, the development process begins anew.

Understanding some of the dynamics and patterns that occur within groups is essential if a facilitator wants to diagnose and describe the current status of any group, predict what might occur in the future, and provide behavior and influence which might help the group move on to a more productive level of development. For the leader of CPS activity it is important to provide appropriate leadership strategies to move the group beyond learning basic skills and how the CPS tools can be organized around components and process. The aim is productively applying these learnings to real challenges and opportunities. Group development combined with an appropriate understanding and application of facilitative leadership strategies can help CPS groups reach higher levels of application (Carew, Parisi-Carew & Blanchard, 1984).

REFERENCES

Bales, R. F., & Strodtbeck, F. L. (1951). Phases in group problem solving. *Journal of Abnormal and Social Psychology, 46,* 485-495.

Benne, K. D., & Sheats, P. (1948). Functional roles of group members. *Journal of Social Issues, 4,* 41-49.

Blake, R. R., & Mouton, J. S. (1964). *The managerial grid.* Houston, TX: Gulf Publishing Co.

Carew, D. K., Parisi-Carew, E., & Blanchard, K. H. (1984). *Group development and situational leadership: A model for managing groups.* Escondido, CA: Blanchard Training and Development.

Conner, D. R. (1993). *Managing at the speed of change: How resilient managers succeed and prosper where others fail.* New York: Villard Books.

Firestien, R. L., & Treffinger, D. J. (1983). Ownership and converging: Essential ingredients of creative problem solving. *Journal of Creative Behavior, 17,* 32-38.

Isaksen, S. G. (1983). Toward a model for the facilitation of creative problem solving. *Journal of Creative Behavior, 17,* 18-31.

Isaksen, S. G. (1992). Facilitating creative problem solving groups. In S. S. Gryskiewicz & D. A. Hills (Eds.), *Readings in innovation* (pp. 99-135). Greensboro, NC: Center for Creative Leadership.

Jay, A. (1977). Rate yourself as a client. *Harvard Business Review, 55,* 84-92.

Lacoursiere, R. B. (1980). *The life cycle of groups: Group developmental stage theory.* New York: Human Service Press.

Maier, N. R. (1970). *Problem solving and creativity: In individuals and groups.* Belmont, CA: Brooks/Cole.

Tuckman, B. W. (1965). Developmental sequence in small groups. *Psychological Bulletin, 63,* 384-399.

Tuckman, B. W. & Jensen, M. A. (1977). Stages of small group development revisited. *Group and Organizational Studies, 2,* 419-427.

VanGundy, A. B. (1984). *Managing group creativity: A modular approach to problem solving.* New York: American Management Association.

Vroom, V. H. (1974). Decision making and the leadership process. *Journal of Contemporary Business, 3,* 47-67.

Vroom, V. H., & Jago, A. G. (1988). Managing participation: A critical dimension of leadership. *Journal of Management Development, 7,* 32-42.

CHAPTER SIX

Encouraging Teamwork in CPS Groups

Scott G. Isaksen
Creativity Research Unit
Creative Problem Solving Group — Buffalo

"The stimulus and support that some individuals need to be open to inspiration and imaginative insight often come from the nurture of groups. There may not be a "group mind" (inspiration and imaginative insight may be gifts only to individuals), but there is clearly a climate favorable to creativity by individuals that the group, as community, can provide."

Robert Greenleaf

Introduction

Facilitators of creative problem solving (CPS) groups have the primary responsibility for managing the balance among process, people, desired outcome and the context surrounding the session (Isaksen & Dorval, 1996). Although the main focus for CPS facilitators is on the process tools and the general "technology" surrounding the framework, there are many other variables to consider. Aside from the actual CPS tools, language, guidelines and framework, facilitators need to know when groups are working productively and how to help them work more effectively. They are generally responsible for moving the agenda forward, refocusing the group, and providing an objective view toward the content of the session. The purpose of this chapter is to provide the facilitator a variety of signposts to consider when working with groups, and how to prepare them to get the most out of working with CPS.

CPS meetings, sessions, and workshops are very often conducted with groups. Groups have been defined in many different ways. Most definitions point out that a group is something more than the simple sum of its members. Others point out that teams are a special class of groups. The following definition was provided by Katzenbach and Smith (1993) and will be used for this chapter:

> *A team is a small number of people with complementary skills who are committed to a common purpose, performance goals, and approach for which they hold themselves mutually accountable. (p. 45)*

One implication of this definition is that it places the work between a facilitator and client within our concern for managing groups. This means that much of the information and material included on managing groups will be relevant when the facilitator is working one-on-one and also when working with small or large groups. The main focus for most of the information in this chapter is the typical small-group CPS session. The usual session includes a facilitator, a client, and 5-7 resource-group members. There are also clear and important implications for when CPS is used beyond the session. For example, when applying CPS as a part of a larger project or program, the characteristics of teamwork can also be targeted. The major focus of this chapter is to outline teamwork as a model for when all the roles are interacting well. In fact, one goal for effective facilitative leadership is the creation and application of teamwork in helping to understand and apply creativity to challenges and opportunities.

There are at least two major ingredients in all human interactions: content and process. This is one of the major dynamic tensions CPS facilitators deal with. Content includes an emphasis on subject matter, or the task on which the group is working. In most interactions, the primary focus of attention is on the content (the "what"). The second ingredient, process, is what happens between and to group members while the group is working. For CPS facilitators this process emphasis includes everything they learned about the CPS tools, language, and framework, as well as the group process.

Group process includes such items as morale, atmosphere, influences, participation, leadership struggles, conflict, competition, cooperation, etc. In most interactions, very little attention is paid to process (the "how"), even when it is the major cause of ineffective group action and decision making. Sensitivity to group processes will better enable members to diagnose group problems early and deal with them more effectively. Since these processes are present in all groups, awareness of them will enhance a member's worth to a group and make that person a more effective participant.

The growing importance of group creativity is being recognized by all types of organizations (Isaksen, 1986). Leaders concerned with the most productive means and guidelines for using groups have frequently attempted to gain some clear indications from research in the social sciences. However, the current status of this literature does not shed significant light on the subject. Hackman and Morris (1975) indicated:

> In sum, there is substantial agreement among researchers and observers of small task groups that something important happens in group interaction which can affect performance outcomes. There is little agreement about just what the "something" is—whether it is more likely to enhance or depress group effectiveness, and how it can be monitored, analyzed, and altered. (p. 49)

Awareness of group processes is especially important for those who take responsibility for facilitating group creative problem solving. The effective leader sees the group as a group—not merely as a collection of individuals (Bradford, 1976). Leaders of groups need to be aware of the group as a whole; the individuals who make up the group itself; and the qualities of the interaction and dynamics among group members. Since the literature on small group behavior offers at best an inconclusive set of guidelines, it will be useful for facilitators to be able to make their own observations of group dynamics.

The remainder of this chapter will include information on the major areas that you, as the CPS facilitator, will need to attend to when working with CPS groups. It focuses on encouraging teamwork in CPS sessions and includes information on characteristics which promote teamwork, as well as a discussion of concerns which often serve as obstacles to effective teamwork. Chapter Seven "Exploring Group Dynamics" focuses on what you need to look for in CPS groups. This includes group dynamics to watch for among and between the individual members of the group, as well as suggestions about ways to establish the appropriate interpersonal and working climate in the sessions.

ENCOURAGING TEAMWORK

Given how important it is to be able to contribute productively as a member of a working group, it is interesting to note the increased interest in developing teamwork skills (Belbin, 1981 a & b; Carnevale, Gainer & Meltzer, 1990; Guzzo & Salas, 1995; Katzenbach & Smith, 1993; Katzenbach, 1998). This section of the chapter will provide some general characteristics which promote teamwork and some tripwires to watch out for when working with groups. The purpose of describing effective teamwork is to help you create similar conditions when working with others using CPS. The goal is to have the client, resource group and facilitator behave more like a team than a loose collection of indifferent individuals.

Identifying Characteristics That Promote Teamwork

There are a variety of ways to differentiate working groups from teams. One senior executive with whom I have worked described groups as individuals with nothing in common except a zip code. Teams, however, were characterized by a common vision. Smith (1996) described a team as "...a small number of people with complementary skills who are mutually committed to a common purpose, a common set of performance goals, and a commonly agreed upon working approach." The following dozen characteristics of productive teams have been formulated from reviewing the work of McGregor (1967), Bales (1988) and Larson & LaFasto (1989).

A Clear Elevating Goal. Having a clear and elevating goal means having understanding, mutual agreement and identification with respect to the primary task a group faces. Active teamwork toward common goals happens when members of a group share a common vision of the desired future state.

Results-Driven Structure. Individuals within groups feel productive when their efforts take place with a minimum of grief. Open communication, clear coordination of tasks, clear roles and accountabilities, monitoring performance, providing feedback, fact-based judgment, efficiency, and strong impartial management combine to create a results-driven structure.

Competent Team Members. Competent teams are comprised of capable and conscientious members. Members must possess essential skills and abilities, a strong desire to contribute, be capable of collaborating effectively and have a sense of responsible idealism. They must have knowledge in the domain surrounding the task (or some other domain which may be relevant) as well as with the process of working together.

Unified Commitment. Having a shared commitment relates to the way the individual members of the group respond. Effective teams have an organizational unity; members display mutual support, dedication and faithfulness to the shared purpose and vision, and a productive degree of self-sacrifice to reach organizational goals.

Collaborative Climate. Productive teamwork does not just happen. It requires a climate which supports cooperation and collaboration. This kind of situation is characterized by mutual trust...trust in the goodness of others. Organizations desiring to promote teamwork must provide a climate in the larger context which supports cooperation.

Standards of Excellence. Effective teams establish clear standards of excellence. They embrace individual commitment, motivation, self-esteem, individual performance and constant improvement. Members of teams develop a clear and explicit understanding of the norms upon which they will rely.

External Support and Recognition. Team members need resources, rewards, recognition, popularity and social success. Being liked and admired as individuals and respected for belonging and contributing to a team is often helpful in maintaining the high level of personal energy required for sustained performance. With the increasing use of cross-functional and inter-departmental teams within larger complex organizations, teams must be able to obtain approval and encouragement.

Principled Leadership. Leadership is important for teamwork. Whether it is a formally appointed leader or leadership of the emergent kind, the people who exert influence and encourage the accomplishment of important things usually follow some basic principles. Principled leadership includes the management of human differences, protecting less able members and providing a level playing field to encourage contributions from everyone. This is the kind of leadership which promotes legitimate compliance to competent authority.

Appropriate Use of the Team. Teamwork is encouraged when the tasks and situations really call for that kind of activity. Sometimes the team itself must set clear boundaries on when and why it should be deployed. One of the easiest ways to destroy a productive team is to overuse it or use it when it is not appropriate to do so.

Participation in Decision Making. One of the best ways to encourage teamwork is to engage the members of the team in the process of identifying the challenges and opportunities for improvement, generating ideas and transforming ideas into action. Participation in the process of problem solving and decision making actually builds teamwork and improves the likelihood of acceptance and implementation.

Team Spirit. Effective teams know how to have a good time, release tension and relax their need for control. The focus at times is on developing friendship, engaging in tasks for mutual pleasure and recreation. This internal team climate extends beyond the need for a collaborative climate.

Embracing Appropriate Change. Teams often face the challenges of organizing and defining tasks. In order for teams to remain productive, they must learn how to make necessary changes to procedures. When there is a fundamental change in how the team must operate, different values may need to be accommodated. Productive teams learn how to use the full spectrum of their members' creativity.

Evading the Tripwires When Managing Groups

There are many challenges to the effective management of groups. We have all seen groups that have "gone wrong." As a group develops, there are certain aspects or guidelines which might be helpful to keep them on track. Hackman (1990) has identified a number of themes relevant to those who design, lead and facilitate groups.

In examining a variety of organizational work groups, he found some "tripwires" that could lead to major mistakes when managing groups. From our own experience, we have identified a number of key contingencies to consider when managing CPS groups.

Group versus Team. One of the mistakes that is often made when managing groups is to call the group a team, but to actually treat it as nothing more than a collection of individuals. This is similar to making it a team "because I said so." It is important to be very clear about the underlying goal structure. Organizations are often surprised that teams do not function too well in their environment. Of course, they often fail to examine the essential ingredient of competition in their rating or review process.

If a team is important, then a cooperative goal structure will be more appropriate than a competitive or individualistic one. The group must be accountable for its outcomes. Reward and recognition systems need to be built around different, and more appropriate, perspectives. If one wants the benefits of teamwork, then teams must be built and developed.

Ends versus Means. Managing the source of authority for groups is a delicate balance. Just how much authority can you assign to the team to work out its own issues and challenges? For the CPS facilitator, the authority issue is handled primarily by the charge given by the client. The outcome of client-facilitator planning during task appraisal, process planning and session planning ought to give a clear direction for the problem-solving efforts of the group.

The group should not be told exactly the kinds of problem statements to generate or the precise qualities of the ideas to be generated. However, group members should be given a clear understanding of the general direction in which the client needs to move. The end, direction or outer limit constraints ought to be specified, but the means to get there ought to be within the authority and responsibility of the group.

People are always ends unto themselves, but during CPS sessions it is the desired outcome of the client that serves as the agreed-upon end.

Structured Freedom. It is a major mistake to assemble a group of people and merely tell them in general terms what needs to be accomplished and let them work out their own details. At times, the belief is that if groups are to be creative, they ought not be given any structure. It turns out that most groups would find a little structure quite enabling, if it were the right kind. Groups generally need a well-defined task. They need to be composed of an appropriately small number to be manageable but large enough to be diverse, and they need clear limits as to the group's authority and responsibility.

In terms of facilitating CPS, the well-defined task can be the result of client-facilitator planning and the preparation of the group to deal effectively with the process technology. The extent to which resource-group members need to be diverse depends greatly on the nature of the task. Finally, the roles within the group insure an adequate understanding of the expected behaviors and responsibilities of the group members.

Structures and Systems Supportive of Teamwork. Often challenging team objectives are set, but the organization fails to provide adequate support in order to make the objectives a reality. In general, high performing teams need a reward system which recognizes and reinforces excellent team performance. They also need access to good quality and adequate information, as well as training and educational support. Good team performance is also dependent on having an adequate level of material and financial resources to get the job done.

Assumed Competence. Many organizations have a great deal of faith in their selection systems. Facilitators cannot assume that the group members have all the competence they need to work effectively as a team simply because they have been selected to join any particular organization. Often it has been a technical set of skills and abilities which has put someone in a position for inclusion within a CPS group. Members will undoubtedly need explicit coaching on skills they need to work well in a team. Coaching and other supportive interventions are best done during the launch, at a natural break in the task or at the end of a performance or review period. It appears that the start-up phase is probably the most important time-frame to provide the necessary coaching or training.

Although the members of a CPS session might all be very competent individuals in general, a facilitator should not assume that all are competent in performing their roles during the session.

Group Orientation. All group members need to have some basic information regarding what they are expected to do. Agreement is necessary regarding the procedures and methods used for group activity. It is also very helpful for group members to be aware of their strengths and limitations in using various tools, as well as the kinds of personal and situational blocks to creative thinking which may surface during the session.

Composition. Some deliberate decisions need to be made regarding the number and type of people to be a part of the session. Heterogeneity of perspectives and experiences as well as homogeneity of levels of power should be considered. Generally, CPS groups should be informed of the criteria used in member selection to prevent unnecessary concern about who makes up the group.

Group Size. Depending on the purposes of the session or meeting, a certain number of participants should be specified. A common mistake is to think that teamwork means that "the more the merrier." We generally recommend that group size be no fewer than five and no more than seven. Larger groups should provide additional facilitators to allow an equivalent ratio or at least allow for working in smaller sub-groups. The facilitator may also want to consider the levels of expertise necessary in dealing with the client's task and insure adequate input and deliberation during the planning meetings prior to group sessions.

   The Structure of the Environment. Structuring the environment includes the physical surroundings as well as the emotional tone of the people. The climate or environment within which the task occurs needs to be conducive to creativity. Group members need to have a certain degree of trust and security to make contributions and engage in open communication. The facilitator has a special challenge to estab-lish a social climate which is characterized by psychological safety and that encour-ages the participants, in order to obtain an internal or intrapersonal climate which overcomes barriers to effective problem solving.

   Some attention must be focused on assuring that the necessary equipment and resources are assembled for the session. This means setting up visuals, flipcharts with plenty of paper and markers, and a means for affixing these papers in a promi-nent place for all to see. In addition, the group should be assembled in a place where it is possible to be comfortable to share ideas and engage in effective communication.

   The purpose of the session, as well as the amount of time to be scheduled, should be explicitly identified for all group members. Is the purpose of the group meeting to identify the initial statement of the problem, to generate ideas, or to develop and evaluate options? A specific process task should be identified and an appropriate amount of time should be set aside for the accomplishment of that task.

   The environment may provide some indications regarding the level of quality needed for the decision, as well as the level of acceptance required for implementa-tion. Some situations may call for a quick, unilateral and autocratic response. Others may necessitate a great deal of inclusion. If the leader lacks the necessary informa-tion and other group members have that information, the leader can increase the quality of the outcome by involving a group. The same is true if the leader does not know what type of information is required or where it is located.

   Involving group members in problem-solving sessions that affect them increases acceptance of the outcome or solution. The facilitator who can analyze the environ-mental considerations so as to structure the appropriate climate can be assured of a greater degree of success in utilizing group resources.

Teamwork and Goal Structures

   There is very clear evidence that if teamwork is desired, then goals that are com-petitive or individualistic should be avoided (Johnson, Maruyama, Johnson, Nelson & Skon, 1981). Groups can be structured so that they will cooperate, compete or act individualistically (Deutsch, 1949; Johnson & Johnson, 2000).

Individualistic goal structures are those where there is no relationship among group members' goal attainments. Group members perceive that obtaining their goals is unrelated to the goal achievement of other members of the same group. An individual's success in swimming fifty yards, for example, is unrelated to whether others swim fifty yards or not.

When working within individualistic goal structures the interaction among group members is likely to be characterized as non-related to work, unnecessary or even as a distraction to accomplishing the tasks at hand. There is really no perceived need for interaction.

Competitive goal structures exist when there is a negative relationship among group members' goal attainments. Group members perceive that they can obtain their goals only if the other members, with whom they are competitively linked, fail to obtain their goal. When one runner wins a race, for example, all other runners in that race fail to win.

When the goal structure is competitive, interaction, communication and information exchange among group members can often be misleading or threatening. Group members do not utilize each others' resources. There is increased fear of failure, low trust, evidence of win-lose conflict and high emotional involvement in and commitment to productivity by the few members who have a chance "to win." There is a tendency to avoid risk taking and divergent thinking.

Cooperative goal structures exist when there is a positive relationship among group members' goal attainments. This happens when group members perceive that they can achieve their goal if and only if the other members with whom they are cooperatively linked obtain their goal. When a team of climbers, for example, reaches the summit of a mountain, the success is experienced by all members of the team.

In groups with cooperative goal structures interaction among members is characterized by effective communication and exchange of information, facilitation of each others' productivity, helping and sharing. Group members use each other's resources. The climate is characterized by high acceptance and support among members, high trust, decreased fear of failure, and a problem-solving orientation to conflict.

People perform better when they are structured for cooperative and collaborative work. In short, productivity increases. Promoting teamwork within CPS groups is not merely a matter of warm-ups, fun and games or team building exercises. Seeking cooperative goal structures and organizing for effective teamwork is best done upon the foundation of a key philosophy. One of the best writers and thinkers about this area is Greenleaf (1998) on the servant as leader. His basic premise is that a leader seeks first to serve. It is just this attitude that establishes a collaborative environment with which cooperative goal structures are likely to flourish.

REFERENCES

Bales, R. F. (1988). *Overview of the SYMLOG system: Measuring and changing behavior in groups.* San Diego, CA: SYMLOG Consulting Group.

Belbin, M. (1981a). *Management teams: Why they succeed or fail.* San Diego, CA: Pfieffer & Co.

Belbin, M. (1981b). *Team roles at work.* San Diego, CA: Pfieffer & Co.

Bradford, L. P. (1976). *Making meetings work: A guide for leaders and group members.* San Diego, CA: University Associates.

Carnevale, A. P., Gainer, L. J., & Meltzer, A. S. (1990). *Workplace basics: The essential skills employers want.* San Francisco: Jossey-Bass.

Deutsch, M. A. (1949). A theory of cooperation and competition. *Human Relations, 2,* 129-152.

Greenleaf, R. K. (1998). *The power of servant leadership* (edited by L. C. Spears). San Francisco: Berrett-Koehler.

Guzzo, R. A., & Salas, E. (1995). (Eds.). *Team effectiveness and decision making in organizations.* San Francisco: Jossey-Bass.

Hackman, J. R. (1990). *Groups that work (and those that don't): Creating conditions for effective teamwork.* San Francisco: Jossey-Bass.

Hackman, J. R., & Morris, C. G. (1975). Group tasks, group interaction process, and group performance effectiveness: A review and proposed integration. In L. Berkowitz (Ed.), *Advances in experimental social psychology - Volume 8* (pp. 45-99). New York: Academic Press.

Isaksen, S. G. (1986). Facilitating small group creativity. In S. S. Gryskiewicz & R. M. Burnside (Eds.), *Creativity Week VIII Proceedings* (pp. 71-84). Greensboro, NC: Center for Creative Leadership.

Isaksen, S. G. & Dorval, K. B. (1996). *Facilitating creative problem solving.* Sarasota, FL: Center for Creative Learning.

Johnson, D. W., & Johnson, F. P. (2000). *Joining together: Group theory and group skills* (7th ed.). Boston: Allyn and Bacon.

Johnson, D. W., Maruyama, G., Johnson, R. T., Nelson, D., & Skon, L. (1981). Effects of cooperative, competitive, and individualistic goal structures on achievement: A meta-analysis. *Psychological Bulletin, 89,* 47-62.

Katzenbach, J. R. (1998). *Teams at the top: Unleashing the potential of both teams and individual leaders.* Cambridge, MA: Harvard Business School Press.

Katzenbach, J. R., & Smith, D. K. (1993). *The wisdom of teams: Creating the high-performance organization.* Cambridge, MA: Harvard Business School Press.

Larson, C. E., & LaFasto, F. M. J. (1989). *Teamwork: What must go right - what can go wrong.* Newbury Park, CA: SAGE Publications.

McGregor, D. (1967). *The professional manager.* New York: McGraw-Hill.

Smith, D. K. (1996). *Taking charge of change: 10 principles for managing people and performance.* Reading, MA: Addison-Wesley.

CHAPTER SEVEN

EXPLORING GROUP DYNAMICS

Scott G. Isaksen
Creativity Research Unit
Creative Problem Solving Group — Buffalo

> "Never doubt that a small group of thoughtful, committed citizens can change the world. Indeed, it is the only thing that ever has."
>
> ◆ **Margaret Mead**

INTRODUCTION

Once the decision has been made to use a group for a CPS session, a skillful facilitator will be able to observe a variety of group dynamics and monitor the working climate in order to make effective choices about tools to use or other approaches to managing behavior. Many very productive CPS facilitators have very little formal background or study in the area of group dynamics. Often they have an excellent intuitive sense about what is going on within a group and what to do to help the members move forward.

The following information has been derived from years of watching excellent intuitive practice of facilitation. The focus has been upon discovering the key factors which need to be managed during a CPS session. The information should not be considered a comprehensive briefing on the field of group dynamics (Brandstätter, Davis, & Schuler, 1978; Dimock, 1987; Forsyth, 1983; Fox, 1988; Francis & Young, 1979;

Galegher, Kraut & Egido, 1990; Hanson, 1981; Kinlaw, 1993; Larson & LaFasto, 1989; Rees, 1991; Worchel, Wood & Simpson, 1992). Its purpose is simply to highlight some key considerations for you to be aware of and watch for when using CPS with groups.

GROUP DYNAMICS

The field of group dynamics was first popularized by Kurt Lewin (1948) and had to do with the study of group behavior. Cartwright and Zander (1968) defined group dynamics as "...a field of inquiry dedicated to advancing knowledge about the nature of groups, the laws of their development, and their interrelations with individuals, other groups, and larger institutions (p. 7)."

There are at least a half-dozen dimensions of group dynamics which are important to consider during CPS sessions, meetings and workshops. Remember that this list is not meant to be exhaustive, but it should be illustrative of the core issues regarding the way individuals within the group are interacting.

Group Roles

Facilitators, clients and resource groups have distinct areas of responsibility. Having all the responsibilities met by the right people is an important and productive dynamic for the CPS group. The facilitator has the major charge for managing process, the client takes primary responsibility for the content outcomes, and the resource group provides alternatives and gives input for the benefit of the client. There are many possible behaviors appropriate for each of these three social roles. There are also many possible ways that the people who hold these roles can interact together in order to obtain a productive result. You will need to be sure during this interaction that the three roles are kept as distinct as possible and that the behavior during the session is appropriate for each. Some things to watch for include:

- ✦ Are you concentrating on the process flow and managing the agenda toward the desired outcomes for the session?

- ✦ Do the client and resource group members interact well with each other?

- ✦ Do the client and resource group members interact well with you?

Group Norms and Membership

Standards or rules may develop in a group to control and guide the behavior of its members. Norms usually express the beliefs or desires of the majority of the group members about what behaviors should or should not take place in the group. These norms may be clear to all members (explicit), be known or sensed by only a few (implicit), or operate completely below the level of awareness of all group members. Some norms help the group to progress and some may hinder productivity.

You can help to establish the explicit norms for the session or interaction by crafting the agenda and task statement appropriately and by clearly establishing the guidelines for the generating and focusing of options. If you can keep the agreed expectations of the outcomes of the session well defined and manage the basic kinds of interaction and behavior by reinforcing appropriate behavior within the guidelines and use the appropriate tools and language, then the norms and expectations for effective membership within the CPS group can be clear to all. Some things to watch for include:

- Are certain topical areas avoided in the group? Who seems to reinforce this avoidance? How do they do it?

- Are group members overly nice or polite to each other? Are only positive feelings expressed? Do members agree with each other too readily? What happens when members disagree?

- Do you see norms operating about participation or the kinds of questions that are allowed, e.g., "If I tell my problem, you have to tell your problem?" Do members feel free to question each other about their feelings? Do questions tend to be restricted to intellectual topics or events outside the group?

A major concern for group members is the degree of acceptance or inclusion they feel in the group. Different patterns of interaction may develop in the group that give clues about the desired degree and kind of membership. In addition, the facilitator may seek various levels of diversity. This diversity could include culture, sex, age, level in the organization, cognitive style, as well as level of expertise or familiarity with the situation. Maintaining membership in the group can be accomplished by establishing clear norms (as described above) and making sure that those invited know why they were chosen to participate. This can be accomplished before the actual session by working with the client when sending out an invitational memo with appropriate background on the task. It can be reinforced by some opening comments during the session. Some things to watch for include:

- Is there any sub-grouping? Do two or three members consistently agree with and support one another, or consistently disagree with or oppose one another?

- Do some people seem to be "outside" the group? Do some members seem to be more "in the group?" How are the "outsiders" treated?

- Do some members move in and out of the group? Under what conditions do they move in or out of the group?

- Are differences in perspective evident among the group members? How are they dealt with?

Emotional Tone

Although much of our concern with facilitating CPS has dealt with the cognitive kinds of knowledge, skill and behavior, some psychologists believe that emotions drive cognition. Emotions can be positive (e.g. love, liking, joy, delight and hope) or negative (e.g. anger, fear, despair, sadness or disgust), strong or weak (i.e. anger can range from rage to irritation), and can help or hinder us. Without emotional energy, sessions and human interaction would be dull at best.

During any group discussion or activity, feelings are generated by the interactions between members. These feelings, however, are seldom discussed. Observers must guess about them based on the tones of voice, facial expressions, gestures, or other nonverbal cues given by members. Facilitators must sometimes demonstrate empathy for the emotions of group members. Some things to watch for include:

+ What signs of emotion do you observe in group members?

+ Do you see any attempts by group members to block the expression of feelings, particularly negative feelings? How is this done? Does anyone do this consistently?

+ Does anyone support or encourage the expression of feelings? How is this done? How is it received?

+ Do the group members appear to have passion for what they are doing?

There are also dynamics which can ensure the general positive emotional tone of the group. These are called maintenance functions. Maintenance functions are important to the morale of the group. They maintain good and harmonious working relationships among the members and create a group atmosphere that enables each member to contribute productively. They ensure smooth and effective teamwork within the group. Some things to watch for include:

+ Who helps others enter the discussion (gate openers)?
+ Who cuts off others or interrupts them (gate closers)?
+ How well do members succeed in getting their ideas across? Do some members seem to be preoccupied or not listening? Are there any attempts by group members to help others clarify their ideas?
+ How are ideas rejected? How do members react when their ideas are not accepted? Do members attempt to support others when they reject their ideas?
+ Does anyone check for feelings in others?

Communication Behaviors

Many of the core dynamics of a CPS session revolve around communication. Most of the actual interaction in a session may, in fact, be through the use of language. This means that although the actual language used during a session should be clear and easy to follow, the facilitator needs to be careful about the appropriate use of CPS-related language. The messages sent need to be clear and consistent (especially with the special vocabulary associated with CPS). During the session, the facilitator needs to avoid the use of jargon or words which have inherent confusion.

Of course, communication behaviors include many more considerations than simply the use of language. The quality of listening (active or reflective) and comprehension of the language is also key. Paying attention to what is said can be complemented by perceiving how it is being said. One of the most powerful means of communication is dialogue (Bohm, 1990) as opposed to discussion. Finally, much communication is without words. Some things to watch for include:

- How does the group respond to the language you are using?
- What kind of non-verbals are group members showing you?
- How are group members listening to you and each other?
- Are group members paying attention to both words and actions?

Influence and Decision-Making

Some people may speak very little, yet capture the attention of the whole group. Others may talk a lot but are generally not listened to by other members. Some group members will, for a variety of reasons, exert more force over the group. This dominance can be caused by many variables including: perceived level of expertise, position power of the individual, seniority, the amount of designated authority, the amount of interest in the task, physical qualities such as attractiveness or size, as well as other aspects.

The CPS facilitator needs to be aware of the varieties of influence taking place within a group. It is the facilitator's role to provide influence by selecting the tools and adjusting their use through techniques and strategies applied during the group session. It is the client's role to influence (through ownership) the directions and qualities of outcomes generated by resource-group members. It is the role of the resource-group members to utilize their unique backgrounds and experiences to influence the variety and breadth of options generated for the client. Some things to watch for include:

- Which members are high in influence (i.e., when they talk, others seem to listen to or follow them)?
- Which members are low in influence (i.e., others do not listen to or follow them)?
- Is there any shift in influence? Who shifts? How?

✦   Do you see any rivalry in the group? Is there a struggle for leadership? What effect does this have on other group members?

✦   What do members do that leads to high influence?

Influence can take many forms. It can be positive or negative; it can enlist the support or cooperation of others or alienate them. How a person attempts to influence another may be the crucial factor in determining how open or closed the others will be toward being influenced. Four styles of influence frequently emerge in groups.

Autocratic.   Does anyone attempt to impose his or her will or values on other group members, or try to coerce them into supporting a decision? Does anyone evaluate or pass judgment on other group members? Do any members block action when it is not moving in the direction they desire? Does anyone push to "get the group organized?"

Peacemaker.   Does anyone eagerly support other group members' decisions? Does anyone consistently try to avoid the expression of conflict or unpleasant feelings by "pouring oil on the troubled waters"? Is any member typically deferential toward other group members — giving them power? Do any members appear to avoid giving negative feedback?

Laissez Faire.   Do any group members attract attention by their apparent lack of involvement in the group? Does any group member go along with group decisions without seeming to commit himself or herself one way or the other? Does anyone seem to be withdrawn and uninvolved, not initiating activity, or participating mechanically and only in response to other members' questions?

Democratic.   Does anyone try to include everyone in a group decision or discussion? Does anyone express his or her feelings and opinions openly and directly without evaluating or judging others? Does this person encourage others to do the same? Do any members appear to be open to feedback and criticism from others? When feelings run high and tension mounts, do some members attempt to deal with the conflict in a problem-solving way?

CPS sessions and interactions may contain periods of time when decisions need to be made. This can be, for instance, when you check in with the group about their readiness to move on, their need for clarity and direction on the task, or even scheduling breaks. The main activity is not so much a general influence process, but a deliberate focus on decision making. Although most of the content-related decision making will be made by the client, there will be opportunities for the entire group to make decisions about a variety of issues.

When making decisions, do group members:

✦   Make a (self-authorized) decision and carry it out without checking with other group members? What effect does this have on other group members?

✦ Drift from topic to topic? Who topic-jumps? Do you see any reason for this in the group's interactions?

✦ Support other members' suggestions or decisions? Does this support result in two members deciding the topic or activity for the group? How does this "hand clasp" procedure affect other group members?

✦ Push a decision through despite other members' objections? Do the majority members call for a vote?

✦ Attempt to get all members to participate in a consensus decision? What effect does this seem to have on the group?

✦ Make contributions that do not receive any kind of response or recognition? What effect does this "plop" have on the members?

Answers to these questions, based on observation of verbal and non-verbal interaction, can help you understand the way power and influence is being handled by any particular group.

Process Flow

Process flow has to do with the linking together of various tools and activities, making successful transitions between them, and laying out a pathway which serves the needed outcomes for the session. These functions illustrate behaviors that are concerned with getting the job done or accomplishing the task that the group has before it. They may deal with how group members reinforce the CPS process agenda or guidelines, in addition to the aspects of group development and dynamics. Some behaviors to watch for include:

✦ Does anyone ask for or make suggestions about the best way to proceed or tackle a problem?

✦ Does anyone attempt to summarize what has been discussed or what has been going on in the group?

✦ Does anyone keep the group on target and prevent topic jumping or going off on tangents?

✦ Does anyone amplify or build on contributions from others?

✦ Are group members asking questions regarding the goal or objectives of the session (orientation)?

✦ Do group members want to know more about their roles, rules and responsibilities to the group (organization)?

✦ Does anyone ask for or give facts, ideas, opinions, feedback, feelings; does anyone search for alternatives (open data flow)?

✦ Is there openness, collaboration and functional competition among group members (problem solving)?

INTERPERSONAL CLIMATE

In addition to the level of energy and the actual process technology used, the facilitator needs to focus attention on the nature and qualities of the interpersonal dynamics and relationships within the group. The categories within which these concerns may fall include the creative climate, maintenance functions, aspects of group membership, the amount of interaction dealing with feelings, as well as group norming issues. As a result of certain decisions, a CPS facilitator may find that the group has changed the characteristic pattern of how the members work and act with each other. Becoming aware of these interpersonal climate variables can provide useful information for the facilitator in making choices about which techniques to use and how much energy to attempt to release. The facilitator builds the space where dialogue, discussion, interaction and working with other tools happens freely (Zohar, 1997).

The way in which a group works creates an observable atmosphere. People may differ in the kind of atmosphere they like in a group. Insight can be gained into the characteristics of a group by observing the general climate and the behavior which forms this atmosphere. For example:

✦ Who seems to prefer a friendly, congenial atmosphere? Is there any attempt to suppress conflict or unpleasant feelings?

✦ Who seems to prefer an atmosphere of conflict and tension?

✦ Do people seem involved and interested? Is the atmosphere one of reward, cooperation, competition, work and/or play, sluggishness, fighting, taking flight, or tension? Which seems most apparent?

Ekvall (1996) and Isaksen, Lauer, Murdock, Dorval & Puccio (1995) have identified a series of dimensions which are important in establishing and maintaining a climate which supports creativity and change. The following nine dimensions are included on the current version of the Situational Outlook Questionnaire (see Isaksen, Lauer & Ekvall, 1999) and are derived from Ekvall's research.

Challenge and Involvement

The climate dimension of challenge and involvement is the degree to which people are involved in daily operations, long-term goals, and visions. High levels of challenge and involvement suggest that people are positively motivated and committed to making contributions to the success of the organization. The climate has a dynamic, electric, and inspiring quality. People find joy and meaningfulness in their work, and therefore, they invest much energy. In the opposite situation, people are not engaged and feelings of alienation and indifference are present. The common sentiment and attitude is apathy and lack of interest in that work and interaction is both dull and listless.

One of the most important categories of group dynamics for CPS facilitators to consider is the level of energy and enthusiasm shown within the group. Although energy may often be considered a function of individual motivation and interest in the problem or challenge, it may be productive to consider the level of participation and degree of influence as well. It is the facilitator's responsibility to ensure evenness of participation and a degree of influence which provides for broad involvement in the group session. The facilitator needs to maintain a productive level of energy, while creating an appropriate balance between the diversity of perspectives on the part of the resource group on the one hand, and the needs of the client on the other.

Level of participation can be both verbal and nonverbal. Although most facilitators may find it easier to observe verbal participation, it should be noted that nonverbal behavior may be more meaningful than verbal behavior in any given situation. Some tasks may affect certain people in different ways. Someone you find to be very active and verbal may respond more introspectively for particular tasks. In addition, it will also be important to consider the style orientation of group members. For example, there may be qualitative differences in the observable level of participation on the part of introverts and extroverts. The key indicator of challenge and involvement during a CPS session is the degree of engagement you can observe. This can be shown as intense internal reflection as well as active and "noisy" participation in the session.

The facilitator participates in the CPS session. However, this participation is focused on providing process input, structure and guidelines rather than contributing options or content. The facilitator may find it helpful to look for differences in the amount of participation among resource-group members and clients. You may find it particularly useful to monitor your own wait time (the time you wait between asking a question and moving on to the next question or activity). Some things to watch for include:

- Who are the high or low participants?
- Do you see any shift in participation, e.g., highs become quiet; lows suddenly become talkative? Do you see any possible reason for this in the group's interaction?
- How are silent people treated? How is their silence interpreted? As consent? Disagreement? Disinterest? Fear?
- Who talks to whom? Do you see any reason for this in the group's interaction?
- Is the client an active participant in the group activity?
- Do group members show emotional involvement in the session?
- Is there a lively level of activity in the group?

Freedom

Freedom is the independence in behavior exerted by the people in an organization. In a climate with much freedom, people are given autonomy to define much of their own work. People are able to exercise discretion in their day-to-day activities. People take the initiative to acquire and share information, to make plans and decisions about their work. In the opposite climate, people work within strict guidelines and roles. People carry out their work in prescribed ways with little room to redefine their tasks.

In the context of managing CPS groups, freedom is at the heart of the descriptive use of CPS. Descriptive application of CPS provides a flexible structure that enables the group to move in the direction it thinks is most appropriate. Prescriptive approaches to CPS limit freedom and require groups to perform in a predetermined approach. Running through the process becomes the goal rather than obtaining the desired content outcome.

As CPS is used in a more descriptive manner, its role as a servant to the content becomes more clear. It provides "structured freedom" for group members and allows for individual differences and multiple pathways for participation of group members. At this point, the process becomes transparent and the emphasis is on task productivity. When trying to establish freedom, it can be helpful to look for:

+ What happens when you check in with the client or group to make real-time decisions about the direction and process flow?
+ What kind of language is being used within the group? Is it natural or heavily laden with jargon?
+ Are multiple pathways being laid out for the group to follow?
+ Do group members demonstrate independence in their behavior?

Trust and Openness

Trust and openness refers to the emotional safety in relationships. When there is a high level of trust, individuals can be genuinely open and frank with one another. People can count on each other for personal support. People have a sincere respect for one another. Where trust is missing, people are suspicious of each other, and therefore, they guard themselves and their ideas closely. In these situations, people find it extremely difficult to communicate with each other openly.

Trust and openness is an important attribute of the interpersonal climate for a CPS group. If people do not perceive that there is emotional safety within the group, it is very unlikely that the session will be productive. The facilitator needs to be convinced that the session is the right thing to do. This is confirmed through pre-work, planning and preparation. The facilitator and client(s) have agreed with the basic ethics and guidelines for the session, especially how confidentiality will be addressed. During the session the appropriate guidelines are established and reinforced for dealing with suspending judgment and using affirmative forms of judgment.

Some things to watch for include:

- ✦ How are people responding to the task and the client's presentation?
- ✦ How is judgment being managed during the session?
- ✦ Is there consistency between the stated plan and the actual behavior?
- ✦ Do group members appear to believe that it is safe to work with each other?

Idea Time

Idea time is the climate dimension which is concerned with the amount of time people can use (and do use) for elaborating new ideas. In the high idea-time situation, possibilities exist to discuss and test impulses and fresh suggestions that are not planned or included in the task assignment. There are opportunities to take the time to explore and develop new ideas. Flexible timelines permit people to explore new avenues and alternatives. In the reverse case, every minute is booked and specified. The time pressure makes thinking outside the instructions and planned routines much more difficult.

The main purpose of a CPS session or interaction is to provide for the necessary idea time for a particular problem or opportunity. The major emphasis is to create deliberate time and space for effective problem solving. This may include the generating of many, varied, and unusual alternatives, or the focusing and developing of novel options. Time is managed so that there is a minimum of general discussion or analysis and a maximum consideration and generation of novel perspectives. Sessions are managed so that if a promising new direction or line of thinking becomes interesting to the client, the group may be guided in this new direction. At times, an appropriate time-out can be called to provide for a needed period of reflection or incubation.

Some things to watch for include:

- ✦ Are group members responding well to the time-frame allotted for the session? Do they see the time they are investing as worthwhile?
- ✦ Is the time during the session being devoted to the generation and consideration of truly new ways of looking at the problem or challenge?
- ✦ Are truly new and fresh perspectives being shared and considered?
- ✦ Do group members take time to incubate or elaborate on ideas?

Playfulness/Humor

Playfulness and humor is the climate dimension concerned with the level of spontaneity and ease displayed within the workplace. A relaxed atmosphere where good-natured jokes and laughter occur often is indicative of this dimension. People can be seen having fun at work. The atmosphere is seen as easy-going and light-hearted. The opposite climate is characterized by gravity and seriousness. The atmosphere is stiff, gloomy and cumbrous. Jokes and laughter are regarded as improper and intolerable.

One of the ways that you know a CPS session is working is that there will be joking, laughter, smiles, and humor. Applying CPS should be fun, but not for fun. The purpose of the session is not to have fun, but to make progress on an issue or opportunity requiring a creative approach. One of the best ways for people to produce a creative approach is to use humor and laughter to release tension. A playful and relaxed atmosphere can be established by showing your own sense of humor, paying attention to the humor of others, having a few playful objects around, and deliberately building in something humorous or playful (like assigning heroic roles to participants).

Some things to watch for include:

✦ Do group members laugh with each other, tell jokes, etc.?

✦ Are group members smiling?

✦ Do people appear to be relaxed?

Conflict

In the context of the climate for creativity, conflict refers to the presence of personal and emotional tensions in the organization. When the level of conflict is high, groups and single individuals dislike and may even hate each other. The climate can be characterized by "interpersonal warfare." Plots, traps, power and territory struggles are usual elements in the life of the organization. Personal differences yield gossip and slander. In the opposite case, people behave in a more mature manner; they have psychological insight and control of impulses. People accept and deal effectively with diversity.

One of the main responsibilities of the CPS facilitator is to limit the amount of conflict and maximize the more productive aspects of tension. Productive tension refers more to increasing debate (idea tension) and reducing personal tension through humor and appropriate management of the group. When and if conflict emerges in the group, the facilitator needs to be able to deal with it effectively. This can include using conflict resolution and negotiation skills. The key is maintaining a content-neutral role, encouraging effective listening and sending, and working to separate the person from the idea.

Some things to watch for include:

◆ Are there personal attacks among members of the group?

◆ Are people talking behind each others' backs?

◆ Does there appear to be a high degree of personal or interpersonal tension between group members?

Idea Support

Idea support refers to the ways new ideas are treated. In the supportive climate, ideas and suggestions are received in an attentive and professional way by bosses, peers, and subordinates. People listen to each other and encourage initiatives. Possibilities for trying out new ideas are created. The atmosphere is constructive and positive when considering new ideas. When idea support is low, the automatic "no" is prevailing. Every suggestion is immediately refuted by a destructive counter-argument. Fault-finding and obstacle-raising are the usual styles of responding to ideas.

The CPS facilitator establishes idea support during a session by recording every alternative and treats each contribution in an accepting manner. The facilitator observes internal and external judgments made by group members, and takes action (verbal and non-verbal) to encourage the sharing and receiving of options.

Some things to watch for include:

◆ Are novel ideas embraced by group members?

◆ Do group members listen well to each other?

◆ To what extent are group members engaging in fault-finding?

Debate

Debate is the climate dimension which deals with the occurrence of encounters and disagreements between viewpoints, ideas, and differing experiences and knowledge. In the debating organization, many voices are heard and people are keen on putting forward their ideas for consideration and review. People can often be seen discussing opposing opinions and sharing a diversity of perspectives. Where debates are missing, people follow authoritarian patterns without questioning.

Although the CPS session is designed to bring together people with diverse viewpoints and perspectives, the facilitator does not actually encourage formal debate between or among group members. You do not want the session to be reduced to a discussion or argument. Instead you can establish a climate where debate is encouraged by managing the process to allow for the generation and consideration of many, varied, and unusual viewpoints. Even when alternatives appear to be in direct opposition, the facilitator treats each the same and records them for later consideration.

Some things to watch for include:

✦ Are different points of view presented and discussed?

✦ Do group members feel free to question each other?

✦ Is there evidence of flexibility of options (or do most of the options fall within a few narrow categories)?

Risk-Taking

Risk-taking is the tolerance of uncertainty and ambiguity expressed in the workplace or situation. In a high risk-taking climate, bold new initiatives can be taken, even when the outcomes are unknown. People feel as though they can "take a gamble" on some of their ideas. People will often "go out on a limb" and be first to put an idea forward. In a risk-avoiding climate, there is a cautious, hesitant mentality. People try to be on the "safe side." They decide "to sleep on the matter." They set up committees and they cover themselves in many ways before making a decision.

In the broadest sense, facilitating CPS is all about deliberately introducing change in the way people work together and increasing the likelihood of novel and useful outcomes. The CPS facilitator supports the client in choosing and considering breakthrough alternatives. The resource group is invited to try new methods, while the facilitator keeps the process as transparent or clear as possible.

Some things to watch for include:

✦ Do group members take chances?

✦ When people share highly novel options, do group members support them?

✦ Are clients deliberately supported when they choose or wish to develop highly novel options?

CONCLUSION

Facilitative leadership implies a group-oriented influence role aimed at assisting people to be more effective and productive in addressing challenges and pursuing opportunities. One of the most important aspects of this role is the deliberate observation and understanding of group dynamics and interpersonal climate.

These factors make a real difference when learning or applying CPS. I have seen people who are new to facilitation put most of their focus on the tools, language and process agenda they have created with their client. Often, ignoring these group factors has led to a less than satisfactory result.

REFERENCES

Bohm, D. (1990). *On dialogue*. Ojai, CA: David Bohm Seminars.

Brandstätter, H., Davis, J. H., & Schuler, H. (1978). *Dynamics of group decisions*. Beverly Hills, CA: SAGE Publications.

Cartwright, D., & Zander, A. (1968). *Group dynamics: Research and theory (third edition)*. New York: Harper & Row.

Dimock, H. G. (1987). *Groups: Leadership and group development*. San Diego, CA: University Associates.

Ekvall, G. (1996). Organizational climate for creativity and innovation. *European Journal of Work and Organizational Psychology, 5*, 105-123.

Forsyth, D. R. (1983). *An introduction to group dynamics*. Monterey, CA: Brooks/Cole Publishing.

Fox, W. M. (1988). *Effective group problem solving: How to broaden participation, improve decision making and increase commitment to action*. San Francisco: Jossey-Bass.

Francis, D., & Young, D. (1979). *Improving work groups: A practical manual for team building*. San Diego, CA: Pfieffer & Company.

Galegher, J., Kraut, R. E., & Egido, C. (Eds.). (1990). *Intellectual teamwork: Social and technological foundations of cooperative work*. Hillsdale, New Jersey: Lawrence Erlbaum Associates.

Hanson, P. G. (1981). *Learning through groups: A trainer's basic course*. San Diego, CA: University Associates.

Isaksen, S. G. & Dorval, K. B. (1996). *Facilitating creative problem solving*. Sarasota, FL: Center for Creative Learning.

Isaksen, S. G., Lauer, K. J., Murdock, M. C., Dorval, K. B., & Puccio, G. J. (1995). *Situational outlook questionnaire: Understanding the climate for creativity and change (SOQ) - A technical manual*. Buffalo, NY: Creative Problem Solving Group - Buffalo.

Isaksen, S. G., Lauer, K. J., & Ekvall, G. (1999). Situational Outlook Questionnaire: A measure of the climate for creativity and change. *Psychological Reports, 85*, 665-674.

Kinlaw, D. C. (1993). *Team-managed facilitation: Critical skills for developing self-sufficient teams*. San Diego, CA: Pfieffer & Co.

Larson, C. E., & LaFasto, F. M. J. (1989). *Teamwork: What must go right - what can go wrong*. Newbury Park, CA: SAGE Publications.

Lewin, K. (1948). *Resolving social conflicts: Selected papers on group dynamics*. New York: Harper.

Rees, F. (1991). *How to lead work teams: Facilitation skills*. San Diego, CA: Pfieffer & Co.

Stacey, R. (1993). Strategy as order emerging from chaos. *Long Range Planning, 26*, 10-17.

Stacey, R. (1996). *Complexity and Management - Working Paper No 1: Creativity in organizations: The importance of mess*. Hertfordshire, UK: Complexity and Management Centre at the University of Hertfordshire.

Treffinger, D. J. (1983). George's group: A creative problem solving case study. *Journal of Creative Behavior, 17*, 39-48

Worchel, S., Wood, W. & Simpson, J. A. (Eds.), (1992). *Group process and productivity.* Newbury Park, CA: SAGE Publications.

Zohar, D. (1997). *Rewiring the corporate brain: Using the new science to rethink how we structure and lead organizations.* San Francisco: Berrett-Koehler.

CHAPTER EIGHT

PLANNING FOR THE UNEXPECTED

Scott G. Isaksen
Creativity Research Unit
Creative Problem Solving Group — Buffalo

> "What definition of 'good' will apply to all the arts? Let us say it is that for the sake of which all else is done... If, then, there is one end and aim of all our actions, this will be the realizable good; if there are several such ends, these jointly will be our realizable goods."
>
> **Aristotle, *Nicomachean Ethics* Book I**

INTRODUCTION

When you work within the broad area of creativity, there will be many opportunities and challenges associated with surprise and spontaneity. About the only thing of which you can be certain is that your plan will change. We refer to this as "preplanned spontaneity".

When learning and applying Creative Problem Solving (CPS) there are a number of concerns that arise. We can put them into two broad categories: those issues and concerns associated with planning and preparing to learn and apply CPS, and those that arise when actually providing services and interaction.

The first part of this chapter will address some concerns that participants in our facilitation development courses frequently raise. The second part will address common, yet surprising, challenges (we call these "curves") that occur when facilitating groups. I have then provided some suggested levels of intervention as well as some general guidelines in order to help you begin thinking about how you might respond to these challenges.

PREPARING FOR SURPRISES

Participants during our facilitator development training courses are frequently asked to think about the likely challenges they will face as they think about returning to work with their new skills. We ask them to generate lists of "What if's" and then to come up with some way to deal effectively with them.

One of the most frequent themes in their lists is dealing with the planning and preparation for applying what they learned. Participants often identify potential challenges in dealing with clients, certain kinds of tasks, and situational or context-related issues.

Interacting withTough Clients

A concern often raised is that the newly-trained facilitator will return to face a client who has an agenda that can be described as hidden, designed to achieve re-venge, or in some way is self-promotional or self-serving. Facilitators envision a client who wants them to construct a session that "discovers" the answer the client already has for the task at hand, or who has little interest in taking any real action, but wants to be seen as doing the right thing.

The basic suggestions these facilitators identify is reinforcing the concept of own-ership with the client. Interest is shown when the client has energy and commitment to give you the time and attention for planning. Influence is shown when the client asserts the appropriate amount of power or decision-making authority. Imagination is shown when the client is open to novelty and avoids "stacking the deck" with his or her own ideas or favorite resource-group members.

When anticipating challenges with clients, newly-trained facilitators often raise the issue of integrity. I have always been amazed by the amount of energy generated from this discussion and how intently facilitators want to know how and when to say no to a prospective client.

This always raises the question of "How do you say no to your boss?" I have heard stories of facilitators who have felt coerced into conducting sessions and managing process for content they did not feel right about. The answers I have heard range from "just say no" to "we all know ways to avoid work without being direct." Our response is that it is less about saying no and more about qualifying, and then appro-priately applying, CPS.

Facing Inappropriate Tasks

Another challenge facilitators foresee is that they may be asked to work on a task or content that they find objectionable to their personal values. Working on the task could mean that a good friend could lose a job, or you might injure or harm people. The facilitator may also find that the content of the task is so close that they have a hard time focusing on the process.

The recommendation that comes up most often to deal with this challenge is to work on maintaining a process-content separation. First, try to maintain your concentration on the process. If the weight of the content is so heavy that it is not possible for the facilitator to maintain focus on the process, then it may be best not to approach the task at all. You may be able to suggest someone else to take on the facilitator role.

Expecting Magic from the Process

Both new and experienced facilitators often face clients (and others) who expect magical results from using a creative approach. I experience this one as well. Clients often start out by telling me they want one or two really big ideas that need to come from a very short session, with people they trust, within a small budget, and quick time-frame. They often have little time or energy for preparation, but spend what little time they do have telling you all about the requirements.

There is no "silver bullet" or quick fix. Sometimes it may feel a little magical when you see the quantity and quality of results from engaging in a creative approach, but these impressive results are more often from good preparation, a technically-sound design, and good people working well together.

The Situation Is Just Not Right

Even well-intentioned facilitators, who anxiously search for opportunities to apply their skills and knowledge, can face a situation that simply will not support creativity. It may be that the task they have been asked to work on is way off strategy or lacks sponsorship. You can find yourself in a situation in which the request sounds right, is issued by a client with the right level of ownership, and the tool or method you want to use is a good one, but the timing is just not right.

I remember being asked by a CEO to conduct a climate assessment on an entire global organization. The measure was good. The sponsor was clear and well intentioned. The strategic need was compelling. However, there had just been a rather large change in key strategic positions throughout the organization. It would have been simply nonsense to go ahead with the survey at that point in time because climate is strongly influenced by leadership. The climate results would have prompted so many unanswerable questions it would not have been worth the effort.

DEALING WITH CURVES

Despite all the precautions taken, unexpected challenges can emerge during an actual CPS session. Sid Parnes and Ruth Noller called these "curves." Our definition of curves are those unexpected and potentially non-productive dynamics or surprising events which place the session's results at risk. If anticipated, most can be dealt with through pre-planning. Those which occur during a session can be dealt with through a variety of levels and kinds of interventions.

The purpose of this section is to describe a few of the likely curves we have seen take place during CPS sessions. We will also outline a number of possible interventions facilitators can take to deal effectively with those unexpected threats to productivity.

LIKELY "CURVES" WHEN APPLYING CPS

When applying CPS in groups it is possible for some rather counter-productive dynamics to develop or occur. These "curves" can occur between the facilitator and the client, while others occur more often among group members. Nearly all the behavior identified above can be considered a curve if it is "overdone" or "underdone."

Role Confusion

One of the most frequent curves we have observed is what we call role muddle. This occurs when the facilitator forgets to focus on the process, the client abandons the content outcomes of the session, or the resource group forgets its responsibility to provide alternatives and begins to take clientship. Whenever the defined social roles for group application become unclear or are not observed, it is very possible for the session to become off track or nonproductive.

+ Do resource-group members attempt to take over the client's ownership?

+ Is the client trying to disown the problem or challenge?

+ Does the client really want the group's help?

+ Do resource-group members take the facilitator's role?

Withdrawal

Whenever participants pull away from the session, verbally or non-verbally, they may be withdrawing their support. You can observe people withdrawing from the activity of the group when they appear to shut down or simply refuse to play.

+ Are group members withdrawing, remaining indifferent, or aloof?

+ Are they engaging in irrelevant side conversations or behavior?

Inappropriate Judgment

The two basic principles within the guidelines for CPS deal with either suspending judgment or applying judgment affirmatively. When judicial or critical thinking occurs at the same time creative thinking is being called forth, problems are likely to result.

✦ Do group members reject or criticize ideas, or each other?

✦ Are people overly positive about the suggestions that only one or a few members share?

Dominating Individuals

Some members of the group may come forward and attempt to over control the generation or focusing efforts of others.

✦ Do group members refuse to cooperate, monopolize or seek unusual amounts of recognition?

✦ Are there attempts to take over the session?

Unexpected Shifts

A variety of unexpected shifts can occur when learning or applying CPS in groups. These can relate to the people, the process or the content. People can arrive late or leave early. The process diagnosis can change and need to be redirected, and certain alternatives can create a major shift in the content and desired outcomes for the group.

✦ Do group members promote a hidden agenda?

✦ Does the client have a hidden agenda?

Sudden Outbursts of Emotional Tension

Occasionally, individuals involved in learning or applying CPS can become very emotional and need to vent their feelings or frustrations.

✦ Do the responses to certain tools or language anger participants?

✦ Are there super-sensitive people in the group?

Conflict between or among Resource-Group Members

At times the natural and productive tension that can occur during a session may become non-productive and result in an outburst of personal tension and conflict between two or more members of the resource group. Conflict of this kind can cause the session to stop and can potentially threaten the well-being of the participants.

+ Are arguments and conflicts taking place?
+ Is the tension primarily focused on people rather than on ideas?

Wandering from the Task at Hand

Although group application of CPS can often include excursions and productive diversions, it is also possible that people can get off track and pursue discussion on a topic totally unrelated to the purpose of the session.

+ Do people engage in discussion on unrelated tasks or issues?
+ Do people in the group shift their attention to distractions?

Logistical Challenges

When the interaction takes a sudden shift in direction, it is possible (and even likely) that the facilitator may need certain resources which were not planned for?

+ Do logistics seem to be a concern?
+ Are the physical arrangements (i.e. equipment, wall space, etc.) taken care of?
+ Are the necessary supplies and materials available?

Interruptions

Fire drills, sudden storms, threatening weather conditions, wild animals suddenly joining your session, and announcements can all occur unexpectedly.

+ Do group members interrupt each other?
+ Are group members literally leaving the room for other chores or phone calls?

LEVELS OF INTERVENTION

Most of the curves and challenges identified above can be most effectively dealt with if guidelines and norms have been explicitly established (stated and agreed upon) before the session begins. If the curves occur, then a variety of levels and kinds of interventions may be used by the facilitator to re-establish the direction of the session. For more detailed information regarding helpful interventions see Heron (1990). We recommend that you start with the more indirect forms of redirecting the session, and then move up to the more direct approaches as necessary. These are outlined below.

Intervening Indirectly

On occasion, you may notice a low level of involvement or that some group members are distant or appear non-involved. In the flow of the session, you might try an indirect approach to increase energy or involvement. You could use some body language such as motioning with your hands or simply providing increased eye contact. You could move more closely to those who are not participating. Verbal behavior could be used to make more targeted invitations for participation by saying: "What do you think?" or "What do you have?" Another indirect way to intercede is to offer the opportunity to rank the group member's level of commitment for the session output thus far. Intervening indirectly includes using gestures, eye contact, and verbal stimulators that are seen as in the process flow of the session.

Reinforcing Norms and Guidelines

At times, all that may be necessary is to remind the group members of the norms you had established or of the guidelines for the particular activity. If you have already tried to softly influence the members through eye contact or a light invitation and you do not see any change, you may need to clarify the basic ground rules that ought to be operating. This can include a general reminder that "We are generating options now, so please defer your judgment." or "Remember that we are not trying to have a discussion, but need to generate as many options as we can for right now."

Intervening Directly

Directly intervening would include a whole range of behaviors designed to put the curve on the table and obtain agreement to move forward on the reason for being together. This could include addressing the group and asking for commitment to proceed, pausing the action to enable a conversation with the person causing the disruption, or verbal behavior like: "I am noticing some judgment here, let's get back to deferring our judgment."

Renegotiating Session Outcomes

If you have tried all the previous ways to redirect behavior and non-productive consequences are still likely, you may need to renegotiate the session outcomes or norms. Doing this will mean stopping the action of the session, pointing out the distraction or curve and its implication, and then stating that the session will not be able to meet its desired outcome as a result. If this creates more favorable conditions, then you can proceed. If that doesn't work, you may simply need to engage in direct conversation with the client to reschedule the session, or suggest that some additional planning may be necessary before scheduling another session.

It is unlikely that you will be able to remain cognizant of all the group dynamics or climate variables while you are in the beginning stage of developing your facilitation skillbase. The material included here is aimed at helping you continue your learning about the complexity of groups and how your role as a CPS facilitator can effect group productivity.

Learning how to deal productively with curves is a continuous challenge (see Treffinger, 1983). Since there is no way to predict exactly what will happen when you get a group together, the idea is to prepare for the unexpected. This has to do with preplanned flexibility or channeled freedom. Stacey (1993) would call CPS groups complex adaptive systems. As such, they would be reliably unpredictable. Stacey (1996) indicated:

> The true role of the leader of a creative system is not to foresee its future and take control of its journey, but to contain the anxiety they are creating and discovering a new future that none could possibly foresee.... The science of complexity leads to a diametrically opposed perspective in which disorder plays a vital role, in tension with order; in which people do not know where they are going over the long term, but through interaction develop, discover and create a new direction through their self organising interaction. The result emerges without prior shared intention. This is a never ending process in which we all play a part and in which the role of our leader is much more to contain the anxiety it all generates than to tell us what to do. (p.23)

The CPS facilitator has many responsibilities and characteristics (see Chapter 3 on *Facilitating CPS*). Generally, the role of the facilitator is to balance the process with the people. A variety of characteristics, abilities and skills can help the facilitator perform this process-oriented leadership function (Isaksen & Dorval, 1996).

Facilitators work with those who have the ownership for sponsoring change to ensure that the results from CPS application will be used. Knowing the characteristics of effective clients can help the facilitator select appropriate sponsors or encourage clients to perform effectively in their role (see Chapter 5 on *Managing Clients and Resource Groups*).

There may be occasions when the facilitator interacts with the client and there is no need to convene a resource group. If a group becomes necessary, the facilitator should be able to encourage teamwork and manage group development (see Chapter 6 on *Encouraging Teamwork in CPS Groups*). Those facilitators who understand group dynamics and can observe the climate of the group will be better off than those who only focus on the technology of the process (see Chapter 7 on *Exploring Group Dynamics*). Being able to watch the dynamics and energy of the group can also help the facilitator deal effectively with those sudden threats to group productivity.

Some Guidelines

These guidelines were originally prepared to guide the professional practices of all those who work for and with CPS-B professionals. Those who work directly for CPS-B include all full and part-time staff. Those who work indirectly include our suppliers, independent contractors, and all those certified by CPS-B on our skillbase. The guidelines represented our effort to become more explicit and deliberate regarding the norms for our behavior as professionals in this field.

You may find these guidelines useful as a "pre-flight checklist" to prepare yourself to deal with many of the unexpected challenges that may arise from your own application of CPS.

Where Did These Guidelines Come from?

I developed an earlier version of these guidelines while I was the director of the Center for Studies in Creativity. As an administrator and a professor, I was concerned about the level of professionalism in the practice of creativity consultants, trainers, and researchers. My colleagues and I had numerous conversations with students and clients and began the drafting process.

The original guidelines were developed to help professionals within the field of creativity:

✦ Establish productive learning environments by outlining suggestions to insure physical and psychological comfort and safety, as well as identifying the needs for confidentiality and disclosure;

✦ Understand some suggested standards regarding basic principles like informed consent, voluntary involvement, and the protection of human rights; and

✦ Identify some specific qualities for professional competence needed by trainers, teachers, researchers, and other professionals within the field of creativity.

These guidelines were *not* presented as a comprehensive statement of ethical practice. Our field will clearly need to make significant advances in setting out its epistemology, ontology, and axiology before these outcomes are possible or even desirable (Isaksen & Murdock, 1993). In the meantime, some sort of preliminary guidelines seemed necessary, as no other field's statement of ethical practice applies completely to our field of work and study. Researchers and practitioners need to have some sort of framework within which to address questions of the "rightness" or "wrongness" of actions and behaviors.

What Are Ethical Guidelines?

There are countless situations for which creativity professionals need to be able to figure out the right thing to do. We will often engage participants who are learning how to facilitate the current version of CPS with the question "What if...?" In response, we often hear about situations these future facilitators have in terms of a few of the more likely situations they will face. Issues like "What if I am asked to facilitate a session by my boss, but I know that the client already has an answer and just wants the group to buy in?" "What if I learn something about a friend in a session and it really affects his life?" "What if I meet people socially after learning about their KAI scores and one of them asks me the score of another?" These, and many other situations, may create challenges to the personal integrity of the individuals involved and have long-term consequences for the professional's future work.

The fact that people make judgments of right and wrong is the basic starting point of ethics (Singer, 1993). Generally speaking, ethics are the rules or guidelines of conduct recognized in respect to a particular class of human actions of a particular group (Ross, 1954; Wolff, 1969).

The word ethics is often used to mean morality. This closeness is reflected in their definitions. For example, Webster's defines morals as "...relating to principles or considerations of right and wrong action or good or bad character; ethical, relating to the study of such principles or considerations."

Morals or ethics refer to generally accepted customs of conduct and practice. Morals refers to generally accepted customs of conduct and right living in a society, and to the individual's practice in relation to these: *the morals of our civilization*. Ethics now implies high standards of honest and honorable dealing, and of methods used, especially in the professions or in business: *the ethics of the medical profession*. In short, ethical guidelines are suggested standards established to guide the behavior of individuals involved in professional activity.

Since a great deal of what we do can be described as involving the social and behavioral sciences, we can look to a few of the disciplines within this area for some guidance. For example, the American Psychological Association (APA) has a number of resources and activities which can be helpful (APA, 1982; 1985; 1986). The APA regularly publishes the Ethical principles of psychologists and code of conduct (APA, 1992). Although these resources are very helpful and informative, they may not cover all the conflicts and ethical dilemmas faced by creativity researchers and practitioners.

Our Role in Establishing These Guidelines

Until 1996, the Center for Studies in Creativity (CSC) had provided us a unique arena within which a broad array of undergraduate and graduate students from various disciplinary and professional backgrounds had come to study creativity and its many applications. Interaction with this diverse collection of individuals was complemented by contact with a variety of professionals within many different kinds of organizations. We were able to work with companies and international organizations, providing many productive experiences and challenges in dealing with basic ethical conflicts and dilemmas. This provided a unique opportunity to expand our contact with other professionals from a variety of disciplines, functions, and cultural backgrounds.

Since the CSC had nearly thirty years of experience dealing with these issues and had the largest collection of full-time doctoral faculty devoted to teaching and research within this area, we took the lead in explicating our ethical principles. In no way were these suggestions to be taken as the final word on ethical practice within our field. Nor did we present ourselves as having the same leverage as the APA in setting the standards and outlining specific procedures for filing, investigating and resolving complaints against those who may not follow these guidelines. No single creativity organization has universal acceptance as being the main source of information on guidelines for best practice.

This statement of guidelines became a working draft of our best thinking regarding these issues. It has been continuously updated and discussed with others in allied disciplines and areas of work. Since 1991, CPS-B has continued the effort and has carried on preparing professionals for high levels of practice as independent consultants or internal facilitators or trainers. In each case, we have had discussions regarding ethical practice. Each time we have certified a facilitator or trainer, we have had conversations about what constitutes ethical practice. This work has been a continuous source of input in the drafting process.

The three main contexts of CPS-B's work (services, research, and development) provide the general headings for the suggestions outlined below. The planning and preparation of services includes the design of educational and training courses, workshops, presentations and other interventions. The delivery and provision of services includes the actual interaction with the participants and clients during the providing of professional services. The third major category of suggestions deals with the use of instrumentation and assessment. The final general category includes a few of the norms for working with each other.

This statement does not replace or limit the effect of international, federal, or state laws within the context of our research or practice. Further, general guidelines like knowing and respecting the boundaries of our competence, maintaining and extending our expertise, respecting others, documenting our work, etc., have yet to be identified and widely agreed upon within our field, but are included in our meaning of best practice.

Planning and Preparing Services

Planning and preparing for services includes the deliberate design and determination of activities, purposes and outcomes for instruction, training and educational operations. The implication is that the reflective practitioner will actually engage in planning and design in order to meet the needs of a particular group or context, as opposed to delivering a canned product. During the planning and preparation of programs, the professional will:

1. Provide a specific program of learning or research based on some well thought out answers to basic questions. It is important to have a clear purpose in mind for the program and to be able to state that purpose clearly. The purpose for the program is clearly stated, as are its goals and objectives. These descriptions are made available to all interested parties.

2. To the extent possible, review their plans with colleagues who have some degree of expertise in the field to engage in intersubjective verification. This means that there is some possibility to exchange views on the collective perception or "common sense" of the design, purpose and approach. Intersubjective verification must involve those who have a similar level of general competence and familiarity with the program or design under review. In a sense, this kind of verification is very similar to the notion of peer review.

3. Spend time engaging in deliberate and explicit planning for the delivery and follow-up of courses, workshops and presentations. Preparing an event in our field always involves some element of risk. It is the responsibility of the professional to make specific plans to recognize and manage this risk in the best interest of the field and the participants. This risk may be contained within the actual program being planned or delivered, or come as a result of the program.

4. Carefully examine their own personal motivations, skills, and competence to assess the appropriateness of the match between these and the requests of clients or participants. This guideline suggests that professionals will make choices deliberately, and with care, to insure a fit between their abilities and the needs of those who request their services. Professionals seek to provide programs that are clearly within their area of competence.

5. Respect the proprietary rights regarding the intellectual property of others. The professional is expected to obtain appropriate permissions, to give credit as to the origin of certain contributions, and make all necessary arrangements before using the materials of others. This guideline also suggests that professionals obtain all necessary certifications and licenses before using the material of others.

Delivering and Providing Services

Many creativity programs, workshops, courses, and services provided by creativity professionals are experiential in nature. They become uniquely open and special environments. This does not mean that there is no room for lecture and formal presentations. Many programs designed for impact actually involve the learner in the learning process. When delivering and providing services, the professional will:

1. Provide a clear statement of the purpose of the program. Care should be taken that individuals, groups or organizations who involve themselves in a

program have a clear understanding of the general goals as well as the specific objectives of the program. (This guideline along with number 2, approaches the issue of "informed consent.")

2. Provide assurance of the freedom from coercion to participate. In short, participants should have the right to refuse to involve themselves or discontinue their involvement at any point during the program. Professionals should make sure participants are aware of their choice and provide a non-punitive and dignified alternative way to exercise their options.

3. Be concerned with protecting participants from discomfort, harm, or danger. Establishing certain precautions for certain activities, screening of participants, and maintaining confidentiality (and limited disclosure) are important suggestions.

4. Work to provide a productive balance between managing the integrity of the design of the program with the well-being of the participants. The professional recognizes the importance of balancing the objectives of the program with the concern for individual respect and courtesy. Explicit decisions need to be made regarding the relative importance of the purposes of the program, versus the participants in the program. The professional recognizes that managing human growth is a complex undertaking and should be dealt with as such.

5. Maintain appropriate awareness of the boundaries of personal competence. It is easy for activities and questions during a program to get to the limits of knowledge and competence. The professional acknowledges the importance and value of these questions, but readily admits when they do not know or should not engage in answering or speculating about these issues. They will at least acknowledge when they are basing their answers or content on research, and when they are speculating or talking on the basis of experience.

6. Make every effort to improve their own competence in providing programs. This suggestion includes continuously engaging in formal learning activities, attending workshops, discussions, reading, and studying to acquire as much knowledge as possible to insure personal competence within the domain of creativity and within other domains.

7. Include some provision for participant follow-up and debriefing the personal application of the key learnings. This guideline focuses on the need to provide supplementary clarification and assistance for participants during learning events. Professionals ought to have some plan to monitor the need for clarification and to understand the consequences of their courses, workshops, and presentations.

8. Refrain from using the unique environments created during services as opportunities to establish "personally intimate" relationships. While we often

make lasting friendships and collegial relationships, we refrain from behaviors and interaction that might damage the professional reputations of participants or place them in difficult positions within their organizations.

Using Instruments and Assessments

We often use formal and informal measures in planning and delivering services. These instruments and assessments have powerful potential to help participants understand and nurture creative talents. When using assessment approaches or instrumentation the professional will:

1. Utilize the best standards and ethical principles of the disciplines involved in such assessment and instrumentation. Therefore, it is suggested that the following sources be consulted to provide the framework from which to draw specific application to our field:

    A. Committee for the protection of human participants in research. (1982). *Ethical principles in the conduct of research with human participants.* Washington, DC: American Psychological Association. (This monograph outlines the APA Ethical Principle Number 9, which covers the area of research with human participants.) A more recent version of these guidelines was published as: Ethical principles of psychologists and code of conduct (1992). *American Psychologist, 47,* 1597 -1611.

    B. *Standards for educational and psychological testing.* (1985). Washington, DC: American Psychological Association. (This publication was prepared by the Committee to Develop Standards for Educational and Psychological Testing of: The American Educational Research Association, The American Psychological Association, and The National Council on Measurement in Education.)

    C. Any other formal statements of policies and procedures of relevant organizations. If none, then at least the "Statement of Research Policy" of the Creative Problem Solving Group - Buffalo.

2. Obtain all necessary and recommended certification and training relating to the administration and interpretation of instruments they use; and stay current with respect to the research and literature related to these assessments.

    Should a professional decide to utilize powerful tools from the behavioral and psychological sciences, they must seek and acquire a professional level of competence in those instruments, assessments or other techniques. They must also refrain from using those resources that are beyond their level of certification or qualification. They also discourage others who seek to use instruments for which they are not qualified.

3.   Professionals use instruments and assessments that:

   A.   Have reasonable evidence of validity

   B.   Have reasonable evidence of reliability

   C.   Have been carefully developed or revised

   D.   Have "legitimate" publications, manuals or user guides to promote effective use. "Legitimate" might mean reviewed, published by a credible provider, or meeting certain standards

4.   Generally, safeguard the dignity and well-being of the participants by carefully considering whether the planned study and design maximizes the yield of generalizable knowledge and minimizes the costs and potential risks to the human beings who participate in it. Specifically, professionals are concerned about:

   A.   **Confidentiality.** Information obtained about the research participant during the course of an investigation is confidential, unless otherwise agreed upon in advance. When the possibility exists that others may obtain access to such information, this possibility, together with plans for protecting confidentiality, is explained to the participant as a part of the procedure for obtaining informed consent.

   B.   **Informed consent.** Participants in a research study must be able to provide informed consent regarding their involvement. This includes supplying full disclosure to and acquiring clear and explicit agreement from potential participants. The investigator has the responsibility to honor all promises contained within the agreement.

   C.   **Voluntary participation.** The investigator must respect the participant's freedom to decline to participate in or withdraw from the research at any time. This requires careful thought when the investigator may be in a position of authority (employee, teacher, client, etc.).

   D.   **Safety from discomfort, harm, or danger.** The investigator protects the participant from physical and mental discomfort, harm and danger that may arise from the research procedures. If risks of such consequences exist, participants are informed.

   E.   **Participant debriefing.** All participants in research are provided information about their results unless specifically informed that this will not occur. The debriefing should also include opportunities to remove any misconceptions or provide clarity regarding the results and their meaning.

   F.   **Removing undesirable consequences.** When research procedures result in undesirable consequences for the individual participant, the investigator has the responsibility to detect and remove or correct them.

G.   **Intersubjective verification.** Research designs and data collection and analysis procedures can be productively shared with peers to confirm and strengthen them.

CONCLUSION

This chapter has provided you with an awareness of some potential challenges you may face when you engage in facilitative leadership. It is a unique kind of leadership and is likely to generate a different set of unexpected reactions and surprises.

Even if you follow all the suggestions and guidelines contained within this chapter, it is still quite possible (and even likely) that you will encounter true tests of your patience, faith and character. All I can say is that pursuing the journey of learning how to be a better facilitative leader is worth the effort.

REFERENCES

American Psychological Association (1982). *Ethical principles in the conduct of research with human participants.* Washington, DC: American Psychological Association.

American Psychological Association (1986). *Guidelines for computer-based tests and interpretations (Committee of Professional Standards and the Committee on Psychological Tests and Assessment).* Washington, DC: American Psychological Association.

American Psychological Association (1992). Ethical principles of psychologists and code of conduct. *American Psychologist, 47,* 1597-1611.

Fagothey, A. (1976). *Right and reason: Ethics in theory and practice.* St. Louis, MO: The C. V. Mosby Co.

Heron, J. (1990). Helping the client: A creative practical guide. London: SAGE Publications.

Isaksen, S. G. & Dorval, K. B. (1996). *Facilitating creative problem solving.* Sarasota, FL: Center for Creative Learning.

Isaksen, S. C. & Murdock, M. C. (1993). The emergence of a discipline: Issues and approaches to the study of creativity. In S. G. Isaksen, M. C. Murdock, R. L. Firestien & D. J. Treffinger (Eds.), *Understanding and recognizing creativity: The emergence of a discipline* (pp. 13-47). Norwood, NJ: Ablex Publishing Co.

Ross, D. (1954). *Kant's ethical theory.* West Port, CT: Greenwood Press.

Singer, P. (1993). *Practical ethics* (2nd ed.). Cambridge, UK: Cambridge University Press.

Stacey, R. (1993). Strategy as order emerging from chaos. *Long Range Planning, 26,* 10-17.

Stacey, R. (1996). *Complexity and Management - Working Paper No 1: Creativity in organizations: The importance of mess.* Hertfordshire, UK: Complexity and Management Centre at the University of Hertfordshire.

Standards for educational and psychological testing. (1985). Washington, DC: American Psychological Association.

Treffinger, D. J. (1983). George's group: A creative problem-solving case study. *Journal of Creative Behavior, 17,* 39-48

Wolff, R. P. (Ed.). (1969). *Foundations of the metaphysics of morals by Immanuel Kant.* New York: Bobbs-Merrill Company.

CHAPTER NINE

GUIDING THE EXPERIENTIAL LEARNING OF CPS

Scott G. Isaksen
Creativity Research Unit
Creative Problem Solving Group — Buffalo

> "Knowledge teaches the mind. Teaching the spirit requires experience."
>
> ◆ **Martin Brokenleg**

INTRODUCTION

Experiential learning is based on the belief that people learn best by doing. Walter & Marks (1981) indicated:

> *Experiential learning is operative when participants are fully involved, when the lessons are clearly relevant to the participants, when individuals develop a sense of responsibility for their own learning, and when the learning environment is flexible, responsive to the participants' immediate needs. (p. 2)*

Creative Problem Solving (CPS) is often (and best) learned and applied through an experiential approach. The learning process starts with preparation on the part of those providing the learning and the participants attending the course. The activities, exercises, lectures and discussions provide opportunities to share content and build skills. Taking an experiential approach reinforces the point that creativity is natural and engaging. It is not just about fun and games but is based on obtaining meaning through reflection on experience.

When it is important to focus on process learnings as well as content outcomes from CPS experiences (as in the development of facilitation expertise), debriefing the activities can be an effective procedure to identify the key insights and insure that these learnings are transferable to other situations. The transfer of these key insights to other CPS activities should not be left to chance. Transfer depends on deliberate development of these applications for future use during CPS activities. This kind of learning can be described by using a model for experiential learning.

A MODEL FOR EXPERIENTIAL LEARNING

Debriefing is only one aspect of experientially learning CPS. There are many different models of behavioral change and experiential learning (Druckman & Swets, 1988; Frederick, 1987; Hannaford, 1995; Palmer, 1981). Figure 1 presents a model for

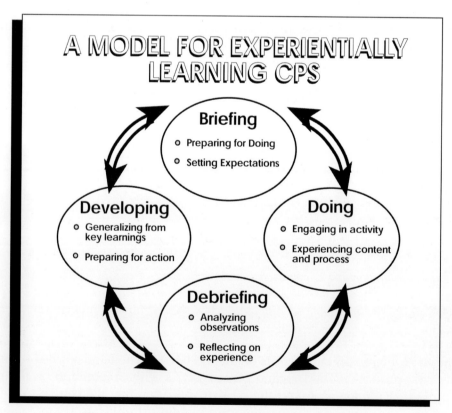

Figure 1: A Model for Experientially Learning CPS

the experiential approach to learning and applying CPS we use in training facilitators and trainers. There are many possible CPS activities which might provide the basis for experiential learning.

Generally, the session, interaction, training event or activity begins with a "briefing" regarding the purpose of the exercise and establishing an appropriate learning environment. The briefing explains what is going to happen and what the participants are going to do. The next stage in experientially learning CPS involves the "doing" and provides the actual experience. This could be a client-facilitator planning meeting, an idea-generation session, or a training session on the dynamic balance between generating and focusing options.

The "debriefing" stage follows the session or event. During debriefing some time and energy is devoted to analyzing what happened and reflecting on the experience. This could include a formal meeting after the first day of a training course, an exercise for the participants following the entire program, an evaluation session conducted by the trainers after a training design meeting, or a closing discussion at the end of a CPS application session. The main questions are focused on *what* happened and *so what*?

Finally, we focus on how to use the results of the analysis conducted during the debriefing stage. This fourth stage is referred to as "developing." This kind of activity may often occur during the time-frame established for debriefing, or it can be an independent outcome or session. For example, if limitations or concerns are raised during the first day of a three-day training program, the developing stage might include some design modifications for implementation during the second day. Developing could also take place a few days following the training session so that new learnings can be transferred to future program designs or materials. The main question during the developing phase of experiential learning is *now what?*

Having a deliberate structure or model to help you guide experiential learning can be helpful in making sure that the activity does not lose its focus. It should be used as a flexible and dynamic guide for managing exercises and activities that have specific learning purposes. It is not some predefined pathway that you must follow in some linear fashion. You can often move back and forth or skip ahead or backward as needed.

Briefing

The briefing aspect of the experiential learning model includes preparing yourself, as well as participants, for engaging in the activity. Part of the briefing stage of experiential learning is being clear about the purpose for the activity. Having an "end in view" is necessary in order to develop a shared vision with the participants of the experience. It also includes helping participants clarify and set their own expectations prior to the activity.

Prepare for doing. Preparation for experientially learning CPS includes planning the design of the learning exercise, identifying learning needs, assessing capabilities of leadership, establishing appropriate objectives and selecting suitable activities. Having, holding and sharing explicit goals and objectives for the experience is what differentiates real experiential learning from mere "games" or activity for its own sake.

Prior to the actual doing of the activity, the environment needs to be adequately prepared. It is important to have adequate time and energy devoted to setting up the context and logistics. Participants also need to be adequately prepared. Informing them about the activity, establishing clear expectations and norms, inviting them to get the full value from the activity, ensuring voluntary participation (providing multiple ways to be involved) and reinforcing key safety and comfort issues are all important considerations for establishing an environment for learning.

Set participants' expectations. Be sure to make some comments to help set the stage for what is about to happen. Introducing the activity includes both the general comments as well as the actual instructions for the exercises. This could include a preview of what is to come, a key quote, or any other action which helps get the participants ready for the experience. For example, a formal time-frame during which expectations are stated and recorded to build the actual agenda for the experience can be a helpful activity. Heightening the anticipation for the experience helps to keep the participants focused and engaged. Establishing the anticipation helps to set appropriate expectations for the activity.

Doing

The doing aspect of CPS experiential learning includes engaging in an activity and experiencing both content and process. The focus is on active involvement and participation in the actual activity.

Encourage full participation and observation. Participants should be encouraged to become fully involved in the experience, as they will be able to take away only that which they invest. Responsibility for experientially learning CPS is shared by the participants as well as the trainers and facilitators. Participants should also be encouraged to use idea systems or journals to record observations, key reactions and behaviors, or feelings experienced during the activity. They should pay attention to their own intentions, motivations and behavior, as well as to others' actions and potential intentions.

Encourage the use of group norms. Early in the experience, you should keep an eye out for behaviors that may be outside the norms. These offer the opportunity to clarify the norms and check on agreement and commitment to follow them.

Some Sample Norms

What we promise to you. We will...

✦ Work to maintain your interest (fun, real examples, etc.);
✦ Schedule reasonable personal time and breaks;
✦ Accommodate a diversity of learning styles and needs (flexibility);
✦ Use appropriate language (clean/concise);
✦ Structure the design to enable you to use CPS on real tasks; and
✦ Listen and respond to your feedback.

To achieve this we need you to...

✦ Engage in the program;
✦ Ask questions if you don't understand;
✦ Stick to the schedule (be punctual);
✦ Accommodate a diversity of learning styles and needs;
✦ Use appropriate language;
✦ Consider what you need to "let go" of to maximize your learning;
✦ Provide constructive feedback when requested; and
✦ Take responsibility for your learning and comfort.

Debriefing

Debriefing is the phase of CPS experiential learning which involves analyzing observations and reactions as well as reflecting on the actual experience. There are many structures which can aid debriefing. Taking notes during the activity ("out" thoughts, reactions, interesting observations, etc.), engaging in a "Taking it Forward" activity (i.e., identifying interesting, useful or intriguing aspects) or conducting an ALUo (Isaksen, Dorval & Treffinger, 1998) on a session are all natural ways to debrief the activity. The focus of attention during debriefing is on the experience itself. Time and energy is devoted to establishing a historical perspective regarding what happened. The emphasis is on conscious observation.

As Nadler (1998) indicated:

> *Reflection is the capacity to go back and analyze—without blame, without attempting to find fault — the elements that contribute to the success or failure of a product or process. Reflection leads to insight, which enables organizations to question their knowledge and beliefs and avoid repeating the same mistakes. It is that collective learning that provides successful organizations with the intellectual capital that becomes a true and unassailable source of competitive advantage. (p. 301)*

Tactics for Asking Questions

✦ Ask one question at a time.
✦ Avoid asking simple yes or no questions.
✦ Pose questions that lack a single right answer (use a balance of divergent or open-ended as well as closed questions).
✦ Avoid leading questions (Don't you think that...?).
✦ Use "wait time" after asking a question and again after hearing the response.
✦ Encourage participant interaction and elaboration.

Use questions to stimulate reflection and learning. Questions are important tools for learning (Dillon, 1988). They are particularly useful for guiding experiential learning. We recommend that you have a plan for the kinds of questions you will ask the participants. Be aware of the tone of your voice, facial expressions, and gestures while asking questions. Remember that questions are used to promote learning and seek understanding. You do not want to be perceived as an interrogator.

There are all sorts of questions you can ask. For example, exploratory questions probe for facts and basic knowledge, while challenge questions examine the assumptions, conclusions and interpretations that people have developed. There are also cause and effect, priority, extension and summary questions (Davis, 1993).

You can also vary the cognitive skills called for your questions. Some questions can call for memory and recall, others can call for evaluation. This relates to the kinds of goals or objectives you have for the experience. We recommend that you refer to Bloom's (1956) system or taxonomy of objectives to help vary the kinds and levels of objectives and questions you use. Whatever questioning approach you choose to take, be sure to be ready to actually listen (and listen generously) to the responses, answers, comments, and even questions that come in response.

Provide time for reflection. One of the key principles in using wait time is that the kinds and levels of responses will improve if given sufficient time. For the creativity field this relates to the value of incubation and the principle of extending your effort.

One of the best ways I know of to even out the participation during debriefing is to build in some deliberate time for reflection. For example, following the exercise you could ask each individual to write down a certain number of responses to a question. You could then go right around a standing circle to insure that each participant has a chance to contribute. You could do this after participants have some additional time for reflection.

Sample Debriefing Questions

◆ What did you observe?
◆ How did you feel about that?
◆ What are some of the advantages...?
◆ What surprised you about...?
◆ What concerns does this raise?
◆ What is really novel about...?
◆ What really struck you about...?
◆ How did you decide what to do?

◆ What were you aware of?
◆ What did you like about what you did?
◆ Share some of the strengths of...
◆ What limitations might exist?
◆ Were there any surprises?
◆ Who had a similar experience?
◆ Why did you do what you did?

◆ What were a few of your most important observations about this exercise?
◆ What do you think about what happened during this activity?

Developing

Following the debriefing of the activity, experiential learning also includes some time and energy devoted to developing practical outcomes which might be transferred to other situations or experiences. The developing phase involves generalizing and applying the key learnings from the experience. Emphasis is upon integrating insights into new behaviors and tasks.

Focus on transfer. It is during this phase of experientially learning CPS that the learning is made practical and prepared for transfer. Specific plans and action steps for future doing can often result from the developing phase. In addition, this phase of experientially learning CPS provides the opportunity for summarizing the key outcomes as well as determining the effectiveness of the learning experience.

In order to focus the learning for transfer you must provide some deliberate time and attention to transforming the insights from the structured learning experience to a more personally meaningful context. In a way, you can close down the previous stage of debriefing by turning the participants' attention to how they might use or apply what they have learned.

Help participants prepare for action. Once the participants have made a few meaningful connections from the experience, you can then help them identify some specific actions they might take to use or apply what they learned. At this point you may have some useful resources or references available to assist the participants in taking their learning forward.

Sample Developing Questions

- ✦ What did you learn or relearn from this exercise?
- ✦ How might you apply this?
- ✦ What do some of these learnings suggest about...?
- ✦ How might you use these learnings?

- ✦ When would you use these?
- ✦ What might we draw or pull from that?
- ✦ What were some of your key learnings?
- ✦ What will you do differently now?

- ✦ What new ways of behaving or operating might be developed on the basis of your learnings?
- ✦ How might you use these key learnings in your role as...?
- ✦ What are you going to do differently as a result of what you learned?

PROCEDURES FOR EXPERIENTIALLY LEARNING CPS

There are many ways to accomplish successful experiential learning. There are also a variety of resources to help you along the way. I will outline a few areas that may be helpful for providing procedures within each of the stages of the experiential learning model.

Briefing

To assist in the briefing stage, you may find information on curriculum and instructional planning to be helpful. A good general resource is Dembo (1981). The main procedures deal with planning and specifying the purpose for the activity, as well as preparing the environment for learning. This can also include contracting for safety and comfort.

Doing

There are many resources which provide possible exercises and suggestions for running the actual activities. Some of these include: Epstein (1996); Fluegelman (1976; 1981); Heermann (1997); Nilson (1993); Rohnke (1984; 1989); Rohnke & Butler (1995); Sikes, (1995); Solem & Pike (1997); Weinstein & Goodman (1980).

Debriefing

Treffinger and Wittig (1990) recommended the use of a framework which focuses upon areas of praise, questions for clarification, areas of concern and amplification or new possibilities. Treffinger and Wittig (1990) provided a variety of benefits and goals for debriefing CPS. From a facilitator's perspective, the benefits of debriefing include:

1. Increased awareness of one's own strengths and needs as a facilitator;

2. Enhanced understanding of the structure and dynamics of CPS and facilitation (learning through experience);

3. Evaluation of the impact or effectiveness of particular activities or strategies;

4. Identification of possible ways to modify techniques or apply varied strategies in future sessions;

5. Increased sensitivity to the impact of facilitators' actions on other group members; and

6. Evaluation of the choices and decisions that were made spontaneously, given more time for reflection and analysis.

From a participant's perspective, the benefits of debriefing include:

1. Increased awareness of the process elements of the session, when isolated from the content demands of the problem or task;

2. Increased understanding of the roles of the facilitator, the client, and the resource-group members in the session;

3. Reflective definition and understanding of the methods and techniques that were used during the session; and

4. Evaluation of the impact or the effectiveness of the session, each person's contributions, and needs that might have been unrecognized or unmet.

Debriefing can be conducted by the leader or can be made the responsibility of the participants. It is possible to build it directly into the design for the learning activity or make it an activity for homework or follow-through. Procedures for debriefing provide some guidance and structure for implementing the model shown in Figure 1. Another procedure is using the ALUo tool (Isaksen, Dorval & Treffinger, 1998; Puccio & Dorval, 1988) for debriefing and developing an exercise or experience. (See the example at the end of this chapter.)

Developing

The Project Adventure approach (Schoel, Prouty, & Radcliffe, 1989) offers one of the best guides for ensuring that activities are effectively processed. One of the main procedures for developing is generalizing from the learning to encourage future application and use. This is very similar to developing a useful theory about what happened and why (Kolb, 1992).

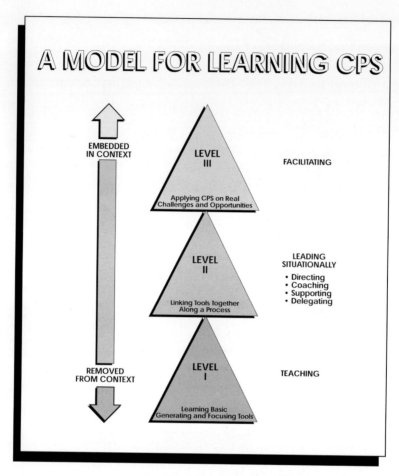

Figure 2:   A Model for Creative Learning

LEVELS OF USE

A number of models have been developed to help guide the learning and application of CPS. Treffinger (1980) provided a model for creative learning targeted toward the teaching of gifted and talented students, which was later validated by Isaksen and Parnes (1985). Isaksen (1988) later modified Treffinger's model to focus it more on learning and applying CPS (see Figure 2).

This model suggested that learning and applying CPS occurs on at least three different levels: Level I — learning some basic generating and focusing CPS tools; Level II — linking CPS tools together and using them in individual stages, components or as an entire process; and Level III — applying CPS on real challenges and opportunities. Treffinger continues to develop this model and the most up-to-date version is available in Treffinger & Feldhusen (1998).

Learning Basic Tools

Level I includes learning some basic generating and focusing CPS tools. The setting could be large-group training during which many small groups would work together independently and as a total group. Teaching and training would characterize the predominant type of leadership, and much of the content would be removed from the actual context of the participants. For example, participants may be given the opportunity to work on case studies or practice problems.

Even at this level, plans can be made to take an experiential approach. Individuals and small groups can be given time to engage in meaningful activity, reflect on the experience and develop and share key learnings. Typically, a "taking it forward" or "taking it home" exercise accomplishes this and pools the reactions, key learnings and applications from the entire group to encourage sharing of perspectives and outcomes.

Practicing Use of Tools

Level II includes linking CPS tools together and using them in individual stages, components or as an entire process. From a skill-development perspective, this level of experientially learning CPS can be based on some diagnosis of both competence and commitment on the part of the individual or group. Based on the level of readiness, the leadership is more situational and the content of the activities begins to become more relevant to the participant.

In a sense, the learner (when ready, willing and able) begins to apply CPS tools and approaches on more realistic challenges and opportunities under the guidance and direction of someone in a leadership role. The benefit of taking an experiential approach at this level is that the leader can obtain a much more accurate diagnosis of competence (ability and skill level) and commitment (degree and kind of motivation) by observing the actual behavior of the participants.

Like any effective coaching interaction, learning can be structured to coincide with the skill deficit and the need. If adequately debriefed and developed, this can encourage the participants to monitor their own learning and empower them to seek assistance or direction when needed.

Applying Tools on Real Challenges

Level III includes applying CPS on real challenges and opportunities. When applying CPS on real challenges the main focus of leadership is facilitation. Of course, the leadership role will be very dynamic at this level as there will be movement to teaching, training and leading in a situational manner.

From an experiential learning perspective, it is during this level that participants operate very close to the content of the challenge or opportunity being addressed. Engaging in debriefing and developing following the actual session helps to achieve an improved balance between content and process. At this level there is an opportunity to approach debriefing from the point of view of resource-group member, client and facilitator.

When the facilitation of small groups is going on within a larger context of a training event, it will also be very useful for table facilitators to gather together following the scheduled length of the day or program and engage in structured debriefing and developing activities. In this way, experiential learning can be designed to take place within the actual small groups as well as within large groups.

It is when a training and facilitation team gather to debrief and develop each day that another level of experiential learning occurs. One of the key benefits from providing an experiential approach to learning is that those responsible for the teaching and planning also have the opportunity to learn and obtain deeper levels of insight regarding the content and process of the event. Having a team commit to work together and share different observations and perspectives enriches the learning even further.

A MODEL FOR LEARNING AND APPLYING CPS

The current model for learning and applying CPS builds on earlier work but also attempts to separate **what** is being learned from **how** it is being learned. Balancing the concern for learning the process with the emphasis on applying the process to meaningful content is a key dynamic for planning and delivering programs to develop creativity.

What is being learned, with respect to CPS, has been identified as a specific set of skills. For example, the CPS "skillbase" at a foundational level includes understanding the basic language of CPS and being able to apply specific creative-thinking and problem-solving tools. At a CPS facilitator level, it includes skills for using a facilitative style of leadership to manage small-group application of CPS. At a CPS trainer level, it includes skills in managing the learning of CPS by multiple small groups against a design and resources for learning. How the CPS skills are learned is what is depicted by the model in Figure 3.

The current model for learning and applying CPS (Isaksen, in press) uses the experiential learning model to manage the balance between an emphasis on learning CPS skills and applying or experiencing them on meaningful content. During the "briefing" aspect of experiential learning, preparation takes place for applying CPS.

As the facilitator or trainer moves a group into the "doing" of an activity, the primary focus is on application. After completing the activity, the application is "debriefed." At this point, the emphasis begins to shift from a focus on applying CPS to one of learning CPS. Individuals analyze and reflect on the CPS application and begin to identify key learnings resulting from the application. These learnings are then "anchored" and made transferable in the "developing" aspect of the model. Here the emphasis is almost entirely focused on learning CPS.

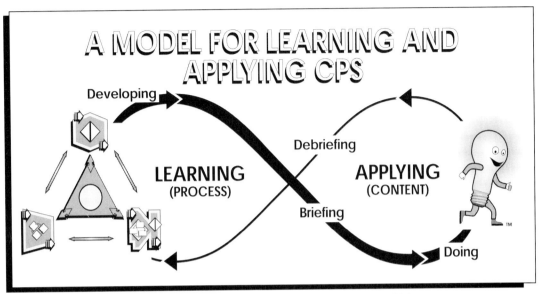

Figure 3: A Model for Learning and Applying CPS

The model is designed to help trainers, practitioners or facilitators manage the amount of time, energy and focus placed on learning and applying CPS. It helps set appropriate expectations for people engaging in CPS to accomplish specific outcomes.

The model does not prescribe a start or end point in the process of learning and applying CPS. It also does not prescribe the amount of time and energy to spend or emphasis to place on learning or application — that depends upon the desired outcome. For example, I once facilitated a meeting with a team working on a critical organizational issue related to safety and morale. The primary purpose of the meeting was to make real progress toward developing a plan of action for handling the critical issue. As a result, the meeting focused 90% on applying the language and tools of CPS to develop the plan of action and about 10% on learning the process language and tools.

I was able to plan what to do in the meeting as well as the amount of time and energy to devote in the meeting toward different activities. It also helped me set the groups' expectations regarding what would happen in the meeting, as well as what would result from the meeting. In this case, the model for learning and applying CPS would have looked more like that presented in Figure 4. The CPS process was used transparently — simple, everyday language was used to guide participants in applying tools. The primary purpose of the interaction was about "giving the group a fish" rather than "teaching them how to fish."

There are other occasions where the emphasis is on learning the tools and language of CPS. Under these conditions we are more mindful and explicit about the strategies and procedures so that the participants can be less dependent on those

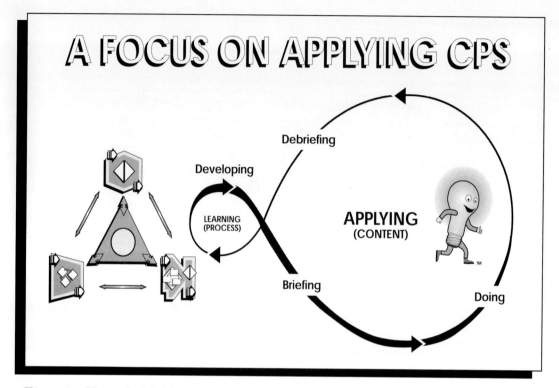

Figure 4: Using the Model for Learning and Applying CPS to Facilitate a Planning Meeting

who are certified facilitators and more independent in their own use of the CPS method. Experiential learning is relevant for both learning and applying CPS.

CONCLUSION

Experiential learning is an important way to learn about many topics, but particularly for those concerned with the learning and applying of CPS. This chapter provided a general model and some resources for experiential learning. It also provided two ways to be clear about the purpose for the activity. One was to consider the level of use: this could range from teaching tools totally removed from any real context to facilitating a group on a real problem. The second way to clarify the purpose was to know if you should be focusing on learning or applying CPS. Finally, a few examples of debriefing are included following the references.

REFERENCES

Bloom, B. S., Engelhart, N. D., Furst, E. J., Hill, W. H. & Krathwohl, D. R. (1956). *Taxonomy of educational objectives - Handbook I: The cognitive domain.* New York: McKay.

Davis, B. G. (1993) *Tools for teaching.* San Francisco: Jossey-Bass.

Dembo, M. H. (1981). *Teaching for learning: Applying educational psychology in the classroom.* Glenview, IL: Scott, Foresman and Company.

Dillon, J. T. (1988). *Questioning and teaching: A manual of practice.* New York: Teachers College Press

Druckman, D. & Swets, J. A. (1988). (Eds.). *Enhancing human performance: Issues, theories and techniques.* Washington, DC: National Academy Press.

Epstein, R. (1996). *Creativity games for trainers: A handbook of group activities for jumpstarting workplace creativity.* New York: McGraw-Hill.

Fluegelman, A. (1976). (Ed.). *The new games book.* Garden City, NY: Dolphin Books.

Fluegelman, A. (1981). (Ed.). *More new games.* Garden City, NY: Dolphin Books.

Frederick, P. J. (1987). Student involvement: Active learning in large classes. In M. G. Weimer (Ed.), *Teaching large classes well* (pp. 45-56). London: Jossey-Bass, Inc.

Hannaford, C. (1995). *Smart moves: Why learning is not all in your head.* Arlington, VA: Great Ocean Publishers.

Heermann, B. (1997). *Building team spirit: Activities for inspiring and energizing teams.* New York: McGraw-Hill.

Isaksen, S. G. (1988). Innovative problem solving in groups: New methods and research opportunities. In Y. Ijiri & R. L. Kuhn (Eds.). *New directions in creative and innovative management - Theory and practice* (pp. 145-168). Cambridge, MA: Ballinger Publishing.

Isaksen, S. G. (in press). The Center for Studies in Creativity: A quarter century of progress. In M. K. Raina (Ed.) *International perspectives in creativity research.*

Isaksen, S. G., & Parnes, S. J. (1985). Curriculum planning for creative thinking and problem solving. *Journal of Creative Behavior, 19,* 1-29.

Isaksen, S. G., Dorval, K. B., & Treffinger, D. J. (1998). *Toolbox for CPS: Basic tools and resources for Creative Problem Solving.* Buffalo, NY: Creative Problem Solving Group - Buffalo.

Kolb, D. G. (1992). The practicality of theory. *The Journal of Experiential Education, 15,* 24-28.

Nadler, D. A. (1998). *Champions of change: How CEOs and their companies are mastering the skills of radical change.* San Francisco: Jossey-Bass.

Nilson, C. (1993). *Team games for trainers: High-involvement games and training aids for developing team skills.* New York: McGraw-Hill.

Palmer, A. B. (1981). Learning cycles: Models of behavioral change. *The 1981 annual handbook for group facilitators* (pp. 147-153). San Diego, CA: University Associates.

Puccio, G. J. & Dorval, K. B. (1988). Affirmative judgment for evaluating performance. *Creative Learning Today*, 2 (1), 3.

Rohnke, K. (1984). *Silver Bullets: A guide to initiative problems, adventure games and trust activities.* Dubuque, IA: Kendall/Hunt Publishing.

Rohnke, K. (1989). *Cowstails and cobras II: A guide to games, initiatives, ropes courses, & adventure curriculum.* Dubuque, IA: Kendall/Hunt Publishing.

Rohnke, K., & Butler, S. (1995). *Quicksilver: Adventure games, initiative problems, trust activities and a guide to effective leadership.* Dubuque, IA: Kendall/Hunt Publishing.

Schoel, J., Prouty, D., & Radcliffe, P. (1989). *Islands of healing: A guide to adventure-based counseling.* Hamilton, MA: Project Adventure, Inc.

Sikes, S. (1995). *Feeding the zircon gorilla.* Tulsa,OK: Learning Unlimited Corporation.

Solem, L. & Pike, B. (1997). *50 creative training closers: Innovative ways to end your training with impact.* San Francisco: Jossey-Bass/Pfeiffer.

Treffinger, D. J. (1980). *Encouraging creative learning for the gifted and talented.* Ventura, CA: Ventura county Schools/LTI.

Treffinger, D. J., & Feldhusen, J. F. (1998). *Planning for productive thinking and learning: A handbook for teachers.* Sarasota, FL: Center for Creative Learning.

Treffinger, D. J. & Wittig, C. W. (1990). Understanding the role of debriefing in creative problem solving. *Creative Learning Today* , 4 (5 and 6), 6-7.

Walter, G. A. & Marks, S. E. (1981). *Experiential learning and change: Theory design and practice.* New York: John Wiley & Sons.

Weinstein, M., & Goodman, J. (1980). *Everybody's guide to noncompetitive play: Playfair.* San Luis Obispo, CA: Impact Publishers.

APPENDIX: AN EXAMPLE OF DEBRIEFING

Experiential learning can be applied in a variety of contexts. The following debriefing example is taken from a real event - attending an International Creativity Conference called INNO '90, held in Finland. We were briefed about the experience in that we received and read conference brochures and had extensive telephone conversations and meetings about the event. The doing aspect took place when we actually attended the conference. We attended a number of cultural events and programs during the three days.

On the way back from the conference, three of us (two colleagues and I) sat together on the plane and "debriefed" the conference. The results of this activity are provided below as an example of a possible outcome from experiential learning.

Advantages

These are aspects of our experience which were seen as positives or strong points.

+ The opportunity to meet and understand people from Finland and the Soviet Union.

+ The opportunity to see a variety of locations (Helsinki, Lappeenranta, Imatra, Leningrad, Vyborg, Pushkin) while participating in one conference.

+ Working on a real challenge of global significance (the problems and opportunities associated with the establishment of a free economic zone in the Vyborg area of Russia).

+ Appreciation for the cultural differences and similarities between and among eastern and western cultures. For example:

  ■ The warmth, character and sincere desire to communicate was common to both.

  ■ Perceptions and behaviors described as "western" differ between the US and Finland.

  ■ The economic way of life, level of English language proficiency (no American spoke Russian), developmental level of understanding of basic business concepts and psychology of work life, and perceptions of equality between males and females were very different.

+ The conference itself provided an historic first step toward broadening cultural understanding.

+ Facilities (food, rooms, equipment) were first class.

+ There was a high level and quality of care and personal attention paid to participants and presenters (which exceeded expectations).

  ■ Tommi (conference host) picked us up at the airport and assisted with hotel selection.

  ■ Hotel reservations were made for us.

  ■ When our hotel room wasn't ready on arrival, Tommi spent time with us and was helpful in providing tourist information.

  ■ Travel arrangements were made from Helsinki to Lappeenranta.

  ■ Bus transportation was well planned and entertaining.

+ In the "East meets West" session, early emphasis on non-verbal communication and interaction helped to overcome cultural barriers.

+ The skill level of the interpreters was excellent; especially those who did so for the first time.

✦ The cultural programs in Finland and Russia were excellent. There was a high level of preparation and concern for providing the best possible experience for the participants.

Limitations

These are aspects of our experience that were opportunities for improvement. We have first identified the challenge and then provided a few suggestions for development. The challenges are phrased in a "How to..." question format to invite ideas or suggestions for overcoming them. We actually overcame each of the limitations as we identified them. Usually, the key limitations can be chosen and then suggestions can be generated to overcome them.

✦ How to improve the Finnish understanding and appreciation of the richness of the Russian culture?

■ More small group and informal interaction, with some opportunity for consistent interaction as well. Perhaps deliberate sessions aimed at understanding different cultural norms and expectations.

■ Encouragement and participation in identifying strengths of Russian culture (A few Finnish participants could not identify a single strength when requested. More Finnish participation in the cultural program).

✦ How to better understand and utilize differences in social structure in the design of the Lappeenranta segment of the conference?

■ Identify key Russian participants and be sure to meet their particular needs.

■ Recognize status issues and behaviors (verbal and nonverbal) and design conference experiences that consider these differences.

✦ How to better design and communicate goals and activities to participants?

■ Pre-work - more accurate information (long and short term; conceptual and specific); participants involved in preparation activities, including style and biographical data exchange.

■ Design experience in light of group development.

■ Provide clear expectations for conference and session outcomes (both process and content).

■ Be sure to follow-up with the conference participants (i.e. send report regarding accomplishments in a timely manner of two to four weeks, be available and respond to follow-up requests).

■ Improve the screening of presenters to be sure that they promote learning and applying appropriate content, rather than selling their services and materials.

✦ How to improve logistics and organization?

■ Handouts and transparencies - Provide graphics and handouts on more readable overhead transparencies. Perhaps two more screens for the translated overheads would have been helpful.

■ More communication and coordination among conference planners (before, during, and after conference).

■ Every session should be planned and interpreted for multiple languages, or declare one formal conference language. It may have been helpful to have more interpreters for small-group work.

■ Adjust the design so that pacing and timing within sessions are more responsive to participants' needs (i.e. comfort breaks, reflection, energy level).

■ Brief participants and presenters on how to respond to simultaneous translation (clarity around time allotment and appropriate behaviors during translation).

■ Make better use of the expertise that was assembled. The US presenters generally had short isolated presentations with very little opportunity for integration into the theme areas. This was a two-way loss; inability to learn from the theme as well as to add value to the thrust of the theme (finding and using strengths).

■ Broaden the diversity of presenters. Few were Russian, all were white males.

■ Let presenters know more details about the design so they are better coordinated and integrated into the main purpose and direction of the conference.

Unique Qualities

These are aspects of the conference that may not have actually been Advantages or Limitations, but clearly identify novel or original features of the event. In a sense, they are the surprises and novel insights we are not ready to analyze or evaluate.

✦ The concept of having a real client work on a real challenge during the implementation during a conference was novel and useful.

✦ The importance and necessity of face-to-face interaction in international relations.

✦ There is a great deal of stress and intensity associated with multiple language communication. Planning and design must accommodate these factors for conferences of this type to be successful.

✦ There is a vast potential within the Russian people for the release of human creativity!

As you can see, the ALUo tool can be readily adapted to support experiential learning. In this case, the focus was not an actual CPS session but an entire conference. Other examples of the use of affirmative judgment are provided by Puccio and Dorval (1988).

AN EXAMPLE OF DEVELOPING

The following is a continuation of our INNO '90 International Creativity Conference example. Here are examples of the "key learnings" or take aways developed as a result of attending the conference. (Please note that these were developed in 1990!)

These are some of the key learnings from the conference activities.

+ We learned of the necessity to balance teaming and learning (using common diversity and supportive tension as building blocks) Respites/dyads.

+ Complex purposes need layered, flexible designs. The next time we plan a major conference or training event, we need to consider the layers needed to manage multiple purposes.

+ Other cultures (without a 50-year tradition of dealing with creativity) will invite "innovators" to take the initiative. All the potential strengths and weaknesses associated with this can be predicted. We need to be careful of whom we invite to our conferences, programs or research meetings. "Many opportunities to see Niagara Falls for the first time."

+ Written papers are important for international presentations. They can be translated for distribution, they provide the opportunity for the presenters to plan their talks and the conference planners to better communicate the focus of the presentation. Whenever we attend a conference, we must submit a paper because they will go where we are unable to go.

+ The Russian contacts we made from the manufacturing and finance sectors were eager to do business with the West. There is enormous potential within the culture, from a natural and human-resource perspective. Although anxious for Western enterprise, the economic infrastructure for a market system is not well developed (unconvertible currency, non-reliable phones, rare fax systems, a poor distribution system and complete lack of customer orientation will offer major challenges.). For example, there is currently a dual distribution system. One is formally and centrally planned but relatively ineffective. There is another way of getting things done which is much more emergent and informal, based on friends, favors and bribes. It is also based on ad hoc entrepreneurs. There are many opportunities for us to support the deliberate use of creativity in many parts of Europe and Asia. We need to consider how to get our information to these parts of the world.

◆ The standard Western approaches to market economy will not be effectively transplanted. Small intermediary steps and gradual adjustment within existing systems will be essential. We need to communicate information about creativity that encourages the use of continuous improvement approaches to managing change.

CHAPTER TEN

MAKING A DIFFERENCE WITH CPS: A SUMMARY OF THE EVIDENCE

Scott G. Isaksen
Creative Research Unit
Creative Problem Solving Group — Buffalo
and
Luc De Schryver
Creativity and Innovation Center — Europe

> "Of making many books there is not end; and much study is a weariness of the flesh. Let us hear the conclusion of the whole matter."
> **Solomon,** *Ecclesiastes 12:12-13*

INTRODUCTION

The purpose of this chapter is to create a road map of a big part of the creativity field for people interested in knowing if there is an actual research base behind that "creativity stuff." Our goal is to take stock of the available evidence in support of learning and applying Creative Problem Solving (CPS). There is much more to creativity than CPS, but it would be a difficult task to take stock of everything ever written on creativity or its enhancement from an all-inclusive perspective.

We saw the challenge as assembling everything we were aware of that provided evidence that learning and applying CPS made a difference. We are certain that we did not collect every shred of evidence. In fact, we invite you to find something that we missed. We will include it in future editions of this book and credit you for the find!

Our experience tells us that organizations, and human resource managers in particular, are overwhelmed by the amount of information available on creativity. This creates a particular problem when they have to deal with this new focus on creativity and innovation. When participants, clients, consultants, academics and students venture into relatively unfamiliar territory, they may be helped along by knowing that there is a foundation underpinning their efforts. We believe that those interested in facilitative leadership in general, and more specifically, the facilitation of Creative Problem Solving, can benefit from being aware of the research and related literature that supports their practice.

This road map starts with some foundational work. In order to know where we are going as a discipline, we first have to know where we are coming from. Although the field of creativity is relatively young, creativity has intrigued many authors and researchers for many decades, even going back to Duff (1767). This foundational work consists of three parts: some historical perspectives, major theoretical approaches, and finally some general philosophical support.

Secondly, we focused on the research and development that is occurring not only in Buffalo, but also in Europe and in other parts of the world. During the last few decades researchers have been building evidence that CPS does have a positive impact on individuals, teams and organizations. This evidence has grown through case studies, the development of programs, and their evaluation, in the United States, England, Belgium, France, the Netherlands and all over the world. Communities to extend this knowledge are being created. An overview of journals, networks and creativity organizations is also provided.

Finally, we focused on some experimental evidence. Researchers, clients, and those in organizations want to have more than a surface understanding of some of the important issues around introducing and nurturing creative behavior and creative output. What are the underlying mechanisms that push individuals, teams, departments and organizations to be innovative? In the last part of this chapter the reader will find references to brainstorming research and impact research. Finally an overview of a wide range of CPS applications and case studies is provided.

The central question that organizes this chapter is "How do we know that training, teaching, learning or applying CPS is worthwhile?" There are numerous ways to know that learning something is worth the effort. We invest our resources in teaching and learning because the content we choose makes sense. We also know that it is worthwhile if it works or makes a real difference in the world. Each of the major subheadings provides a basic assertion to answer the central question. These are followed with a short narrative to explain the assertion, and then a series of references to support it.

To make your use of this resource a little easier, we have organized our nine basic answers to this central question. The page numbers follow the category to make it easier for you to turn directly to the section of interest.

1. A solid and explicit conceptual foundation exists (pages 191-203)

    Historical approaches
    Major theoretical approaches
    General philosophical support

2. Continuous research and development occurs (pages 204-208)

    Buffalo-based foundational work
    Other evidence

3. Formal courses are available (page 209)

4. Courses and programs have been evaluated (pages 210-212)

5. Communities exist to advance knowledge (pages 213-217)

    Edited collections
    Published bibliographies
    Scholarly review and syntheses
    Dedicated journals

6. Communities exist to advance practice (pages 218-220)

    Networks
    Creativity organizations

7. There is a documented need (pages 221-223)

    The nature of knowledge
    The importance of creative-thinking skills
    Skills more transferable than knowledge
    Situations may demand creativity
    Creative thinking can be enjoyable
    Creativity is natural
    Builds on knowledge

8. There is experimental evidence (pages 224-242)

    Foundational evidence
    Brainstorming research
    Experimental evidence of course impact

9. CPS has been widely applied (pages 242-248)

    Special populations

    Case studies

1. A Solid and Explicit Conceptual Foundation Exists

There is a wealth of evidence to support the teaching and learning of CPS from conceptual, theoretical and philosophical viewpoints. Support for teaching and learning creativity comes from a variety of sources. CPS fits a conceptual context of an identified domain (creativity) and there is sufficient knowledge to inform the subdomain. There is a long-term history to the concept, numerous theoretical foundations and an established philosophical literature.

Historical Perspectives

There is a great deal of mythology associated with the concept of creativity. Most of the mythology has some historical basis. Some believe that creativity is magical, mysterious, or linked with madness. These myths have their basis in history. First, from the point of view of the Greeks and Romans as an act of divine inspiration, then later as a unique gift from heredity or special talent.

God's Gift of Genius

The earliest thinkers to take up the subject of creativity explained it as a gift from God (or the gods). The Greeks had Homer's poetry that supported the idea of the bicameral mind. According to this view the mind had two chambers, one of which was for the gods to provide original insights and inspiration. All creative thoughts came from the gods or through the mediation of a muse. The other was reserved for humans to translate or express this inspiration into words or deeds. This point of view is exemplified in Homer's tales in which the characters could accomplish great acts, but only as directed by the gods.

The creative process was explained as a gift from above. Creative accomplishments carried out by humans were products of divine inspiration. Many early thinkers also believed that the mind's chamber for creative inspiration also contained madness when the muse's spirit was present.

It is no wonder that the concept of creativity is laced with notions of mysticism and madness. See:

Stein, M. I. (1983). Creativity in Genesis. *Journal of Creative Behavior, 17,* 1-8.

And Dodds, E. R. (1951). *The Greeks and the irrational.* Berkeley, CA: University of California Press.

Giftedness and Eminence

Although there is certainly evidence that people produced creatively during the Roman era and the Middle Ages, it was the Renaissance and the beginning of humanism during which creativity was considered more of a human characteristic. The early investigation into creativity as a human characteristic began during the eighteenth century. The major focus was on understanding the nature of giftedness and eminence. The major thrust was to explain creativity as an inherited gift.

Today we can see the full spectrum of thinking about giftedness. On the one end we have the most exceptional humans who have left lasting imprints on the world. On the other end of the spectrum we have those concerned with nurturing and developing the creative talents that can best be described as day-to-day.

Albert, R. S. (Ed.). (1983). *Genius and eminence: The social psychology of creativity and exceptional achievement*. New York: Pergamon Press.

Albert R.S., & Runco, M. A. (1986). The achievment of eminence: A model based on a longitudinal study of exceptionally gifted boys and their families. In R. J. Sternberg & J. E. Davidson (Eds.), *Conceptions of Giftedness*. New York: Cambridge University Press.

Duff, W. (1767). *An essay on original genius and its various modes of exertion in philosophy and the fine arts: Particularly in poetry*. London: E. & C. Dilly.

Dunn, R., Dunn, K., & Treffinger, D. (1992). *Bringing out the giftedness in your child: Nurturing every child's unique strengths, talents, and potential*. New York: John Wiley & Sons.

Eysenck, H. J. (1995). *Genius: The natural history of creativity*. Cambridge, UK: Cambridge University Press.

Feldhusen, J. F. (1992). *Talent identification and development in education*. Sarasota, FL: Center for Creative Learning.

Feldhusen, J. F., & Treffinger, D. J. (1985). *Creative thinking and problem solving in gifted education*. Dubuque, IA: Kendall Hunt.

Galton, F. (1870). *Hereditary genius*. London: AppletonCentury Crofts.

Getzels, J. W. (1987). Creativity, intelligence, and problem finding: Retrospect and prospect. In S. G. Isaksen (Ed.), *Frontiers of creativity research: Beyond the basics* (pp. 88-102). Buffalo, NY: Bearly Limited.

Goertzel, M. G., Goertzel, V., & Goertzel, T. G. (1978). *Three hundred eminent personalities*. San Francisco: Jossey-Bass.

Gowan, J. C., Khatena, J., & Torrance, E. P. (1979). *Educating the ablest: A book of readings on the education of gifted children*. Itasca, IL: Peacock Publishers.

McCluskey, K. W., & Walker, K. D. (1986). *The doubtful gift: Strategies for educating gifted children in the regular classroom*. Kingston, Canada: Frye & Co.

Seagoe, M. V. (1975). *Terman and the gifted*. Los Altos, CA: William Kaufmann.

Simonton, D. K. (1984). *Genius, creativity & leadership: Historiometric studies*. Cambridge, MA: Harvard University Press.

Simonton, D. K. (1987). Genius: The lessons of historiometry. In S. G. Isaksen (Ed.), *Frontiers of creativity reearch: Beyond the basics* (pp. 66-87). Buffalo, NY: Bearly Limited.

Simonton, D. K. (1988). *Scientific genius: A psychology of science.* New York: Cambridge University Press.

Simonton, D. K. (1994). *Greatness: Who makes history and why?* New York: Guilford Press.

Treffinger, D. J. (1998). From gifted education to programming for talent development. *Phi Delta Kappan, 79,* 752-755.

MAJOR THEORETICAL APPROACHES

Even those early thinkers who believed that divine inspiration was the source of human creativity had some notion of how the creative process actually worked within humans. Aristotle was one of the earliest to posit that great insights resulted from peoples' own thoughts. His view was that the mind consisted of ideas, thoughts and images, each of which were associated with each other. Thinking was a process of moving from one thought to another by way of a chain of associations. He was one of the first to promote a particular theory of how creative thinking happens.

This was a central development in the history of the concept of creativity as our current focus has expanded to consider the nurture as well as the nature of creative talents. New developments in the cognitive sciences have dramatically impacted the basic philosophy upon which much of our view of the Western world is built (Lakoff & Johnson, 1999).

The following table provides five major categories of theoretical support for creative problem solving. Within each of these major categories, there are a number of sub-categories that relate to the general area of theory. Following each of these there are a few selected references that illustrate the theory.

I. Cognitive, Rational, and Semantic

This first category of theories groups views that consider creativity as rational with an emphasis on phases or semantic or verbal concepts or associations. Within the cognitive, rational, and semantic theories we include several specific approaches: they are Creative Problem Solving (Osborn, 1963; Parnes, Noller & Biondi, 1977); cognitive abilities (e.g., Guilford, 1959, 1967; Sternberg, 1994, Torrance, 1962, 1963; Ward, 1997); associative theories (e.g., Koestler, 1964; deBono, 1978); gestalt theories (e.g., Koffka, 1935; Wertheimer, 1945); and theories focusing on language, thinking and metacognition (e.g., Upton, 1941; Vygotsky, 1978; Chomsky, 1998).

A.	Phasal	1.	Dewey (1933)
		2.	Hadamard (1945)
		3.	Kingsley & Garry (1957)
		4.	Osborn (1963)
		5.	Parnes, Noller & Biondi (1977)

		6.	Polya (1945)
		7.	Rossman (1931)
		8.	Wallas (1926)
B.	Cognitive Abilities	1.	Bruner, Goodnow & Austin (1956)
		2.	Gagné & Briggs (1974)
		3.	Gardner (1993)
		4.	Guilford (1959)
		5.	Guilford (1967)
		6.	Sternberg (1994)
		7.	Torrance (1962)
		8.	Torrance (1963)
		9.	Torrance (1974)
		10.	Ward (1997)
C.	Associative	1.	Arieti (1976)
		2.	Koestler (1964)
		3.	Mednick (1962)
		4.	Mednick & Mednick (1964)
		5.	Rothenberg (1971)
		6.	deBono (1978)
D.	Gestalt	1.	Koffka (1935)
		2.	Kohler (1925)
		3.	Wertheimer (1945)
E.	Language, Thinking and Metacognition	1.	Chomsky (1998)
		2.	Flavell (1979)
		3.	Frawley (1997)
		4.	Kitchener (1983)
		5.	Metcalfe & Shimamura (1994)
		6.	Ogden & Richards (1927)
		7.	Upton (1941)
		8.	Vygotsky (1978)

II. Personality and Environmental

In this second category theorists emphasize the affective nature of creative talent, rather than the cognitive abilities stressed in the first category. These theorists are concerned with the personality traits or characteristics of the creative person. Within this group we find theories that emphasize personality traits (e.g., Barron, 1969; MacKinnon, 1962; Gruber, 1981); parental practices, social and cultural settings (e.g., Stein, 1953); transactualization (Taylor, 1972); affective/cognitive integration (Williams, 1966); and behavioral or stimulus-response models (e.g., Maltzman, 1960; Skinner, 1976; Thorndike, 1898).

A. Personality traits or characteristics
1. Anderson (1959)
2. Barron (1969)
3. Gruber (1981)
4. MacKinnon (1962)

B. Parental practices, social and cultural setting
1. Crutchfield (1962)
2. Eisner (1964)
3. Stein (1953)

C. Transactualization
1. Taylor (1972)

D. Affective/Cognitive
1. Williams (1966)

E. S-R or Behavioristic
1. Hull (1934)
2. Maltzman (1960)
3. Skinner (1976)
4. Staats (1968)
5. Thorndike (1898)

III. Third Force Psychology

This family of approaches focuses on the human potential for self-realization, personal growth and fulfillment. They see creativity as developing throughout life. Theories in this category include self-actualization approaches (e.g., Fromm, 1959; Maslow, 1959) and biological and personal growth approaches (e.g., Sinnot, 1959; Csikszentmihalyi, 1996)

A. Self-actualization, self-realization, and psychological growth
1. Fromm (1959)
2. Maslow (1959)
3. May (1975)
4. Rogers (1969)

B. Biological and personal growth
1. Csikszentmihalyi (1996)
2. Land (1973)
3. Maturana & Varela (1998)
4. Sinnott (1959)
5. Wallace & Gruber (1989)

IV. Psychoanalytic or Psychodynamic

The psychoanalytic view of creativity stems from the work of Freud. He believed that creativity originates in conflict of the conscious, reality-bound processes with unsatisfied, unconscious biological drives. He called this defense mechanism sublimation. Others believed that another defense mechanism–regression–was the primary cause for creativity (Kris, 1952); "regression in the service of the ego". Schachtel (1959) critiqued this view and believed that the main motivation at the root of creative experience is an individual's need to belong to the world around him. Another approach based on Freud's work is Jung's point of view. Jung pointed out that great inventions and other new achievements were not solely the result of personal experiences but also from a deeper source. He called this source of vague memories of the experiences of the whole human race the "collective unconscious" (Jung, 1959).

A. Freudian; emphasis on   1. Freud (1925)
    conflict, sublimation

B. Emphasis on regression,   1. Kris (1952)
    preconscious activity   2. Kubie (1958)
                               3. Weissman (1968)

C. Perceptual dynamics   1. Schachtel (1959)
                               2. Thurstone (1944)

D. Aesthetic   1. Jung (1959)

V. Psychedelic

The psychedelic approaches to creativity emphasize the importance of expanding the awareness of consciousness of the mind. The aim is to help the person to be more creative by opening vast new horizons of untapped resources and experiences (e.g. Erikson, 1964; Naranjo & Ornstein, 1971).

A. Existential and non-   1. Barron (1956)
    rational aspects   2. Houston (1973)
                               3. Krippner & Murphy (1973)
                               4. Weil (1972)

B. Altered States of   1. Aaronson & Osmond (1970)
    Consciousness   2. Harmon (1969)
                               3. Lilly (1972)
                               4. Masters & Houston (1972)
                               5. Mogar (1969)
                               6. Tart (1969)

C. Expansion of   1. Anderson & Savary (1972)
    Consciousness   2. Erikson (1963)
                               3. Gowan (1974)
                               4. Karlins & Andrews (1972)
                               5. Naranjo & Ornstein (1971)
                               6. Payne (1973)

D. Spiritual   1. Briskin (1998)
                               2. Handy (1998)
                               3. Whyte (1994)

VI. New Sciences

The new sciences are calling into question many of the assumptions derived from the Newtonian view of the universe. Two key themes in this emerging area of philosophical support include the complexity and chaos theories.

A. Complexity
1. Gell-Man (1994)
2. Stacey (1996)
3. Wheatley & Kellner-Rogers (1996)

B. Chaos
1. Masterpasqua & Perna (1997)
2. Zohar & Marshall (1994)

References

Aaronson, H. H. & Osmond, H. (1970). *Psychedelics.* New York: Anchor.

Anderson, M. & Savary, L. (1972). *Passages: A guide for pilgrims of the mind.* New York: Harper & Row.

Anderson, H. H. (Ed.). (1959). *Creativity and its cultivation.* New York: Harper and Row.

Arieti, S. (1976). *Creativity: The magic synthesis.* New York: Basic Books.

Barron, F. (1969). *Creative person and the creative process.* New York: Holt, Rinehart and Winston.

Barron, F. (1956). Current work at the Institute of Personality Assessment and Research. In C. W. Taylor, (Ed.), *The third research conference on the identification of creative scientific talent* (pp. 72-76). Salt Lake City, UT: University of Utah Press.

Briskin, A. (1998). *The stirring of the soul in the workplace.* San Francisco: Berrett-Koehler.

Bruner, J. S., Goodnow, J. J., & Austin, G. A. (1956) *A study of thinking.* New York: John Wiley.

Chomsky, N. (1998). *On language: Chomsky's classic works in one volume.* New York: The New Press.

Crutchfield, D. (1962). Conformity and creative thinking. in H. Gruber, G. Terrell, and H. Wertheimer (Eds.), *Contemporary approaches to creative thinking.* New York: Atherton.

Csiksentmihalyi, M. (1996). *Creativity: Flow and the psychology of discovery and invention.* New York: Harper Collins.

Dewey, J. (1933). *How we think: A restatement of the relation of reflective thinking to the educative process.* Lexington, MA: D.C. Health and Company.

deBono, E. (1978). *Teaching thinking.* Harmondsworth: Pelican Books.

Eisner, E. W. (1964). *Think with me about creativity.* Dansville, KY: Owen.

Erikson, E. H. (1963). *Childhood and society.* New York: Norton.

Flavell, J. H. (1979). Metacognition and cognitive monitoring: A new era of cognitive developmental inquiry. *American Psychologist, 34,* 906-911.

Frawley, W. (1997). *Vygotsky and cognitive science: Language and the unification of the social mind and computational mind.* Cambridge, MA: Harvard University Press.

Freud, S. (1925). *Creativity and the unconscious.* New York: Harper and Row.

Fromm, E. (1959). The creative attitude. In H. H. Anderson (Ed.), *Creativity and its cultivation* (pp. 44-54). New York: Harper and Row.

Gagné, R. M. & Briggs, L. J. (1974). *Principles of instructional design.* New York: Holt, Rinehart and Winston.

Gardner, H. (1993). *Creating minds.* New York: Basic Books.

Gell-Mann, M. (1994). *The quark and the jaguar: Adventures in the simple and the complex.* New York: W. H. Freeman and Company.

Gowan, J.C. (1974). *Development of the psychedelic individual.* Northridge, CA: Author.

Gruber, H. E. (1981). *Darwin on man: A psychological study of scientific creativity.* Chicago: University of Chicago Press.

Guilford, J. P. (1959). Three faces of intellect. *American Psychologist, 14 (8),* 469-479.

Guilford, J. P. (1967). *The nature of human intelligence.* New York: McGraw-Hill.

Hadamard, J. (1945). *An essay on the psychology of invention in the mathematical field.* Princeton, NJ: Princeton University Press.

Handy, C. (1998). *The hungry spirit: Beyond capitalism – A quest for purpose in the world.* New York: Broadway Books.

Harmon, W.W. et al. (1969). Psychedelic agents in creative problem solving: A pilot study. In C. T. Tart (Ed.), *Altered states of consciousness* (pp. 455-472). New York: John Wiley.

Houston, Jean. (1973). The psychonaut program: An exploration into some human potentials. *Journal of Creative Behavior,7,* 253-278.

Hull, C. (1934). The concept of the habit-family hierarchy and maze learning. Part I. *Psychological Review, 41,* 33-54.

Jung, C.G. (1959). The archetypes and the collective unconscious. In *Collected Works.* New York: Pantheon.

Karlins, M. and Andrews, L. M. (1972). *Biofeedback.* Philadelphia: Lippincott.

Kingsley, H.L. and Garry, R. (1957). *The nature and conditions of learning.* Englewood Cliffs, NJ: Prentice Hall.

Kitchener, K. S. (1983). Cognition, metacognition, and epistemic cognition. *Human Development, 26,* 222-232.

Koestler, A. (1964). *The act of creation.* New York: Macmillan.

Koffka, K. (1935). *Principles of gestalt psychology.* New York: Harcourt, Brace.

Kohler, W. (1925). *The mentality of apes.* New York: Harcourt, Brace.

Krippner, S., & Murphy, G. (1973). Humanistic psychology and parapsychology. *Journal of Humanistic Psychology, 13,* 4-24.

Kris, E. (1952). *Psychoanalytic exploration in art.* New York: International University Press.

Kubie, L. S. (1958). *Neurotic distortion of the creative process.* Lawrence, KS: University of Kansas Press.

Lakoff, G. & Johnson, M. (1999). *Philosophy in the flesh: The embodied mind and its challenge to Western thought.* New York: Basic Books.

Land, G. (1973). *Grow or die: The principle of transformation.* New York: Random House.

Lilly, J. (1972). *The center of the cyclone.* New York: Julian Press.

MacKinnon, D. W. (1962). The nature and nurture of creative talent. *American Psychologist, 17,* 484-495.

Maltzman, I. (1960). On the training of originality. *Psychological Review, 67,* 229-242.

Maslow, A. (1959). Creativity in self-actualizing people. In H. H. Anderson (Ed.), *Creativity and its cultivation* (pp. 83-95). New York: Harper and Row.

Masterpasqua, F. & Perna, P. A. (Eds.). (1997). *The psychological meaning of chaos: Translating theory into practice.* Washington, DC: American Psychological Association.

Masters, R. & Houston, J. (1972). *Mindgames.* New York: Dell.

Maturana, H. R., & Varela, F. J. (1998). *The tree of knowledge: The biological roots of human understanding.* Boston: Shambala.

May, R. (1975). *The courage to create.* New York: Norton.

Mednick, S. A. (1962). The associative basis of the creative process. *Psychological Review, 69,* 220-232.

Mednick, S. A. & Mednick, M. T. (1964). An associative interpretation of the creative process. In C.W. Taylor (Ed.), *Widening horizons in creativity* (pp. 54-68). New York: John Wiley.

Metcalfe, J., & Shimamura, A. P. (1994). *Metacognition: Knowing about knowing.* Cambridge, MA: MIT Press.

Mogar, R E. (1969). Current status and future trends in psychedelic (LSD) research. In C. T. Tart (Ed.), *Altered states of consciousness* (pp. 391-408). New York: John Wiley.

Naranjo, C. & Ornstein, R. E. (1971). *On the psychology of meditation.* New York: Viking.

Ogden, C. K., & Richards, I. A. (1927). *The meaning of meaning: A study of the influence of language upon thought and of the science of symbolism.* New York: Harcourt, Brace & Co.

Osborn, A. F. (1963). *Applied imagination.* New York: Charles Scribners.

Parnes, S. J.; Noller, R. B.; & Biondi, A. M. (1977). *Guide to creative action.* New York: Charles Scribners.

Payne, B. (1973). *Getting there without drugs.* New York: Viking.

Polya, G. (1945). *How to solve it: A new aspect of mathematical method.* Princeton, NJ: Princeton University Press.

Rogers, C. R. (1969). *Freedom to learn: A view of what education might become.* Columbus, OH: C. E. Merrill Publishing Co.

Rossman, J. (1931). *The psychology of the inventor.* Washington: Inventors Publishing.

Rothenberg, A. (1971). The process of Janusian thinking in creativity. *Archives of General Psychiatry, 24,* 195-205.

Rothenberg, A. (1979). *The emerging goddess: The creative process in art, science and other fields.* Chicago: Chicago University Press.

Schachtel, E. C. (1959). *Metamorphosis.* New York: Basic Books.

Sinnott, E. (1959). The creativeness of life. In H. H. Anderson, (Ed.), *Creativity and its cultivation* (pp. 12-29). NY: Harper and Row.

Skinner, B. F. (1976). A behavioral model of creation. In A. Rothenberg & C. R. Hausman (Eds.), *The creativity question* (pp. 267-273). Durham, NC: Duke University Press.

Staats, A. W. (1968). *Learning language and cognition.* New York: Holt, Rinehart and Winston.

Stacey, R. D. (1996). *Complexity and creativity in organizations.* San Francisco: Berrett-Koehler.

Stein, M. I. (1953). Creativity and culture. *Journal of Psychology, 36,* 311-322.

Sternberg, R. J. (1994). *Thinking and problem solving: Handbook of perception and cognition.* San Diego, CA: Academic Press.

Tart, C. T. (Ed.). (1969). *Altered states of consciousness.* New York: John Wiley.

Taylor, I. A. (1972). *A theory of creative transactualization.* Buffalo, NY: Creative Education Foundation.

Thorndike, E. L. (1898). Animal intelligence: An experimental study of the associative process in animals. *Psychological Review Monograph Supplements, 2,8.*

Thurstone, L. L. (1944). A factorial study of perception. *Psychometrika Monographs.* Vol. 4.

Torrance, E. P. (1962) *Guiding creative talent.* Englewood Cliffs, NJ: Prentice-Hall.

Torrance, E. P. (1963). Conditions for creative growth. In E. P. Torrance (Ed.)., *Education & the creative potential.* (pp. 16-33). Minneapolis, MN: The University of Minnesota Press.

Torrance, E. P. (1974). *Torrance tests of creative thinking: Norms and technical manual.* Lexington, MA: Personnel Press/Ginn Zerox.

Upton, A. (1941). *Design for thinking: A first book in semantics.* Palo Alto, CA: Pacific Books.

Vygotsky, L. S. (1978). *Mind in society: The development of higher psychological processes.* Cambridge, MA: Harvard University Press.

Wallace, D. B., & Gruber, H. E. (1989). *Creative people at work: Twelve cognitive case studies.* New York: Oxford University Press.

Wallas, G. (1926). *The art of thought.* New York: Harcourt, Brace and Company.

Ward, T. B., Smith, S. M., & Vaid, J. (Eds.). (1997). *Creative thought: An investigation of conceptual structures and processes.* Washington, DC: American Psychological Association.

Weil, A. (1972). *The natural mind*. Boston: Houghton-Mifflin.

Weissman, P. (1968). Psychological comcomitants of ego functioning in creativity. *International Journal of Psycho-Analysis, 49,* 464-469.

Wertheimer, M. (1945). *Productive thinking*. New York: Harper & Brothers.

Wheatley, M. J., & Kellner-Rogers, M. (1996). *A simpler way*. San Francisco: Berrett-Koehler.

Whyte, D. (1994). *The heart aroused: Poetry and the preservation of the soul in corporate America*. New York: Doubleday.

Williams, F. E. (Ed.). (1966). Seminar on productive thinking in education. *Proceedings of the first seminar on Productive Thinking in Education*. St. Paul, MN: Creativity & National Schools Project, Macalester College.

Zohar, D., & Marshall, I. (1994). *The quantum society: Mind, physics, and a new social vision*. New York: William Morrow and Company.

General Philosophical Support

The following selection of references provides a sampling of additional kinds of philosophical support available in the literature.

Brophy, D. R. (1998). Understanding, measuring, and enhancing individual creative problem-solving efforts. *Creativity Research Journal, 11,* 123-150.

Carkhuff, R. R. (1981). *Toward actualizing human potential*. Amherst, MA: Human Resources Development Press.

Combs, A. (1962). *Perceiving, behaving, becoming: A new focus for education*. Washington, DC: Association for Supervision and Curriculum Development.

Dewey, J. (1938). *Experience & education*. New York: Collier Books.

Dewey, J. (1944). *Democracy and education: An introduction to the philosophy of education*. New York: The Free Press.

Getzels, J. W. (1964). Creative thinking, problem solving and instruction. In E. Hilgard (Ed.), *Theories of learning and instruction: 63rd Yearbook on the NSEE* (Part 1, pp. 240-267). Chicago: University of Chicago Press.

Gowan, J. C., Khatena, J., & Torrance, E. P. (1981). *Creativity: Its educational implications (Second edition)*. Dubuque, IA: Kendall-Hunt.

Guilford, J. P. (1962). Creativity: Its measurement and development. In S. J. Parnes & H. F. Harding (Ed.), *A source book for creative thinking* (pp. 151-167). New York: Charles Scribners & Sons.

Guilford, J. P. (1987). Creativity research: Past, present and future. In S. G. Isaksen (Ed.), *Frontiers of creativity reearch: Beyond the basics* (pp. 33-65). Buffalo, NY: Bearly Limited.

Hausman, C. R. (1984). *A discourse on novelty and creation*. Albany, NY: State University of New York Press.

Hausman, C. R. (1987). Philosophical perspectives on the study of creativity. In S. G. Isaksen (Ed.), *Frontiers of creativity reearch: Beyond the basics* (pp. 380-389). Buffalo, NY: Bearly Limited.

Isaksen, S. G. & Parnes, S. J. (1983). Curriculum planning for creative thinking and problem solving. *Journal of Creative Behavior, 19,* 1-29.

Isaksen, S. G. (1988). Educational implications of creativity research: An updated rationale for creative learning. In K. Grønhaug & G. Kaufmann (Eds.), *Innovation: A cross-disciplinary perspective* (pp. 167-203). Oslo, Norway: Norwegian University Press.

Isaksen, S. G. (1995). On the conceptual foundations of creative problem solving: A response to Magyari-Beck. *Creativity and Innovation Management, 4, 52-63.*

Isaksen, S. G., & Murdock, M. C. (1990). The outlook for the study of creativity: An emerging discipline? *Studia Psychologica, 32,* 53-77.

Isaksen, S. G., & Murdock, M. C. (1993). The emergence of a discipline: Issues and approaches to the study of creativity. In S. G. Isaksen, M. C. Murdock, R. L. Firestien, & D. J. Treffinger (Eds.), *Understanding and recognizing creativity: The emergence of a discipline* (pp. 13-47). Norwood, NJ: Ablex.

James, W. (1896). *The principles of psychology.* New York: Henry Holt & Co.

Locke, J. (1964). *An essay concerning human understanding.* New York: The New American Library.

Maslow, A. H. (1968). *Toward a psychology of being (Second edition).* New York: Van Nostrand Reinhold Co.

Maier, N. R. (1970). *Problem solving and creativity: In individuals and groups.* Belmont, CA: Brooks/Cole.

May, R. (1959). The nature of creativity. In H. H. Anderson (Ed.). *Creativity and its cultivation* (pp. 55-68). New York: Harper & Row.

Rogers, C. R. (1959). Toward a theory of creativity. In H. H. Anderson (Ed.). *Creativity and its cultivation* (pp. 69-82). New York: Harper & Row.

Runco, M. A., & Albert, R. S. (Eds.). (1990). *Theories of creativity.* Newbury Park, CA: SAGE Publications.

Stein, M. I. (1975). *Stimulating creativity (Volumes I and II).* New York: Academic Press.

Torrance, E. P. (1963). *Education and the creative potential.* Minneapolis, MN: University of Minnesota Press.

Torrance, E. P., & Myers, R. E. (1970). *Creative learning and teaching.* New York: Dodd, Mead & Co.

Treffinger, D. J. (1995). Creative problem solving: Overview and educational implications, *Educational Psychology Review, 7 (3),* 301-312.

Treffinger, D. J., Isaksen, S. G., & Firestien, R. L. (1983). Theoretical perspectives on creative learning and its facilitation: An overview. *The Journal of Creative Behavior, 17(1),* 9-17.

Vanosmael, P. & De Bruyn, R. (1984). *Handboek voor Creatief Denken* (Manual for Creative Thinking). Antwerpen/ Amsterdam: De Nederlandsche Boekhandel.

Whitehead, A. N. (1929). *The aims of education and other essays.* New York: The Free Press.

2. CONTINUOUS RESEARCH AND DEVELOPMENT OCCURS

An important way to know that CPS is worth the effort and makes a difference is that there is an established and defined tradition of research and development that is continuously growing. One of the critical reasons to approach the deliberate teaching and learning of creativity and creative problem solving is that there is a wealth of material and available information. There is a growing domain of knowledge.

BUFFALO-BASED FOUNDATIONAL WORK

Our work in creative problem solving has a rich Buffalo-based tradition. The research and development started with the work of Alex Osborn and then extended to Sidney Parnes, Ruth Noller and others. Impact research has been conducted across numerous organizations, including the University of Buffalo, Buffalo State College, the Creative Education Foundation and the Creative Problem Solving Group - Buffalo.

Osborn's Works

Early work in creative problem solving was begun by Alex Osborn, founder of the Creative Education Foundation. A few of his key works include:

Osborn, A. F. (1942). *How to think up.* New York: McGraw-Hill.

Osborn, A. F. (1948). *Your creative power: How to use imagination.* New York: Charles Scribner's Sons.

Osborn, A. F. (1952a). *Wake up your mind: 101 ways to develop creativeness.* New York: Charles Scribner's Sons.

Osborn, A. F. (1952b). *How to become more creative: 101 rewarding ways to develop your potential talent.* New York: Charles Scribner's Sons.

Osborn, A. F. (1953*). Applied imagination: Principles and procedures of creative thinking.* New York: Charles Scribner's Sons.

Osborn, A. F. (1957). *Applied imagination: Principles and procedures of creative thinking (Revised edition).* New York: Charles Scribner's Sons.

Osborn, A. F. (1963). *Applied imagination: Principles and procedures of creative problem solving (Third edition).* New York: Charles Scribner's Sons.

Osborn, A. F. (1967). *Applied imagination: Principles and procedures of creative problem solving (Third revised edition).* New York: Charles Scribner's Sons.

Instructional Materials

This work was complemented by the early development of a program of research design to test the effectiveness of instruction in creative studies. The materials of Osborn were soon complemented by a variety of instructional material including:

Feldhusen, J. F., & Treffinger, D. J. (1977). The role of instructional material in teaching creative thinking. *Gifted Child Quarterly, 7*, 351-357.

Feldhusen, J. F., & Clinkenbeard, P. R. (1986). Creativity instructional materials: A review of research. *Journal of Creative Behavior, 20*, 153-182.

Isaksen, S. G., Dorval, K. B., & Treffinger, D. J. (1994). *Creative approaches to problem solving*. Dubuque, IA: Kendall-Hunt.

Isaksen, S. G. & Treffinger, D. J. (1985). *Creative problem solving: The basic course*. Buffalo, NY: Bearly Limited.

Joyce, M., Isaksen, S., Davidson, F., Puccio, G., Coppage, C., & Muruska, M. A. (1997). *An introduction to creativity (Second edition)*. Acton, MA: Copley Publishing.

Keller-Mathers, S., & Puccio, K. (1998). *Big tools for young thinkers: Using creative problem solving with primary students*. Sarasota, FL: Center for Creative Learning.

Noller, R. B., Parnes, S. J., & Biondi, A. M. (1976). *Creative actionbook: Revised edition of creative behavior workbook*. New York: Scribners.

Parnes, S. J. (1966). *Programming creative behavior* (title VII project number 5-0716 national defense education act). Buffalo State University of New York: Albany: Research Foundation of State University of New York.

Parnes, S. J. (1967). *Creative behavior guidebook*. New York: Scribners.

Parnes, S. J. (1967). *Creative behavior workbook*. New York: Scribners.

Parnes, S. J. (Ed.). (1992). *Sourcebook for creative problem solving*. Buffalo, New York: Creative Education Press.

Parnes, S. J. (1997). *Optimize the magic of your mind*. Buffalo, New York: Bearly Limited.

Parnes, S. J., Noller, R. B., & Biondi, A. M. (1977). *Guide to creative action: Revised edition of creative behavior guidebook*. New York: Scribners.

Puccio, K., Keller-Mathers, S., & Treffinger, D. J. (1998). *Adventures in real problem solving: Facilitating creative problem solving with primary students (Grades K-3)*. Sarasota, FL: Center for Creative Learning.

Treffinger, D. J., Isaksen, S. G., & Firestien, R. L. (1982). *Handbook of creative learning*. Sarasota, FL: Center for Creative Learning.

These core instructional materials were supplemented by the work of other authors. The Buffalo-based instructional program was complemented by the work of other scholars and developers from its inception. These included:

Gordon, W. J. J. (1961). *Synectics: The development of creative capacity*. New York: Harper & Row.

Gordon, W. J. J., Poze, T., & Reid, M. (1971). *The metaphorical way of learning and knowing: Applying Synectics to sensitivity and learning situations.* Cambridge, MA: Porpoise Books.

Prince, G. M. (1970). *The practice of creativity: A manual for dynamic group problem solving.* New York: Harper & Row.

Treffinger, D. J., & Huber, J. R. (1975). Designing instruction for creative problem solving: Preliminary objectives and learning hierarchies. *Journal of Creative Behavior, 9,* 260-266.

Treffinger, D. J., Sortore, M. R., & Cross, J. A. (1993). Programs and strategies for nurturing creativity. In K. Heller, F. Monks, & H. Passow (Eds.), *International handbook of research and development of giftedness and talent* (pp. 555-567). New York: Pergamon.

Upton, A. (1961). *Design for thinking: A first book in semantics.* Palo Alto, CA: Pacific Books.

Upton, A. & Samson, R. W. (1961). *Creative analysis.* New York: E. P. Dutton & Co.

Cognitive Styles Project

This project was initiated at the Center for Studies in Creativity and based on the early experimental findings that certain individuals seemed to benefit from the courses more than other, characteristically different individuals. The cognitive styles project continues through the work of other scholars and within other academic programs.

Braun, C. L. (1997). *Rogers, Weber, and Merton: Theoretical links to the KAI subscales and Adaption-Innovation theory.* Unpublished master's project. Center for Studies in Creativity, State University College at Buffalo.

Corbett-Whitier, C. (1986). *The relationship of learning style preferences by high school gifted students on the Torrance Tests of Creative Thinking.* Unpublished master's project. Center for Studies in Creativity, State University College at Buffalo.

Dorval, K. B. (1990). *The relationships between level and style of creativity and imagery.* Unpublished master's thesis. Center for Studies in Creativity, State University College at Buffalo.

Grivas, C. C. (1996). *An exploratory investigation of the relationship of cognitive style with perceptions of creative climate.* Unpublished master's project. Center for Studies in Creativity, State University College at Buffalo.

Hurley, C. A. (1993). *The relationship between the Kirton Adaption-Innovation style and the use of creative problem solving.* Unpublished master's project. Center for Studies in Creativity, State University College at Buffalo.

Isaksen, S. G. (1987). Introduction: An orientation to the frontiers of creativity research. In S. G. Isaksen (Ed.), *Frontiers of creativity reearch: Beyond the basics* (pp. 1-26). Buffalo, NY: Bearly Limited.

Isaksen, S. G. & Dorval, K. B. (1993). Toward an improved understanding of creativity within people: The level-style distinction. In S. G. Isaksen, M. C. Murdock, R. L. Firestien & D. J. Treffinger (Eds.), *Understanding and recognizing creativity: The emergence of a discipline* (pp. 299-330). Norwood, New Jersey: Ablex Publishing.

Isaksen, S. G., Dorval, K. B., & Kaufmann, G. (1992). Mode of symbolic representation and cognitive style. *Imagination, Cognition and Personality, 11,* 271-277.

Isaksen, S. G. & Kaufmann, G. (1990). Adaptors and innovators: A discriminant analysis of the perceptions of the psychological climate for creativity. *Studia Psychologica, 32,* 129-141.

Isaksen, S. G., & Puccio, G. J. (1988). Adaption-innovation and the Torrance Tests of Creative Thinking: The level-style issue revisited. *Psychological Reports, 63,* 659-670.

McEwen, P. A. (1986). *Learning styles: Ability and creativity.* Unpublished master's project. Center for Studies in Creativity, State University College at Buffalo.

Murdock, M. C., Isaksen, S. G. & Lauer, K. L. (1993). Creativity training and the stability and internal consistency of the Kirton Adaptive-Innovative Inventory. *Psychological Reports, 72,* 1123-1130.

Pershyn, G. (1992). *An investigation into the graphic depiction of natural creative problem solving processes.* Unpublished masters thesis. Center for Studies in Creativity, State University College at Buffalo.

Puccio, G. P. (1987). *The effect of cognitive style on problem defining behavior.* Unpublished masters thesis. State University College at Buffalo, Center for Studies in Creativity.

Schoonover, P. F. (1996). *The preference for and use of creative problem solving tools among adaptors and innovators.* Unpublished doctoral dissertation, Walden University, Minneapolis, Minnesota.

Teft, M. (1990). *A factor analysis of the TTCT, MBTI, and KAI: The creative level-style issue re-examined.* Unpublished master's thesis. Center for Studies in Creativity, State University College at Buffalo.

Wheeler, J. W. (1995). *An exploratory study of preferences associated with creative problem solving.* Unpublished master's project. State University College at Buffalo, Center for Studies in Creativity.

Wittig, C. V. (1985). *Learning style preferences among third graders high or low on divergent thinking and feeling variables.* Unpublished master's thesis. State University College at Buffalo, Center for Studies in Creativity.

Zilewicz, E. P. (1986). *Cognitive styles: Strengths and weaknesses when using creative problem solving.* Unpublished master's project. State University College at Buffalo, Center for Studies in Creativity.

OTHER EVIDENCE

There is a variety of additional evidence that supports the program developed in Buffalo and provides insight into improving instructional approaches.

Abell, S. K. (1990). The problem-solving muse. *Science and Children*, October, 27-29.

Basadur, M. (1993). Impacts and outcomes of creativity in organizational settings. In S. G. Isaksen, et al. (Eds.), *Nurturing and developing creativity: The emergence of a discipline* (pp. 278-313). Norwood, NJ: Ablex.

Britz, A. (1995). *History, development and current applications of the Creative Problem Solving model.* Unpublished master's project. Darmstadt Technological Institute and the Creative Problem Solving Group - Buffalo.

Bruce, B. (1991). *Impact of creative problem solving training on management behavior.* Unpublished masters project. Center for Studies in Creativity, State University College at Buffalo.

Burns, M. G. (1983). A comparison of three creative problem-solving methodologies (brainstorming, personal analogy, forced relationship). *Dissertation Abstracts International, 45*, 341A.

Buyer, L. (1988). Creative problem solving: A comparison of performance under different instructions. *Journal of Creative Behavior, 22, (1)*, 55-61.

Feldhusen, J. F. , & Clinckenbeard, P. R. (1986). Creativity instructional materials: A review of research. *Journal of Creative Behavior, 20*, 153-182.

Foucar-Szocki, D. (1982). *Possible predictors of effectiveness in the facilitation of creative problem solving.* Unpublished master's project. Center for Studies in Creativity, State University College at Buffalo.

Isaksen, S. G., & Dorval, K. B. (1993). Changing views of creative problem solving: Over 40 years of continuous improvement. *International Creativity Network, 3*, 1-6.

Isaksen, S. G., Dorval, K. B., Noller, R. B., & Firestien, R. L. (1993). The dynamic nature of creative problem solving. In S. S. Gryskiewicz (Ed.), *Discovering creativity: Proceedings of the 1992 International Creativity and Networking Conference* (pp. 155-162). Greensboro, NC: Center for Creative Leadership.

Zogona, S. V., Willis, J. E., & MacKinnon, W. J. (1966). Group effectiveness in creative problem-solving tasks: An examination of relevant variables. *Journal of Psychology, 62*, 111-137.

3. Formal Courses Are Available

There are now many colleges and universities that offer formal courses on creativity. In addition, numerous private organizations offer training courses and programs. The Alden Dow Creativity Center at Northwood University provides an annual conference for those who teach college courses on creativity. Degree programs are offered by the Center for Studies in Creativity (Buffalo State College), the College of St. Thomas (St. Paul, Minnesota), University of Santiago de Compostela (Santiago, Spain), Manchester Business School (Manchester, UK), The University of Malta, The Open University (UK) and the Technical University of Delft (The Netherlands) among other locations. See the following studies for more details:

Johansson, B. (1975). *Creativity and creative problem-solving courses in United States industry.* Special project funded by the Center for Creative Leadership. Greensboro, North Carolina.

McDonough, P. & McDonough, B. (1987). A survey of American colleges and universities on the conducting of formal courses in creativity. *Journal of Creative Behavior, 21,* 271-283.

Montogomery, D., Bull, K. S., & Baloche, L. (1992). College level creativity course content. *Journal of Creative Behavior, 26,* 228-234.

Treffinger, D. J., & Gowan, J. C. (1971). An updated representative list of methods and educational programs for stimulating creativity. *Journal of Creative Behavior, 5,* 127-139.

van Geffen, L. (1997). Creative problem solving: The development of a CPS course at the University of Twente. In T. Rickards, et al. (Eds.), *Creativity and innovation impact* (pp. 43-48). Maastricht, The Netherlands: The European Association for Creativity and Innovation.

4. COURSES AND PROGRAMS HAVE BEEN EVALUATED

It is not enough to know that there are courses and programs available to teach CPS. To know if CPS is worthwhile, there must be evidence that these courses and programs are evaluated. Most academic programs go through regular evaluation from certifying and accrediting agencies. There is also additional evidence that courses have an impact.

Baloche, L., Montgomery, D., Bull, K. S., & Salver, B. K. (1992). Faculty perceptions of college creativity courses. *Journal of Creative Behavior, 26,* 222-227.

Bowman, K. L. (1973). *An assessment of attitude and behavior change in a summer workshop in creative education.* Unpublished master's thesis. Lehigh University.

Buijs, J. (1993). Creativity and innovation in the Netherlands: Project Industrial Innovation and its implications. In S. G. Isaksen, et al. (Eds.), *Nurturing and developing creativity: The emergence of a discipline* (pp. 237-257). Norwood, NJ: Ablex.

Burstiner, I. (1970). *Effects of a workshop in creative thinking for secondary school department chairmen on their perceptions of supervisory activities on problem-solving and on creativity test scores.* Unpublished master's thesis. St. John's University.

David, F. (1975). *A study in the nurturing of creative ability.* Unpublished master's thesis. University of Pittsburgh.

De Cock, C. (1991). *The impact of creativity training programs.* Unpublished master's thesis. Faculty of Business Administration, Manchester Business School. Manchester, England.

Efros, F. (1985). *Effects of Synectics training on undergraduates' problem-solving skills and attitudes.* Unpublished master's thesis, Kansas State University, Manhattan, Kansas.

Firestien, R. L., & Lunken, H. P. (1993). Assessment of the long-term effects of the master of science degree in creative studies on its graduates. *Journal of Creative Behavior, 27, (3),* 188-199.

Gerry, R., De Veau, L., & Chorness, M. (1957, September). *A review of some recent research in the field of creativity and the examination of an experimental creativity workshop* (project 56-24). Lackland, TX: Lackland Air Base, Training Analysis and Development Division - Officer Military Schools.

Golovin, R. W. (1993, November). *Creativity enhancement as a function of classroom structure: Cooperative learning vs. the traditional classroom.* Paper presented at Mid-South Educational Research Association, New Orleans, LA.

Gordon, S. C. (1979). *The effects of a creative thinking skills program on fourth grade students.* Unpublished doctoral dissertation. Oklahoma State University.

Heiberger, M. A. (1983). *A study of the effects of two creativity-training programs upon the creativity and achievement of young, intellectually-gifted students.* Unpublished doctoral dissertation. University of Tulsa.

Heppner, P. P. (1984). Training in problem solving for residence hall staff: Who is most satisfied? *Journal of College Student Personnel, 25,* 357-360.

Hudson-Davies, R., & Moger, S. (1997). Assessing the impact of creativity training in marketing education: A before and after examination of performance outcomes. In T. Rickards, et al. (Eds.), *Creativity and innovation impact* (pp. 109-115). Maastricht, The Netherlands: The European Association for Creativity and Innovation.

Keller-Mathers, S. (1991). *Impact of creative problem solving training on participants' personal and professional lives: A replication and extension.* Unpublished master's project. Center for Studies in Creativity, State University College at Buffalo.

Keong, L. C., Soon, L. G. (1996). Factors affecting managers and executives' attitude towards creativity training. *Research & Practice in Human Resource Management, 4,* 67-88.

Korth, W. L. (1972). *Training in creative thinking: The effect on the individual of training in the "Synectics" method of group problem solving.* Unpublished master's thesis. University of North Carolina.

Lyles, M. A., & Mitroff, I. (1980). Organizational problem formulation: An empirical study. *Administrative Science Quarterly, 25,* 102-119.

Lunken, H. P. (1990). *Assessment of long-term effects of the master of science degree in creative studies on its graduates.* Unpublished master's project. Center for Studies in Creativity, State University College at Buffalo.

Mason, J. G., Jr. (Instructor). (1957, January-April). *Comparison of two courses in creative thinking for dissimilar groups.* (Available from the Center for Studies in Creativity, Buffalo State College, Buffalo, NY).

Neilson, L. (1990). *Impact of creative problem solving training: An in-depth evaluation of a six day course in creative problem solving.* Unpublished master's thesis. Center for Studies in Creativity, State University College at Buffalo.

Pugh, R. H. (1968). *Effect of in-service training and workshops for teachers on students' ability to think creatively.* Unpublished master's thesis. Iowa State University.

Rinehart, B. C. (1978). *An in-service training program for elementary school teachers in reading instruction for the gifted and creative student.* Unpublished master's thesis. Saint Louis University.

Roberts, R. C., Dodge, L. B., & Bjelland, R. (1964). *Evaluation of a pilot demonstration project in developing creative problem solving in selected elementary students.* University of Montana, Missoula, MT.

Rookey, T. J. (1972). *The impact of an intervention program for teachers on creative attitude and creative ability of elementary pupils.* Unpublished master's thesis. Lehigh University.

Rosenberger, N. (1978). *A study of directed instruction, self-instruction and no instruction in creative teaching and problem solving and their effect upon the behavior of preservice elementary teachers during student teaching in mathematics.* Unpublished master's thesis. University of Colorado.

Saner, Y. J. (1990). *The effects of training in collaborative skills on productivity and group interaction in creative problem solving groups.* Unpublished master's thesis. Center for Studies in Creativity, State University College at Buffalo.

Shepardson, C. A. (1990). *Cooperative learning, knowledge and student attitudes as influences on student CPS involvement: An exploratory study.* Unpublished master's thesis. Center for Studies in Creativity, State University College at Buffalo.

Simberg, A. L., Shannon, T. E. (1959). *The effects of AC creativity training on the AC suggestion program.* AC Spark Plug Division, General Motors Corporation.

Treffinger, D. J., Cross, J. A., Feldhusen, J. F., Isaksen, S. G., Remle, R. C., & Sortore, M. R. (1994). *Productive thinking Volume I: Foundations, criteria and reviews.* Dubuque, IA: Kendall/Hunt Publishing.

Vehar, J. R. (1994). *An impact study to improve a five-day course in facilitating creative problem solving.* Unpublished master's project. Center for Studies in Creativity, State University College at Buffalo.

Wesenberg, P. (1983). An assessment of a creativity course. UMIST Management Sciences Department, Manchester UK. (Unpublished doctoral dissertation)

Winsemius, A. C. (1995). *A summary of the internship of Albert C. Winsemius with the Creative Problem Solving Group-Buffalo.* Unpublished internship report from the University of Amsterdam and the Creative Problem Solving Group-Buffalo.

Wu, M., & Hsieh, W. (1997). A study of creative thinking for a course of circuit design of hydraulics and pneumatics. In T. Rickards, et al. (Eds.), *Creativity and innovation impact* (pp. 117-121). Maastricht, The Netherlands: The European Association for Creativity and Innovation.

Young, D. E. (1975). *Perceptions of the persistence of effects of training in creative problem-solving.* Unpublished master's thesis. Center for Studies in Creativity, State University College at Buffalo.

Zelina, M. (1982). Program rozvoja tvorivosti ziakov: Konstrukcia a vysledky pouzitia (Pupils' Creativity Development Program: Construction and results). *Ceskoslovenska psychologia, 2,* 122-136.

5. Communities Exist to Advance Knowledge

One way of knowing if something is worthwhile is to examine whether or not there have been communities of researchers, scholars and other academics who have judged the area worthy of investigation. Evidence of this sort can be found in the number of edited collections available within the field, the emergence of bibliographies and the existence of scholarly reviews and syntheses. These edited collections have often been the results of actual working conferences.

Edited Collections

The literature is both established and growing. We have many edited collections available as good sources for a variety of viewpoints in the emerging field. A sampling of such collections from the past 40 years is included below.

Anderson, H. H. (Ed.). (1959). *Creativity and its cultivation.* New York: Harper.

Boden, M. (Ed.). (1994). *Dimensions of creativity.* Cambridge, MA: The MIT Press.

Charnes, A. & Cooper, W. W. (Eds.). (1984). *Creative and innovative management: Essays in honor of George Kozmetsky.* Cambridge, MA: Ballinger.

Feldman, D. H., Csikszentmihalyi, M., & Gardner, H. (Eds.). (1994). *Changing the world: A framework for the study of creativity.* Westport, CT: Praeger.

Ghiselin, B. (Ed.). (1952). *The creative process.* New York: The New American Library.

Glover, J. A., Ronning, R. R., & Reynolds, C. R. (Eds.). (1989). *Handbook of creativity.* New York: Plenum Press.

Grønhaug, K., & Kaufmann, G. (Eds.). (1988). *Innovation: A cross-disciplinary perspective.* Oslo, Norway: Norwegian University Press.

Gryskiewicz, S. S., & Hills, D. A. (Eds.). (1992). *Readings in innovation.* Greensboro, NC: Center for Creative Leadership.

Henry, J. (Ed.). (1991). *Creative management.* London: SAGE.

Henry, J., & Walker, D. (Eds.). (1991). *Managing innovation.* London: SAGE.

Ijiri, Y., & Kuhn, R. L. (Eds.). (1988). *New directions in creative and innovative management.* Cambridge, MA: Ballinger.

Isaksen, S. G. (Ed.). (1987). *Frontiers of creativity research: Beyond the basics.* Buffalo, NY: Bearly Limited.

Isaksen, S. G., Murdock, M. C., Firestien, R. L., & Treffinger, D. J. (Eds.). (1993). *Nurturing and developing creativity: The emergence of a discipline.* Norwood, NJ: Ablex.

Isaksen, S. G., Murdock, M. C., Firestien, R. L., & Treffinger, D. J. (Eds.). (1993). *Understanding and recognizing creativity: The emergence of a discipline.* Norwood, NJ: Ablex.

Kuhn, R. L. (Ed.). (1985). *Frontiers in creative and innovative management.* Cambridge, MA: Ballinger.

Kuhn, R. L. (Ed.). (1988). *Handbook for creative and innovative managers.* New York: McGraw-Hill.

Parnes, S. J. (Ed.). (1992). *Sourcebook for creative problem solving.* Buffalo, NY: Creative Education Foundation Press.

Parnes, S. J. & Harding, H. (Eds.). (1962). *A source book for creative thinking.* New York: Scribners.

Puccio, G. J., & Murdock, M. C. (Eds.). (1998). *Creativity assessment: Readings and resources.* Buffalo, NY: Creative Education Foundation.

Rothenberg, A. & Hausman, C. R. (Eds.). (1976). *The creativity question.* Durham, NC: University Press.

Runco, M. A., & Pritzker, S. (Eds.). (1999). *Encylopedia of creativity.* New York: Academic Press.

Stein, M. I., & Heinze, S. J. (Eds.). (1960). *Creativity and the individual: Summaries of selected literature in psychology and psychiatry.* Glencoe, IL: The Free Press.

Sternberg, R. J. (Ed.). (1988). *The nature of creativity: Contemporary psychological perspectives.* NY: Cambridge University Press.

Sternberg, R. J. (Ed.). (1999). *Handbook of creativity.* New York: Cambridge University Press.

Sternberg, R. J., & Davidson, J. E. (Eds.). (1995). *The nature of insight.* Cambridge, MA: MIT Press.

Taylor, I. A. & Getzels, J. W. (Ed.). (1975). *Perspectives in creativity.* Chicago: Aldine.

Taylor, C. W. (Ed.). (1963). *Widening horizons in creativity.* New York: Wiley.

Taylor, C. W. & Barron, F. (Eds.). (1963*). Scientific creativity: Its recognition and development.* New York: Wiley.

Tuerck, D. G. (Ed.). (1987). *Creativity and liberal learning: Problems and possibilities in American education.* Norwood, New Jersey: Ablex Publishing.

Vernon, P. E. (Ed.). (1970). *Creativity.* New York: Penguin Books.

Ward. T. B., Smith, S. M., & Vaid, J. (Eds.). (1997). *Creative thought: An investigation of conceptual structures and processes.* Washington, DC: American Psychological Association.

Published Bibliographies

Bibliographies provide important evidence that there is value in creativity as a subject. Some scholars invest deliberate time in taking stock of the available literature and helping others to increase their access to these resources.

De Bruyn, K. & De Bruyn R. (1988). *Creativity in education, learning, school: A selective bibliography.* Antwerpen, Belgium: COCD.

Isaksen, S. G. (1988). Selected books on creativity. In S. J. Parnes *Visionizing: State of the art processes for encouraging innovative excellence* (pp. 349-355). East Aurora, NY: DOK Publishers.

Parnes, S. J., & Brunelle, E. A. (1967). The literature of creativity (part I). *Journal of Creative Behavior, 1,* 52-109.

Stievater, S. M. (1977). Books on creativity and problem solving. In S. J. Parnes, R. B. Noller & A, M. Biondi *Guide to creative action* (pp. 288 - 314). New York: Scribners.

Treffinger, D. J. (1977). Methods, techniques and educational programs for stimulating creativity: 1975 revision. In S. J. Parnes, R. B. Noller & A, M. Biondi *Guide to creative action* (pp. 248 - 259). New York: Scribners.

Treffinger, D. J., Feldhusen, J. F., Isaksen, S. G., Cross, J. A., & Sortore, M. R. (1994). *Handbook of productive thinking - Volume I: Rationale, criteria and reviews.* Sarasota, FL: Center for Creative Learning.

Treffinger, D. J., Sortore, M. R. & Cross, J. A. (1993). Programs and strategies for nurturing creativity. In K. Heller, F. Monks, & H. Passow (Eds.), *International handbook of research and development of giftedness and talent* (pp. 555-567). New York: Pergamon.

Razik, T. A. (1965). *Bibliography of creativity studies and related areas.* Buffalo, NY: Creative Education Foundation and the State University of New York at Buffalo.

The Journal of Creative Behavior also regularly publishes a bibliography of current dissertations, theses and books on the topic of creativity. Susan Stievater has provided this service to the Journal and the Buffalo State College's special Creative Studies Collection housed within Butler Library.

Scholarly Reviews and Syntheses

Edited collections and bibliographies are tools for the emerging field of inquiry and practice. The process of creating them encourages interaction and collaboration. This literature is being read, critiqued and developed by a variety of scholars.

Adams, D., & Hamm, M. (1989). Creativity, basic skills and computing: A conceptual intersection with implications for education. *Journal of Creative Behavior, 23,* 258-262.

Cohn, C. (1984). Creativity training effectiveness: A research synthesis. *Dissertation Abstracts International, 45,* 2501A.

Dacey, J. S., & Lennon, K. H. (1998). *Understanding creativity: The interplay of biological, and social factors – The latest research for students, parents, teachers, parents, trainers and managers.* San Francisco: Jossey-Bass.

Hunsaker, S. L. (1992). Toward an ethnographic perspective on creativity research. *Journal of Creative Behavior, 26,* 235-241.

Isaksen, S. G., Puccio, G. J., & Treffinger, D. J. (1993). An ecological approach to creativity research: Profiling for creative problem solving. *Journal of Creative Behavior, 27,* 149-170.

Isaksen, S. G., Stein, M. I., Hills, D. A., & Gryskiewicz, S. S. (1984). A proposed model for the formulation of creativity research. *Journal of Creative Behavior, 18,* 67-75.

Kabanoff, B., & Bottger, P. (1991). Effectiveness of creativity training and its relation to selected personality factors. *Journal of Organizational Behavior, 12,* 235-248.

MacKinnon, D. W. (1987). Some critical issues for future research in creativity. In S. G. Isaksen (Ed.), *Frontiers of creativity reearch: Beyond the basics* (pp. 120-130). Buffalo, NY: Bearly Limited.

Mansfield, R. S., Busse, T. V., & Krepelka, E. J. (1978). The effectiveness of creativity training. *Review of Educational Research, 48, (4),* 517-536.

Meichenbaum, D. (1975). Enhancing creativity by modifying what subjects say to themselves. *American Educational Research Journal, 12 (2),* 129-145.

Moore, J. G., Weare, J. L., Woodall, F. E., & Leonard, R. L. (1987). Training for thinking skills in relation to two cognitive measures. *Journal of Research and Development in Education, 20, (2),* 59-65.

Nečka, E., & Kubiak, M. (1989). Can training influence metaphorical thinking, creativity and level of dogmatism? *Creativity and Innovation Yearbook, 2,* 95-110.

Nečka, E. (1984). The effectiveness of Synectics and brainstorming as conditioned by socio-emotional climate and type of task. *Polish Psychological Bulletin, 15(1),* 41-50.

Nečka, E. (1985). The use of analogy in creative problem solving. *Polish Psychological Bulletin, 16(4),* 245-255.

Renner, V. & Renner, J. C. (1971). Effects of a creativity training program on stimulus preferences. *Perceptual Motor Skills, 33,* 872-874.

Ripple, R. E., & Dacey, J. (1970). The facilitation of problem solving and verbal creativity by exposure to programmed instruction. *Psychology in the Schools, 4,* 240-245.

Rose, L. H., & Lin, H. T. (1984). A meta-analysis of long-term creativity training programs. *Journal of Creative Behavior, 18, (1),* 11-22.

Schubert, D. S. P., Wagner, M. E., & Schubert, H. J. P. (1977). Interest in creativity training by birth order and sex. *Journal of Creative Behavior, 11, (2),* 144-145.

Seghini, J. B. (1979). *The longitudinal effects of creativity training.* Unpublished master's thesis. University of Utah.

Smith, G. F. (1998). Idea-generation techniques: A formulary of active ingredients. *Journal of Creative Behavior, 32,* 107-133.

Solomon, C. M. (1990). Creativity training. *Personnel Journal, May,* 65-71.

Souder, W. E., & Ziegler, R. W. (1977). A review of creativity and problem solving. *Research Management, 20(4),* 35-42.

Souder, W. E., & Ziegler, R. W. (1988). A review of creativity and problem solving techniques. In R. Katz (Ed.), *Managing professionals in innovative organizations: A collection of readings* (pp. 267-279). Cambridge, MA: Ballinger Publishing.

Treffinger, D. J. (1986). Research on creativity. *Gifted Child Quarterly, 30,* 15-19.

Dedicated Journals

There are numerous journals dedicated to the review and publication of an emerging periodical literature on creativity. These include: *The Journal of Creativity and Innovation Management* (since March of 1992), *The Journal of Creative Behavior* (since Winter of 1967), and the *Creativity Research Journal* (since December of 1988), among others. A report in the August 17, 1996 edition of *The Economist* indicated that there were at least six other academic journals dedicated to the study of creativity as a topic.

6. COMMUNITIES EXIST TO ADVANCE PRACTICE

There is an international community of practitioners emerging with people working within networks and a variety of creativity organizations. Many of these individuals and groups explore and develop best practice.

NETWORKS

There is a growing community of practitioners and researchers who have creativity as their main focus or domain. One of the original networks stems from those who gather each June in Buffalo for the Annual Creative Problem Solving Institute (Grube,1971; Parnes, 1977). As of 1996, a report in the August 17th edition of *The Economist* indicated that there were seven annual conferences each year on the topic of creativity. See:

Grube, T. F. (1971). To make a difference in five days: A commentary on the Annual Creative Problem Solving Institute. *Journal of Creative Behavior, 5,* 74-75.

Parnes, S. J. (1977). CPSI-The general system. *Journal of Creative Behavior, 11,* 1-11.

For example, the PRISM Network provides an International Innovation and Creativity Networking Conference (ICINC) every other year somewhere within North America.

Sample PRISM publications include:

Bédard, J. (Ed.). (1994). *Proceedings of the 1994 International Creativity and Innovation Networking Conference: Trans-sphere.* Québec, Canada: Réseau international de créativité et innovation.

Gryskiewicz, S. S. (Ed.). (1993). *Discovering creativity: Proceedings of the 1992 International Creativity & Innovation Networking Conference.* Greensboro, NC: Center for Creative Leadership.

Sample publications from the European group that was cooperating with PRISM (The European Association for Creativity and Innovation) include:

Colemont, P., Grøholt, P., Rickards, T., & Smeekes, H. (Eds.). (1988). *Creativity and innovation: Towards a European Network.* Dordrecht, Netherlands: Kluwer Academic.

Geschka, H., Moger, S., & Rickards, T. (1994). *Creativity and innovation: The power of synergy.* Darmstadt, Germany: Geschka & Partner Unternehmensberatung.

Additional networks across the world are also making progress. See:

Gryskiewicz, S. S. (1992). Networks: Nurturing the field of creativity. *Creativity and Innovation Management, 1,* 214-215.

Stein, M. I. (Ed.). (1999). *Creativity's Global Correspondents – 1999.* Delray Beach, FL: Winslow Press.

Xu, F. & Xu, F. (1998). Letter from China: A survey of creativity research. *Creativity and Innovation Management, 6,* 249-253.

CREATIVITY ORGANIZATIONS

There are numerous organizations that focus entirely on understanding or developing creativity and innovation. The following is a representative list.

American Association for Creativity (Wilmington, DE) offers an annual conference and publishes a newsletter. (www.becreative.org)

Center for Creative Change (UK) collaborates with CPS-B.

Center for Creative Leadership (Greensboro, North Carolina, established 1970) offers courses and services on creativity and innovation. (www.ccl.org)

Center for Creative Learning (Sarasota, Florida) established by Donald Treffinger to work with educators and schools. Has a network of associates and publishes materials and newsletter. (www.creativelearning.com)

Center for the Development of Creative Thinking (COCD, Antwerp, Belgium) founded by Pros Vanosmael and Roger De Bruyn from the University of Antwerp.

Center for Research in Applied Creativity (Ontario, Canada) is an academic unit within MacMaster University conducting applied research and services to organizations, founded by Min Basadur.

Center for Research on Creativity and Innovation (University of Colorado at Colorado Springs) is a center within the College of Business. (www.uccs.edu/~creative)

Center for Scientific and Technical Creativity (CSTC) an academic unit of the University of Hochiminh City, Vietnam, offers on a regular basis courses on the "Methodology of Creativity".

Center for Studies in Creativity (Buffalo, New York, established 1967) an academic unit of the State University of New York offers an undergraduate minor and a M. Sc. degree as well as supports the Creative Studies Collection at Butler Library. (www.buffalostate.edu/~creatcnt/)

Creative Education Foundation (Buffalo, New York, established 1954 by Alex Osborn) offers an Annual Creative Problem Solving Institute and publishes the Journal of Creative Behavior. (www.cef-cpsi.org)

Creative Problem Solving Group - Buffalo (Buffalo, New York, established 1984) offers a variety of services, conducts research and development on CPS. CPS-B also publishes an occasional Communiqué. (www.cpsb.com)

Creativity and Innovation Center - Europe (Brussels, Belgium, established 1992) collaborates with CPS-B.

European Association for Creativity and Innovation (Enschede, The Netherlands) hosts international conferences and encourages networking. (www.eaci.net)

Innovation Network - (Denver, Colorado) provides a network of people who have professional experience in innovation and creativity. They provide a referral service, host conferences, and provide professional services. (http://www. thinksmart.com)

National Collegiate Inventors and Innovators Alliance (Amherst Massachusetts), an organization that offers occasional conferences for those in higher education.

National Inventive Thinking Association – provides information on creativity applied to invention and organizes an annual conference in cooperation with the US Patent and Trademark Office. (www.newhorizons.org/ofc_nita)

Torrance Center for Creative Studies (Athens, Georgia) is a center within the Department of Educational Psychology at the University of Georgia. It offers advanced graduate work, numerous programs and conferences. (www.coe.uga.edu/edpsych/docs1/gifted/docs1/torrance.html)

7. There Is a Documented Need

There is demand, interest and need for learning and using CPS at an individual, group or team and organizational level. Aside from many references in the popular press, more formal rationales for creative learning have also been provided (Isaksen, 1988; Treffinger & Feldhusen, 1998), but they still provide only a basic answer to the question about the need for learning and applying creative problem solving.

The Nature of Knowledge

The accumulation of factual information is growing to the point that total comprehensive awareness is not feasible. More comprehensive states of awareness are possible within selected specific disciplines. This may lead to isolated learning of static information. Data can be "looked up", skills of creative problem solving cannot.

Botkin, J. W., Elmandjra, M., & Malitza, M. (1979). *No limits to learning: Bridging the human gap.* Oxford, UK: Pergamon Press.

Raths, L. E., Wasserman, S., Jonas, A., & Rothstein, A. M. (1967). *Teaching for thinking: Theory and application.* Columbus, OH: Charles E. Merril Publishing.

Raven, J. (1984). *Competence in modern society: Its identification, development and release.* London, UK: H. K. Lewis & Co.

The Importance of Creative-Thinking Skills

Since the world is changing so rapidly and it is impossible to predict accurately what knowledge or information will be needed, it is important to focus on the development of skills which help individuals become more adaptable to new and changing circumstances. This focus can help shape alternative images of future circumstances.

European Commission (1997). *Building the European information society for us all: Final policy report of the high-level expert group.* Luxembourg: Office for Official Publications of the European Communities.

Isaksen, S. G. (1988). Educational implications of creativity research: An updated rationale for creative learning. In K. Grønhaug & G. Kaufmann (Eds.), *Innovation: A cross-disciplinary perspective* (pp. 167-203). Oslo, Norway: Norwegian University Press.

Isaksen, S. G. & Treffinger, D. J. (1991). Creative learning and problem solving. In A. L. Costa (Ed.), *Developing minds - Programs for teaching thinking: Volume Two* (pp. 89-93). Alexandria, VA: Association for Supervision and Curriculum Development.

Mohan, M. (1973). Is there a need for a course on creativity in teacher education? *Journal of Creative Behavior, 7,* 175-186.

Sternberg, R. J., & Lubart, T. I. (1996). Investing in creativity. *American Psychologist, 51*, 677-688.

Treffinger, D. J., & Feldhusen, J. F. (1998). *Planning for productive thinking and learning: A handbook for teachers.* Sarasota, FL: Center for Creative Learning.

SKILLS MORE TRANSFERABLE THAN KNOWLEDGE

The ability and facility of using knowledge are more generalizable and more widely applicable than memorization of data. Skills and abilities are more permanent and related to the process of solving problems.

Baer, J. (1994). Divergent thinking is not a general trait: A multidomain training experiment. *Creativity Research Journal, 7*, 35-46.

Cole, H. P. (1972). *Process education: The new direction for elementary and secondary schools.* Englewood Cliffs, New Jersey: Educational Technology Publications.

Gordon, J., & Zemke, R. (1986). Making them more creative. *Training, 23*, 30-45.

Nickerson, R. S., Perkins, D. N., & Smith, E. E. (1985). *The teaching of thinking.* Hillsdale, New Jersey: Lawrence Erlbaum Associates.

SITUATIONS MAY DEMAND CREATIVITY

There are many situations where there is no immediate or single right answer. These frequent, real-life conditions clearly call for a creative type of thinking.

Carnevale, A. P., Gainer, L. J., & Meltzer, A. S. (1991). *Workplace basics: The essential skills employers want.* San Francisco: Jossey-Bass.

Centre for Educational Research and Innovation (1974, 1978). *Creativity of the school: Conclusions for a programme of enquiry.* Paris: OECD.

Heinelt, G. (1974). *Kreative Lehrer, kreative Schuler: wie die Schule kreativität fordern kann* (Creative teachers, creative students: ways for the school to stimulate creativity). Freiburg, Germany: Herderbücherei.

Jean, G. (1977). *Pour une pédagogie de l'imaginaire* (For a pedagogy of the imaginitive). Tournai, Belgium: Casterman.

Treffinger, D. J. (1996). *Creative problem solving and school improvement.* Sarasota, FL: Center for Creative Learning.

CREATIVE THINKING CAN BE ENJOYABLE

Learning that calls for the student to actively produce, rather than passively recall, is more motivating. These situations encourage commitment by providing opportunities for learners to follow through on intrinsically-motivated tasks. This increases motivation and relevance for learning.

Lieberman, J. (1977). Playfulness: its relationship to imagination and creativity. New York: Academic.

Gardner, J. W. (1981). *Self-renewal: The individual and the innovative society (Revised edition)*. New York: W. W. Norton & Co.

Treffinger, D. J., & Sortore, M. R. (1990). Creative problem solving: The need, the process, the metamorphosis. *The Prufrock Journal of Secondary Gifted Education, 2*, 6-15.

Creativity Is Natural

All students benefit from involvement in creative learning. There may be varying levels and styles in the responses, but everyone can use the level or style they have when provided with the appropriate opportunity.

deBono, E. & Lane, A. (1972). *Children solve problems*. New York: Harper.

Gloton, R. & Clero, C. (1971). *L' activité créatrice chez l'enfant* (The child and its creative activity). Tournai: Casterman.

Grainger, R. D. (1991). Ways to nurture your creativity. *American Journal of Nursing, 91*, 14-17.

Hesbois, E. (1977). *La créativité chez l'enfant, ou l'enfant et son potentiel de rénovation* (Creativity within children, or children and their potential for renewal). Bruxelles: De Boeck.

Krause, R. (1977). *Produktives Denken bei Kindern: Untersuchungen über Kreativität* (Productive thinking within children: some creativity research). Weinheim, Germany.

Wanninger, G. R. (1981). *Kreativität bei Kindern in Leistings- und Sozialbereich: ein theoretischer und empirisher Beitrag* (Creativity with children related to achievement and social interactions: a theoretical and empirical contribution). Unpublished Doctoral Dissertation. Universität Würzburg, Germany.

Builds on Knowledge

Creative learning is not an "either/or" situation. You cannot focus purely on creativity. All creativity has a context and data surrounding that context. Creative learning uses traditional content as raw material to be used when there is some relevance and need. The focus on process is not entirely independent or exclusive of content, and may actually increase the retention and transfer of learned data.

Tuma, D. J. & Reif, F. (1980). *Problem solving and education: Issues in teaching and research.* Hillsdale, New Jersey: Lawrence Erlbaum Associates

8. THERE IS EXPERIMENTAL EVIDENCE

A critical way of knowing if CPS is worthwhile is the extent to which there is experimental evidence surrounding the development, training and application of CPS methods, guidelines and tools. This evidence is categorized into foundational, brainstorming, and experimental evidence of course impact.

FOUNDATIONAL EVIDENCE

The early instructional program in creative problem solving was developed at the University of Buffalo and it was moved to Buffalo State College in 1967. A series of published reports provided early evidence of the efficacy of the instructional program.

Meadow, A. & Parnes, S. J. (1959). Evaluation of training in creative problem solving. *Journal of Applied Psychology, 43,* 189-194.

Noller, R. B., & Parnes, S. J. (1972). Applied creativity: The Creative Studies Project. Part III - The curriculum. *Journal of Creative Behavior, 6,* 275-293.

Parnes, S. J. (1961). Effects of extended effort in creative problem solving. *Journal of Educational Psychology, 52, 3,* 117-122.

Parnes, S. J. (1962). Can creativity be increased? In S. J. Parnes & H. F. Harding (Ed.), *A source book for creative thinking* (pp. 185-191). New York: Charles Scribners & Sons.

Parnes, S. J. (1964). Research on developing creative behavior. In C. W. Taylor (Ed.), *Widening horizons in creativity* (pp. 145-169). New York: Wiley.

Parnes, S. J. (1966). *Programming creative behavior.* (Grant number 7-42-1630-213). Buffalo, NY: State University of New York at Buffalo, U. S. Department of Health, Education and Welfare.

Parnes, S. J. (1970). Programming creative behavior. *Child Development, 41,* 2-12.

Parnes, S. J. (1972). Programming creative behavior. In C. W. Tyler (Ed.), *Climate for creativity* (pp. 193-227). New York: Pergamon.

Parnes, S. J. (1973). Evaluation of training in creative problem solving. In M. Goldfried & M. Merbaum (Eds.), *Behavior change for self control.* New York: Holt, Rinehart & Winston.

Parnes, S. J. (1974). Applied imagination and the production of original verbal images. *Perceptual and Motor Skills, 138,* 130.

Parnes, S. J. (1976). Creativity development. In S. Goodman (Ed.), *Handbook on contemporary education* (pp. 498-501). Princeton, NJ: Reference Development Corp.

Parnes, S. J. (1978). The creative studies project at Buffalo State College. In M. K. Raina (Ed.), *Creativity research: International perspectives* (pp. 272-274). New Delhi, India: National Council for Educational Research and Training.

Parnes, S. J. (1987). The creative studies project. In S. G. Isaksen (Ed.). *Frontiers of creativity research: Beyond the basics* (pp. 156-188). Buffalo, NY: Bearly Limited.

Parnes, S. J., & Meadow, A. (1960). Evaluation of persistence of effects produced by a creative problem-solving course. *Psychological Reports, 7*, 357-361.

Parnes, S. J., & Noller, R. B. (1971). The creative studies project: Raison d'etre and introduction. *Journal of Research and Development in Education, 4*, 63-66.

Parnes, S. J., & Noller, R. B. (1972). Applied creativity: The Creative Studies Project. Part 1 - The development. *Journal of Creative Behavior, 6*, 11-20 (a).

Parnes, S. J., & Noller, R. B. (1972). Applied creativity: The Creative Studies Project. Part II - Results of the two-year program. *Journal of Creative Behavior, 6*, 164-186 (a).

Parnes, S. J., & Noller, R. B. (1973). Applied creativity: The Creative Studies Project. Part IV - Personality findings and conclusions. *Journal of Creative Behavior, 7*, 15-36.

Reese, H. W., Parnes, S. J., Treffinger, D. J., & Kaltsounis, G. (1976). Effects of a creative studies program on structure-of-intellect factors. *Journal of Educational Psychology, 68*, 401-410.

Brainstorming Research

Brainstorming is one of the most researched of the tools within the CPS framework. The following are actual studies (mostly published), some papers, and unpublished theses and dissertations. They provide a foundation for understanding the conditions for effective brainstorming.

Basadur, M. (1979). *Training in creative problem solving: Effects of deferred judgment and problem finding and solving in an industrial research organization.* Unpublished doctoral dissertation, University of Cincinnati, OH.

Basadur, M. (1982). Research in creative problem solving training in business and industry. In S. S. Gryskiewicz, & J. T. Shields (Eds.), *Creativity Week 4, 1981 Proceedings.* (pp. 40-59). Greensboro, NC: Center for Creative Leadership.

Basadur, M., & Finkbeiner, C. T. (1983). *Identifying attitudinal factors related to ideation in creative problem solving* (Research and Working Paper Series #207). Hamilton, Ontario: McMaster University, Faculty of Business.

Basadur, M., & Finkbeiner, C. T. (1983). *Measuring preference for ideation in creative problem solving* (Research and Working Paper Series #208). Hamilton, Ontario: McMaster University, Faculty of Business.

Basadur, M., & Finkbeiner, C. T. (1985). Measuring preference for ideation in creative problem-solving training. *Journal of Applied Behavioral Science, 21*(1), 37-49.

Basadur, M., Graen, G. B., & Green, S. G. (1982). Training in creative problem solving: Effects on ideation and problem finding and solving in an industrial research organization. *Organizational Behavior and Human Performance, 30*, 41-70.

Basadur, M., Graen G. B., & Scandura, T. A. (1985). Improving attitudes toward creative problem solving among manufacturing engineers (Research and Working Paper Series #237). Hamilton, Ontario: McMaster University, Faculty of Business.

Basadur, M., Graen, G. B., & Scandura, T. A. (1985). Training effects on attitudes toward divergent thinking among manufacturing engineers. *Journal of Applied Psychology, 71*(4), 612-617.

Bayless, O. L. (1967). An alternate pattern for problem solving discussion. *Journal of Communication, 17,* 188-197.

Bottger, P. C., & Yetton, P. W. (1987). Improving group performance by training in individual problem solving. *Journal of Applied Psychology, 72*(4), 651-657.

Bouchard, T. J., Jr. (1969). Personality, problem-solving procedure, and performance in small groups. *Journal of Applied Psychology Monograph, 53*(1 Part 2), 1-29.

Bouchard, T. J., Jr. (1972). A comparison of two group brainstorming procedures. *Journal of Applied Psychology, 56*(5), 418-421.

Bouchard, T. J., Jr. (1972). Training, motivation, and personality as determinants of the effectiveness of brainstorming groups and individuals. *Journal of Applied Psychology, 56*(4), 324-331.

Bouchard, T. J., Jr. Barsaloux, J., & Drauden, G. (1974). Brainstorming procedure, group size, and sex as determinants of the problem-solving effectiveness of groups and individuals. *Journal of Applied Psychology, 59*(2), 135-138.

Bouchard, T. J., Jr., & Hare, M. (1970). Size, performance, and potential in brainstorming groups. *Journal of Applied Psychology, 54*(1), 51-55.

Bouchard, T. J., Jr., Drauden, G., & Barsaloux, J. (1974). A comparison of individual, subgroup, and total group methods of problem solving. *Journal of Applied Psychology, 59*(2), 226-227.

Bray, R. M., Kerr, N. L., & Atking, R. S. (1978). Effects of group size, problem difficulty, and sex on group performance and member reactions. *Journal of Personality and Social Psychology, 36*(11), 1224-1240.

Brilhart, J. K., & Jochem, L. M. (1964). Effects of different patterns on outcomes of problem-solving discussion. *Journal of Applied Psychology, 48*(3), 175-179.

Brown, V., & Paulus, P. B. (1996). A simple dynamic model of social factors in group brainstorming. *Small Group Research, 27,* 91-114.

Burns, M. G. (1983). *A comparison of three creative problem-solving methodologies.* Unpublished doctoral dissertation (Microfilm No. DA 8411 924), University of Denver, Denver, CO.

Buyer, L. S. (1988). Creative problem solving: A comparison of performance under different instructions. *Journal of Creative Behavior, 22*(1), 55-61.

Camacho, L. M. & Paulus, P. B. (1995). The role of social anxiousness in group brainstorming, *Journal of Personality and Social Psychology, 68*(6), 1071-1080.

Cohen, D., Whitmyre, J. W., & Funk, W. H. (1960). Effect of group cohesiveness and training upon creative thinking. *Journal of Applied Psychology, 44*(5), 319-322.

Collaros, P. A., & Anderson, L. R. (1969). Effect of perceived expertness upon creativity of members of brainstorming groups. *Journal of Applied Psychology, 53*(2), 159-163.

Comadena, M. E. (1984). Brainstorming groups: Ambiguity tolerance, communication apprehension, task attraction, and individual productivity. *Small Group Behavior, 15*(2), 251-264.

Connolly, T., Routhieaux, R. L., & Schneider, S. K. (1993). On the effectiveness of group brainstorming: Test of one underlying cognitive mechanism. *Small Group Research, 24*(4), 490-503.

Cox, R. S. (1977). Rewarding instructions vs. brainstorming on creativity test scores of college students. *Psychological Reports, 41*(3), 951-954.

Cox, R. S., Nash, W. R., & Ash, M. J. (1976, April). Instructions for three levels of reward and creativity test scores of college students. *Psychological Reports, 38*, 411-414.

Diehl, M., & Stroebe, W. (1991). Productivity loss in idea-generating groups: Tracking down the blocking effect. *Journal of Personality and Social Psychology, 61*(3), 392-403.

Dillon, P. C., Graham, W. K., & Aidells, A. L. (1972). Brainstorming on a "hot" problem; Effects of training and practice on individual and group performance. *Journal of Applied Psychology, 56*(6), 487-490.

Dirkes, M. A. (1974). *The effect of divergent thinking experiences on creative production and transfer between mathematical and nonmathematical domains.* Unpublished doctoral dissertation (University Microfilms No. 74-29), Wayne State University, Ann Arbor, Michigan.

Ekvall, G. & Parnes, S. J. (1989). Creative problem solving methods in product development - a second experiment. *Creativity and Innovation Yearbook, 2*, 122-142.

Ekvall, G. (1981). *Creative problem solving methods in product development - A comparative study.* (Report no. 1). P.O. Box 5042, S-102 41 Stockholm: FArådet- The Swedish Council for Management and Work Life Issues.

Ekvall, G., & Parnes, S. J. (1984). *Creative problem solving methods in product development - A second experiment* (Report no. 2). P.O. Box 5042, S-102 41 Stockholm: FArådet- The Swedish Council for Management and Work Life Issues.

Firestien, R. L. (1979). *Effects of brainstorming or short-term incubation on divergent production in problem-solving.* Unpublished Master's thesis, State University of New York, College at Buffalo, Buffalo, NY.

Firestien, R. L. (1990). Effects of creative problem solving training on communication behaviors in small groups. *Small Group Research, 21*(4), 507-521.

Firestien, R. L., & McGowan, R. J. (1988). Creative problem solving and communication behavior in small groups. *Creativity Research Journal, 1*(1), 106-114.

Freedman, J. L. (1965). Increasing creativity by free-association training. *Journal of Experimental Psychology, 69*(1), 89-91.

Furnham, A. & Yazdanpanahi, T. (1995). Personality differences and group versus individual brainstorming, *Personality and Individual Differences, 19(1),* 73-80.

Glover, J. A., & Chambers, T. (1978). The creative production of a group: Effects of small group structure. *Small Group Behavior, 9*(3), 387-392.

Gryskiewicz, S. S. (1980). *A study of creative problem solving techniques in group settings.* Unpublished doctoral dissertation, University of London.

Gryskiewicz, S. S. (1984). *Uniformity pressure revisited: An evaluation of three creative problem-solving techniques in an industrial setting.* Paper presented at the Ninety-Second Annual Convention of the American Psychological Association, Toronto, Canada.

Gryskiewicz, S. S. (1987). Predictable creativity. In S. G. Isaksen, (Ed.), *Frontiers of creativity research: Beyond the basics* (pp. 305-313). Buffalo, NY: Bearly Limited.

Gryskiewicz, S. S. (1988). Trial by fire in an industrial setting: A practical evaluation of three creative problem solving techniques. In K. Grønhaug, & G. Kaufmann (Eds.), *Innovation: A cross-disciplinary perspective* (pp. 205-232). Oslo, Norway: Norwegian University Press.

Harkins, S. G. (1987). Social loafing and social facilitation. *Journal of Experimental Social Psychology, 23,* 1-18.

Harkins, S. G., & Jackson, J. M. (1985). The role of evaluation in eliminating social loafing. *Personality and Social Psychology Bulletin, 11*(4), 457-465.

Harkins, S. G., & Petty, R. E. (1982). Effects of task difficulty and task uniqueness on social loafing. *Journal of Personality and Social Psychology, 43*(6), 1214-1229.

Harkins, S. G., Latané, B., & Williams, K. (1980). Social loafing: Allocating effort or taking it easy? *Journal of Experimental Social Psychology, 16,* 457-465.

Hyams, N. B., & Graham, W. K. (1984, August). Effects of goal setting and initiative on individual brainstorming. *The Journal of Social Psychology, 123*(Second Half) 283-284.

Jablin, F. M. (1981). Cultivating imagination: Factors that enhance and inhibit creativity in brainstorming groups. *Human Communication Research, 7*(3), 245-258.

Jablin, F. M., & Sussman, L. (1978). An exploration of communication and productivity in real brainstorming groups. *Human Communication Research, 4*(4), 329-337.

Jablin, F. M., Seibold, D. R., & Sorenson, R. L. (1977, Summer). Potential inhibitory effects of group participation on brainstorming performance. *Central States Speech Journal, 28,* 113-121.

Karau, S. J., & Williams, K. D. (1993). Social loafing: A meta-analytic review and theoretical integration. *Journal of Personality and Social Psychology, 65*(4), 681-706.

Klimoski, R. J., & Karol, B. L. (1976). The impact of trust on creative problem solving groups. *Journal of Applied Psychology, 61*(5), 630-633.

Latané, B., Williams, K., & Harkins, S. (1979). Many hands make light the work: The causes and consequences of social loafing. *Journal of Personality and Social Psychology, 37*(6), 822-832.

Lewis, A. C., Sadosky, T. L., & Connolly, T. (1975). The effectiveness of group brainstorming on engineering problem solving. *IEEE Transactions on Engineering Management, 22*(3), 119-124.

Lindgren, H. C., & Lindgren, L. (1965). Creativity, brainstorming, and orneriness: A cross cultural study. *Journal of Social Psychology, 67,* 23-30.

Madsen, D. B., & Finger, J. R., Jr. (1978). Comparison of a written feedback procedure, group brainstorming, and individual brainstorming. *Journal of Applied Psychology, 63*(1), 120 - 123.

Maginn, B. K., & Harris, R. J. (1980). Effects of anticipated evaluation on individual brainstorming performance. *Journal of Applied Psychology, 65*(2), 219-225.

Meadow, A., & Parnes, S. J. (1959). Evaluation of training in creative problem solving. *Journal of Applied Psychology, 43*(3), 189-194.

Meadow, A., Parnes, S. J., & Reese, H. (1959). Influence of brainstorming instructions and problem sequence on a creative problem solving test. *Journal of Applied Psychology, 43*(6), 413-416.

Necka, E. (1984). The effectiveness of Synectics and brainstorming as conditioned by socio-emotional climate and type of task. *Polish Psychological Bulletin, 15*(1), 41-50.

Necka, E. (1985). The use of analogy in creative problem solving. *Polish Psychological Bulletin, 16*(4), 245-255.

Offner, A. K., Kramer, T. J. & Winter, J. P. (1996). The effects of facilitation, recording, and pauses on group brainstorming. *Small Group Research*, 27(2), 283-298.

Oxley, N. L. & Dzindolet, M. T. (1996). The effects of facilitators on the performance of brainstorming groups. *Journal of Social Behavior & Personality*, 11(4), 633-646.

Parloff, M. B., & Handlon, J. H. (1964). The influence of criticalness on creative problem solving in dyads. *Psychiatry, 52*, 117-122.

Parnes, S. J., & Meadow, A. (1959). Effects of "brainstorming" instructions on creative problem solving by trained and untrained subjects. *Journal of Educational Psychology, 50*(4), 171-176.

Parnes, S. J., Meadow, A., & Reese, H. (1959). Influence of brainstorming instructions and problem sequence on a creative problem solving test. *Journal of Applied Psychology, 43*(6), 413-416.

Paulus, P. B., Dzindolet, M. T., Poletes, G. & Camacho, L. M. (1993). Perception of performance in group brainstorming: The illusion of group productivity. *Personality and Social Psychology Bulletin*, 19(1), 78-89.

Paulus, P. B., Larey, T. S. & Ortega, A. H. (1995). Performance and perceptions of brainstormers in an organizational setting. *Basic and Applied Social Psychology, 17*(1&2), 249-265.

Restle, F., & Davis, J. H. (1962). Success and speed of problem solving by individuals and groups. *Psychological Review, 69*, 520-536.

Rickards, T. (1975). Brainstorming: An examination of idea production rate and level of speculation on real managerial situations. *R & D Management, 6*(1), 11-14.

Rickards, T., Aldridge, S., & Gaston, K. (1988). Factors affecting brainstorming: Towards the development of diagnostic tools for assessment of creative performance. *R & D Management, 18*(4), 309-320.

Riegel, K., F., Riegel, R., M., & Levine, R. S. (1966). An analysis of associative behavior and creativity. *Journal of Personality and Social Psychology, 4*(1), 50-56.

Rowatt, W. C., Nesselroade, Jr., K. P., Beggan, J. K. & Allison, S. T. (1997). Perceptions of brainstorming in groups: The quality over quantity hypothesis. *Journal of Creative Behavior, 31*(2), 131-150.

Sappington, A. A., & Farrar, W. E. (1982). Brainstorming vs. critical judgment in the generation of solutions which conform to certain reality constraints. *Journal of Creative Behavior, 16*(1), 68-73.

Sheppard, J. A. (1993). Productivity loss in performance groups: A motivation analysis. *Psychological Bulletin*, 113(1), 67-81.

Stroebe, W., Diehl, M., & Abakoumkin, G. (1992). The illusion of group effectivity. *Personality and Social Psychology Bulletin, 18*, 643-650.

Sutton, R. I. & Hargadon, A. (1996). Brainstorming groups in context: Effectiveness in a product design firm. *Administrative Science Quarterly*, 41, 685-718.

Szymanski, K., & Harkins, S. G. (1992). Self-evaluation and creativity. *Personality and Social Psychology Bulletin, 18*(3), 259-265.

Telem, M. (1988). Information requirements speculation I: Brainstorming collective decision-making approach. *Information Processing and Management*, 24(5), 549-557.

Telem, M. (1988). Information requirements specification II: Brainstorming collective decision-making technique. *Information Processing and Management*, 24(5), 559-566.

Thornburg, T. H. (1991). Group size and member diversity influence on creative performance. *Journal of Creative Behavior, 25*(4), 324-333.

Torrance, E. P. (1970). Influence of dyadic interaction on creative functioning. *Psychological Reports, 26*, 391-394.

Triandis, H. C., Hall, E. H., & Ewen, R. B. (1965, February). Member heterogeneity and dyadic creativity. *Human Relations*, 18(1), 33-55.

Turner, W. M., & Rains, R. D. (1965). Differential effects of "brainstorming" instructions upon high and low creative subjects. *Psychological Reports*, 17, 753-754.

Warren, T. F., & Davis, G. A. (1969). Techniques for creative thinking: An empirical comparison of three models. *Psychological Reports*, 25, 207-214.

Weisskopf-Joelson, E., & Eliseo, T. S. (1961). An experimental study of the effectiveness of brainstorming. *Journal of Applied Psychology*, 45(1), 45-49.

Williams, K., Harkins, S., & Latané, B. (1981). Identifiability as a deterrent to social loafing: Two cheering experiments. *Journal of Personality and Social Psychology, 40*(2), 303-311.

Zagona, S. V., Willis, J. E., & MacKinnon, W. J. (1966). Group effectiveness in creative problem-solving tasks: An examination of relevant variables. *Journal of Psychology, 62*, 111-137.

Electronic Brainstorming

One of the more recent trends in the brainstorming literature is the use of electronic means to encourage group decision-making support systems. This is more commonly referred to as electronic brainstorming.

Aiken, M. & Riggs, M. (1993). Using a group decision support system for creativity. *Journal of Creative Behavior*, 27(1), 28-35.

Bar, J. (1988). Computer-aided creativity: A systematic technique for new-product idea-generation. *Creativity & Innovation Yearbook*, 1, 20-29.

Benbasat, I., & Lim, L. H. (1993). The effects of group, task, context, and technology variables on the usefulness of group support systems: A meta-analysis of experimental studies. *Small Group Research* 24 (4), 430-462.

Chidambaram, L., & Jones, B. (1993). Impact of communication medium and computer support on group perceptions and performance: A comparison of face-to-face and dispersed meetings. *MIS Quarterly, 17*, 465-491.

Connolly, T., Jessup, L. M. & Valacich, J. S. (1990). Effects of anonymity and evaluative tone on idea generation in computer-mediated groups. *Management Science, 36*, 689-703.

Cooper, W. H., Gallupe, R. B., Pollard,S., & Cadsby, J. (1998). Some liberating effects of anonymous electronic brainstorming. *Small Group Research, 29*, 147-178.

Dennis, A., & Gallupe, R. B. (1993). A history of group support system empirical research: Lessons learned and future decisions. In L.M. Jessup & J.S. Valacich (eds.) *Groups Support Systems New Perspectives* (pp. 59-77).

Dennis, A. R. & Valacich, J. S. (1994). Group, sub-group, and nominal group idea generation: New rules for a new media? *Journal of Management, 20*(4), 723-736.

Dennis, A. R. & Valacich, J. S. (1993). Computer brainstorms: More heads are better than one. *Journal of Applied Psychology, 78*, 531-537.

Dennis, A. R., Valacich, J. S., Connolly, T., & Wynne, B. E. (1996). Process structuring in electronic brainstorming. *Information Systems Research, 7*, 268-277.

Dennis, A. R., Valacich, J. S., Carte, T. A., Garfield, M. J., Haley, B. J., & Aronson, J. E., (1997). Research report: The effectivenss of multiple dialogues in electronic brainstorming. *Information Systems Research, 8*, 203-211.

Gallupe, R. B., Bastianutti, L. M. & Cooper, W. H. (1991). Unlocking brainstorms. *Journal of Applied Psychology, 76*(1), 137-142.

Gallupe, R. B., & Cooper, W. H. (Fall, 1993). Brainstorming electronically. *Sloan Management Review, 23*, 27-36.

Gallupe, R. B., Cooper, W. H., Grisé, M., & Bastianutti, L. M. (1994). Blocking electronic brainstorms. *Journal of Applied Psychology*, 79(1), 77-86.

Gallupe, R. B., Dennis, A. R., Cooper, W. H., Valacich, J. S., Bastianutti, L. M., & Nunamaker, J. F. (1992). Electronic brainstorming and group size. *Academy of Management Journal, 35*, 350-369.

Gavish, B., Gerdes, Jr., J. & Shridhar, S. (1995). CM²: a distributed group decision support system. *IIE Transactions, 27*(6), 722-733.

Herschel, R. T. (1994). The impact of varying gender composition on group brainstorming performance in a GSS environment. *Computers in Human Behavior, 10*(2), 209-222.

McFadzean, E. (1997). Improving group productivity with group support systems and creative problem solving techniques. *Creativity and Innovation Management, 6(4)*, 218-225.

Nunamaker, J. F. Jr. (1997). Future research in group support systems: Needs, some questions and possible directions. *International Journal of Human-Computer Studies, 47*, 357-385.

Nunamaker, J. F., Jr., Allegate, L. M., & Konsynski, B. R. (1987). Facilitating group creativity: Experience with a group decision support system. *Journal of Management Information Systems, 3*(4), 5-19.

Nunamaker, J. F., Jr., Vogel, D. R., & Konsynski, B. R. (1989). Interaction of task and technology to support large groups. *Decision Support Systems, 5*(2), 139-152.

Paulus, P. B., Larey, T. S., Putnam, V. L., Leggett, K. L. & Roland, E. J. (1996). Social influence processes in computer brainstorming. *Basic and Applied Social Psychology, 18*(1), 3-14.

Roy, M. C., Gauvin, S. & Limayem, M. (1996). Electronic group brainstorming: The role of feedback on productivity. *Small Group Research, 27*(2), 215-247.

Siau, K. L. (1995). Group creativity and technology. *Journal of Creative Behavior, 29,* 201-216.

Siau, K. L. (1996). Electronic creativity techniques for organizational innovation. *Journal of Creative Behavior, 30*(4), 283-292.

Smith, C. A., & Hayne, S. C. (1997). Decision making under time pressure: An investigation of decision speed and decision quality of computer-supported groups. *Management Communication Quarterly, 11(1)*, 97-126.

Sosik, J. L., Avolio, B. J., & Kahai, S. S. (1998). Inspiring group creativity: Comparing anonymous and identified electronic brainstorming. *Small Group Research, 29(1)*, 3-31.

Sosik, J. L., Kahai, S. K., & Avolio, B. J. (1998). Transformational leadership and dimensions of creativity: Motivating idea generation in computer-mediated groups. *Creativity Research Journal, 11,* 111-122.

Valacich, J. S., Dennis, A. R., & Connolly, T. (1994). Idea generation in computer-based groups: A new ending to an old story. *Organizational behavior and human decision processes, 57*(3), 448-467.

Valacich, J. S., Dennis, A. R., & Nunamaker, J. F., Jr. (1991). Electronic meeting support: The group systems concept. *International Journal of Man-Machine Studies, 34,* 261-282.

Valacich, J. S., Dennis, A. R., & Nunamaker, J. F. (1992). Group size and anonymity effects on computer-mediated idea generation. *Small Group Research, 23*(1), 49-73.

Extended Effort

An area of interest within brainstorming is what it takes to increase the productivity of a session. One key concept is that of managing the energy during ideation to push for even greater quantity. The following studies provide insight into this area.

Basadur, M., & Thompson, R. (1986). Usefulness of the ideation principle of extended effort in real world professional and managerial creative problem solving. *Journal of Creative Behavior, 20*(1), 23-34.

Gerlach, V. S., Schutz, R. E., Baker, R. L., & Mazer, G. E. (1964). Effects of variations in test directions on originality response. *Journal of Educational Psychology, 55*, 79-83.

Parnes, S. J. (1961). Effects of extended effort in creative problem solving. *Journal of Educational Psychology, 52*(3), 117-122.

Paulus, P. B., & Dzindolet, M. T. (1993). Social influence processes in group brainstorming. *Journal of Personality and Social Psychology, 64*, 575-586.

Individual Versus Group

A major area of interest within the domain of brainstorming research is the influence of groups and individuals. There is a growing empirical literature that is helping to answer the question whether groups or individuals are more productive when generating options.

Bartunek, J. M. & Murninghan, J. K. (1984). The nominal group technique: Expanding the basic procedure and underlying assumptions. *Group & Organization Studies, 9*(3), 417-432.

Brophy, D. R. (1998). Understanding, measuring, and enhancing individual creative problem-solving efforts. *Creativity Research Journal, 11*, 123-150.

Brophy, D. R. (1998). Understanding, measuring, and enhancing collective creative problem-solving efforts. *Creativity Research Journal, 11*, 199-229.

Campbell, J. P. (1968). Individual versus group problem solving in an industrial sample. *Journal of Applied Psychology, 52*(3), 205-210.

Dunnette, M. D., Campbell, J. P., & Jaastad, K. (1963). The effect of group participation on brainstorming effectiveness for two industrial samples. *Journal of Applied Psychology, 47*(1), 30-37.

Graham, W. K. (1977). Acceptance of ideas generated through individual and group brainstorming. *Journal of Social Psychology, 101*, 231-234.

Graham, W. K., & Dillion, P. C. (1974). Creative supergroups: Group performance as a function of individual performance on brainstorming tasks. *Journal of Social Psychology, 93*, 101-105.

Green, T. B. (1975). An empirical analysis of nominal and interacting groups. *Academy of Management Journal, 18*(1), 63-73.

Hall, E. J., Mouton, J. S., & Blake, R. R. (1963). Group problem solving effectiveness under conditions of pooling vs. interaction. *Journal of Social Psychology, 59,* 147-157.

Harari, O., & Graham, W. K. (1975). Tasks and task consequences as factors in individual and group brainstorming. *Journal of Social Psychology, 95,* 61-65.

Hegedus, D. M., & Rasmussen, R.V. (1986). Task effectiveness and interaction process of a modified nominal group technique in solving an evaluation problem. *Journal of Management, 12(4),* 545-560.

Putnam, L.L., & Stohl, C. (1996). Bona fide groups: an alternative perspective for communication and small group decision making. In R. Y. Hirokawa, & M. S. Poole, (Eds.), *Communication and group decision-making (second edition)*(pp. 147-178). Thousand Oaks, CA: SAGE Publications

Rotter, G. S., & Portugal, S. M. (1969). Group and individual effects in problem solving. *Journal of Applied Psychology, 53*(4), 338-341.

Street, W. R. (1974). Brainstorming by individuals, co-acting and interacting groups. *Journal of Applied Psychology, 59*(4), 433-436.

Taylor, D. W., Berry, P. C., & Block, C. H. (1958). Does group participation when using brainstorming facilitate or inhibit creative thinking? *Administrative Science Quarterly, 6,* 22-47.

Triandis, H. C., Bass, A. R., Ewen, R. B., & Mikesell, E. H. (1963). Team creativity as a function of the creativity of the members. *Journal of Applied Psychology, 47*(2), 104-110.

Van de Ven, A. H., & Delbecq, A. L. (1971). Nominal versus interacting group processes for committee decision-making effectiveness. *Academy of Management Journal, 14*(2), 203-212.

Literature Reviews

There are also separate studies that provide reviews of previous research studies and point out trends and key issues.

Beaton, E. M. (1990). *A critical review and analysis of empirical brainstorming research.* Unpublished master's project, Buffalo State College, Buffalo, NY.

Diehl, M., & Stroebe, W. (1987). Productivity loss in brainstorming groups: Toward the solution of a riddle. *Journal of Personality and Social Psychology, 53*(3), 497-509.

Isaksen, S. G. (1998). *A review of brainstorming research: Six critical issues for inquiry.* Creativity Research Unit Monograph (#302). Buffalo, NY: Creative Problem Solving Group - Buffalo.

Jablin, F. M., & Siebold, D. R. (1978). Implications for problem solving groups of empirical research on "brainstorming": A critical review of the literature. *Southern Speech Communications Journal, 43*(4), 327-356.

Lamm, H., & Trommsdorff, G. (1973). Group versus individual performance on tasks requiring ideation proficiency (brainstorming): A review. *European Journal of Social Psychology, 3*(4), 361-388.

Mullen, B., Johnson, C., & Salas, E. (1991). Productivity loss in brainstorming groups: A meta-analytic integration. *Basic and Applied Social Psychology, 12*(1), 3- 23.

Nunamaker, J. F., Briggs, R. O., Mittleman, D. D., Vogel, D. R. & Balthazard, P. A. (1997). Lessons from a dozen years of group support systems research: A discussion of lab and field findings. *Journal of Management Information Systems, 13*, 163-207.

Parnes, S. J. (1963). The deferment-of-judgment principle: A clarification of the literature. *Psychological Reports, 12*, 521-522.

Ruback, R. B., Dabbs, J. M., Jr., & Hopper, C. H. (1984). The process of brainstorming: An analysis with individual and group vocal parameters. *Journal of Personality and Social Psychology, 47*(3), 558-567.

Stein, M. I. (1974). *Stimulating creativity* (See chapter 13 on brainstorming, pp. 25-141). NY: Academic Press.

Stroebe, W., & Diehl, M. (1991). You can't beat good experiments with correlational evidence: Mullen, Johnson, and Salas's meta-analytic misinterpretations. *Basic and Applied Social Psychology, 12*(1), 25-32.

General Brainstorming Literature

In addition to the formal studies cited above, the following literature refers to brainstorming in its more popular form.

Allen, M. S. (ND). *The role of brainstorming in creative problem solving.* (Available from the Center for Studies in Creativity, Buffalo State College, New York).

Alter, U., Geschka, H., Schaude, G. R., & Schliksupp, H. (1973). *Methoden und organisation der Ideenfindung* (Mehods for and structuring of Idea Finding). Frankfurt am Main, Germany: Batelle-Institut.

Bandrowski, J. F. (1984, May). Igniting creativity: A strategic process. *Planning Review,* 18-23.

Barr, V. (1988). The process of innovation: Brainstorming and story boarding. *Mechanical Engineering, 110*, 42-46.

Bouchard, T. J., Jr. (1971). Whatever happened to brainstorming? *Journal of Creative Behavior, 5*(3), 182-189.

Bouchard, T. J., Jr. (1977). Whatever happened to brainstorming? In S. J. Parnes, R. B. Noller, & A. M. Biondi, *Guide to Creative action, part 3.* (pp. 189-192). New York, Charles Scribner's Sons.

Burger, H. G. (1976). On the cultural-materialist model of imagination: Haiku, not brainstorm. *Current Anthropology, 17*(4), 757-758.

Carroll, B. (1991, March). Shaping the future with FPS. *Gifted Child Today, 14*(2), 6-8.

Chapman, J. L. (1957, October 10 & 11). *Introduction to brainstorming* (presented at the Edison Electric Institute Housepower Workshop, Philadelphia, PA). (Available from the Center for Studies in Creativity, Buffalo State College, Buffalo, NY).

Clark, J. W. (1959, Spring). *A brain dusting introduction to brainstorming* (prepared for the Tennessee Valley Authority, Office of Power, class in creative problem solving, Chattanooga, TN). (Available from the Center for Studies in Creativity, Buffalo State College, Buffalo, NY).

Conway, H. A., & McGuinness, N. W. (1986). Idea generation in technology-based firms. *Journal of Product Innovation Management, 4*, 276-291.

Couger, J. D. (1990). Ensuring creative approaches to information system design. *Managerial and Decision Economics, 11*, 281-295.

Davis, G.A. & Roweton, W.E. (1968). Using idea checklists with college students: Overcoming resistance. *Journal of Psychology, 70*, 221-226.

Dunnette, M. D. (1964). Are meetings any good for solving problems? *Personnel Administration, 27*(2), 12-16.

Elam, J. J., & Mead, M. (1987). Designing for creativity: Considerations for DSS development. *Information and Management, 13*(5), 215-222.

Fernald, L. W. & Nickolenko, P. (1993). The creative process: Its use and extent of formalization by corporations. *Journal of Creative Behavior, 27*(3), 214-220.

Gale, J., Dotson, D., Huber, M., Nagireddy, C., Manders, C. & Young, K. (1995). A new technology for teaching/learning marital and family therapy. *Journal of Marital and Family Therapy, 21*(2), 183-191.

Gryskiewicz, S. S. (1980). Creative problem solving: Are individuals still superior to groups? Some creative thinking about brainstorming. *Planned Innovation, 3*(1), 3-5.

Howard, N. (1980). Business probes the creative spark. *Dunn's Review, 115*(1), 32-38.

Judson, L. (1957, June). Got a problem? Brainstorm it! *The Rotarian.*

Krippner, S., & Hughes, W. (1970, June). Genius atzzzz workzzzzzzz. *Psychology Today, 32*, 40-43.

Kuhn, I. (1958, March 8). *Brainstorming fading out.* Newark Star Ledger.

Leclef, F. (1994). 132 managers talk about creativity consultants. In H. Geschka, S. Moger, & T. Rickards (Eds.), *Creativity and innovation: The power of synergy* (pp. 45-49). Darmstadt, Germany: Geschka & Partner Unternehmensberatung.

Malone, M. (1983). The force. In S. S. Gryskiewicz, & J. Shields (Eds.), *Creativity Week 5, 1982 Proceedings* (pp. 128-142). Greensboro, NC: Center for Creative Leadership.

Mamis, R. A. (1985, October). The gang that doesn't think straight. *Inc.,* 108-111.

Mattimore, B. W. (1991, October). Brain-storming. *Success,* 22-28.

McGarvey, R. (1990). Creative thinking. *USAir, 12*(6), 34-41.

McPherson, J. H. (1985). Innovation and creativity: Linking good minds together can spur ideas and bring results. *International Management, 40*(2), 59.

Michel, L. (1990, April). Be creative! It can pay off. *Business/New York,* 46-47.

Neuhaus, C. (1997). Creating an e-mail brainstorm. *Library Administration & Management, 11*, 217-221.

Parnes, S. J. (1962). Do you really understand brainstorming? In S. J. Parnes, & H. F. Harding (Eds.), *A source book for creative thinking* (pp. 283-290). New York: Charles Scribner's Sons.

Proctor, T. (1986). Brain: The computer program that brainstorms. *Simulation & Games, 17*(4), 485-491.

Reis, R., & Tabio, G. (1984, July). Brainstorming - radio's hot new problem - solver. *Radio Only*, 39-41.

Reiter-Palmon, R., Mumford, M. D., Boes, J. O., & Runco, M. A. (1997). Problem construction and creativity: The role of ability, cue consistency, and active processing. *Creativity Research Journal, 10*, 25-32.

Reiter-Palmon, R., Mumford, M. D., & Threfall, K. V. (1998). Solving everyday problems creatively: The role of problem construction and personality type. *Creativity Research Journal, 11*, 213-226.

Rickards, T. (1973). Brainstorming in an R & D environment. *R & D Management, 3*(3),

Rostan, S. M. (1994). Problem finding, problem solving, and cognitive controls: An empirical investigation of critically acclaimed productivity. *Creativity Research Journal, 7*, 97-110.

Runco, M. A., & Chand, I. (1994). Problem finding, evaluation thinking, and creativity. In M. A. Runco (Ed.), *Problem Finding, Problem Solving, and Creativity* (pp. 40-76). Norwood, NJ: Ablex.

Saltzman, A., & Baig, E. C. (1990, October 29). Plugging in to creativity. *U.S. News and World Report*,

Thiagarajan, S. (1988). Beyond brainstorming. *Training & Development Journal, 42*(9) 57-60.

Thiagarajan, S. (1991). Take five for better brainstorming. *Training & Development Journal, 28*(2), 37-42.

True, R. (1971). A few notes on the word "brainstorm". *Journal of Creative Behavior, 5*(1), 70-72.

Zemke, R. (1993). In search of. . . good ideas. *Training, 30*(1), 46-52.

EXPERIMENTAL EVIDENCE OF COURSE IMPACT

Beyond the foundational experimental evidence and the large accumulation of empirical research on brainstorming, there have been numerous efforts dedicated to explore and document the impact of specific courses on creativity and creative problem solving.

Anderson, R. C., & Anderson, R. M. (1963). Transfer of originality training. *Journal of Educational Psychology, 54, (6)*, 300-304.

Baer, J. M. (1988). Long-term effects of creativity training with middle school students. *Journal of Early Adolescence, 8, (2)*, 183-193.

Baer, J. (1996). The effects of task-specific divergent-thinking training. *Journal of Creative Behavior, 30*, 183-187.

Basadur, M. S. (1979). Training in creative problem solving: Effects on deferred judgment and problem finding and solving in an industrial research organization. *Dissertation Abstracts International, 40*, 5855B.

Basadur, M. S. (1982). Research in creative problem solving training in business and industry. In S. S. Gryskiewicz and J. T. Shields (Eds.), *Creativity Week IV, 1981 Proceedings* (pp. 40-59). Greensboro, NC Center for Creative Leadership.

Basadur, M. (1986, September). *Catalyzing interfunctional efforts to find and creatively solve important business problems.* Working Paper No. 261. McMaster University. Ontario, Canada

Basadur, M. S. (1987). Needed research in creativity for business and industrial applications. In S. G. Isaksen (Ed.), *Frontiers of Creativity Research: Beyond the basics* (pp. 390-416). Buffalo, NY: Bearly Limited.

Basadur, M. (1997). Organizational development interventions for enhancing creativity in the workplace. *Journal of Creative Behavior, 31*, 59-71.

Basadur, M. S., Graen, G. B., & Green, S. G. (1982). Training in creative problem solving: Effects in an industrial research organization. *Organizational Behavior and Human Performance, 30*, 41-70.

Basadur, M. S., Graen, G. B., & Scandura, T. A. (1986). Training effects on attitudes toward divergent thinking among manufacturing engineers. *Journal of Applied Psychology, 71*, 612-617.

Basadur, M. S., & Thompson, R. (1986). Usefulness of the ideation principle of extended effort in real world professional and managerial creative problem solving. *Journal of Creative Behavior, 20, (1)*, 23-34.

Basadur, M. S., Wakabayashi, M., & Graen, G. B. (1990). Individual problem-solving styles and attitudes toward divergent thinking before and after training. *Creativity Research Journal, 3, (1)*, 22-32.

Basadur, M. S., Wakabayashi, M., & Takai, J. (1992). Training effects on the divergent thinking attitudes of Japanese managers. *International Journal of Intercultural Relations, 16, (3)*, 329-345.

Beleff, N. (1968). *An experiment to increase ideational fluency gain scores of ninth grade students through brainstorming and questioning methods, developmental exercises, and social studies content.* Unpublished master's thesis. Indiana University.

Biles, B. R. (1976). CPS training for graduate and professional students. *Dissertation Abstracts International, 37*, 4220A.

Blocker, L. P. (1971). *Effect of in-service training for teachers on the creative production of students.* Unpublished master's thesis, United States International University.

Buckeye, D. A. (1968). *The effects of a creative classroom environment on the creative ability of prospective elementary mathematics teachers.* Unpublished master's thesis, Indiana University.

Buijs, J., & Nauta, K. (1991). Creativity training at the Delft school of industrial design engineering. In T. Rickards, P. Colemont, P. Grøholt, M. Parker & H. Smeekes (Eds.), *Creativity and Innovation: Learning from practice* (pp. 249-252). Delft, The Netherlands: Innovation Consulting Group - TNO.

Callahan, C., & Renzulli, J. (1974). Development and evaluation of a creativity training program. *Exceptional Children, 41,* 44-45.

Chen, S. (1993). The effects of creative problem solving training courses on verbal creative thinking, science ability, and science-related attitudes of senior high school students. *Chinese Journal of Psychology, 35, (1),* 33-42.

Chislett, L. M. (1994). Integrating the CPS and Schoolwide Enrichment Models to enhance creative productivity. *Roeper Review, 17,* 4-7.

Clinton, B. J., & Torrance, E. P. (1986). S.E.A.M.: A training program for developing problem identification skills. *Journal of Creative Behavior, 20,* 77-80.

Cohn, C. M. G. (1984). *Creativity training effectiveness: A research synthesis.* Unpublished doctoral dissertation(University Microfilms No. DA8424639), Arizona State University, Tucson, AZ.

Cramond, B., Martin, C. E., & Shaw, E. L. (1988, April). *An investigation of the application of training in creative problem solving to content area problems.* Paper presented at the annual meeting of the American Educational Research Association, New Orleans, LA.

Cramond, B., Martin, C. E., & Shaw, E. L. (1990). Generalizability of creative problem solving procedures to real-life problems. *Journal for the Education of the Gifted,* 13(2), 141-155.

Cramond, B. L., Shaw, E. L., & Martin, C. E. (1987, April). *An investigation of the application of training in creative problem solving to scientific problems.* Paper presented at the meeting of the National Association for Research in Science Teaching, Washington, DC.

Curry, J. A. (1985). *A study to evaluate the effects of using the creative problem solving process in conjunction with the training model of the National/State Leadership Training Institute on the Gifted and the Talented.* Unpublished doctoral dissertation. University of Georgia, Athens, GA.

DiClaudio, J. (1991). Praise, praise and more praise: Designing a creative environment in a health care setting. *Leadership and Organization Development Journal, 12,* 28-31.

Firestien, R. L., & McCowan, R. J. (1992). Effects of creative problem solving training on quality of ideas generated in small groups: A working paper. In L. Novelli (Ed.), *Collected research papers from the 1992 International Creativity and Networking Conference* (pp. 44-51). Greensboro, NC: Center for Creative Leadership.

Fontenot, N. A. (1993). Effects of training in creativity and creative problem finding upon business people. *Journal of Social Psychology, 133,* 1, 11-22.

Glenn, R. E. (1997, February). SCAMPER for student creativity. *The Education Digest, 62,* 67-68.

Golovin, R. W. (1993*). Creativity enhancement as a function of classroom structure: Cooperative learning vs. the traditional classroom.* Paper presented at the meeting of the Mid-South Educational Research Association, New Orleans,LA.

Gelman, M. (1976). *An investigation of the effectiveness of a creativity enhancement program.* Unpublished master's thesis. Temple University.

Haley, G. L. (1984). Creative response styles: The effects of socioeconomic status and problem-solving training. *Journal of Creative Behavior, 18,* 25-40.

Hequet, M. (1992, February). Creativity training gets creative. *Training,* 41-46.

Kabanoff, B., & Bottger, P. (1991). Effectiveness of creativity training and its relation to selected personality factors. *Journal of Organizational Behavior, 15,* 235-248.

Khatena, J. (1969*). The training of creative thinking strategies and its effects on originality.* Unpublished master's thesis. University of Georgia.

Klau, E. (1981). The effects of a 3-day workshop in creative problem solving on selected aspects of problem-solving ability in graduate students of social work. *Dissertation Abstracts International, 42,* 1796A.

Kramer, D. E., & Bayern, C. D. (1984). The effects of behavioral strategies on creativity training. *Journal of Creative Behavior, 18,* 23-24

Leopold, W. D. (1973). *Creativity and education: Some theories and procedures to enhance the development of creativity within a classroom setting.* Unpublished master's thesis. University of Massachusetts.

Maltzman, I. (1960). On the training of originality. *Psychological Review, 67(4),* 229-242.

Maltzman, I., Bogartz, W., & Berger, L. (1958). A procedure for increasing word association originality and its transfer effects. *Journal of Experimental Psychology, 56,* 392-398.

McDonald-Schwartz, L. (1991). *A preliminary experimental evaluation of creative problem solving curriculum resources.* Unpublished master's project. Center for Studies in Creativity, State University College at Buffalo.

Michell, P. C. (1987). Creativity training: Developing the agency-client interface. *European Journal of Marketing, 21,* 44-56.

Moore, J. G., Weare, J. L., Woodall, F. E., & Leonard, R. L. (1987). Training for thinking skills in relation to two cognitive measures. *Journal of Research and Development in Education, 20,* 59-65.

Renner, V., & Renner, J. C. (1971). Effects of a creativity training program on stimulus preferences. *Perceptual and Motor Skills, 33,* 872-874.

Runco, M. A., & Basadur, M. (1993). Assessing ideational and evaluative skills and creative styles and attitudes. *Creativity and Innovation Management, 2,* 166-173.

Ryan, E. G., & Torrance, E. P. (1967). Training in elaboration. *The Journal of Reading, 11,* 27-32.

Sanfilippo, J. A. (1992). *An assessment: Models of teaching and creative problem-solving style.* Unpublished doctoral dissertation (Microfilms order No. DA9322942), West Virginia University.

Schack, G. D. (1993). Effects of a creative problem-solving curriculum on students of varying ability levels. *Gifted Child Quarterly, 37, (1),* 32-38.

Schoenfeld, A. H. (1980). Teaching problem-solving skills. *American Mathematical Monthly, 87 (10),* 794-805.

Shivley, J. E., Feldhusen, J. F., & Treffinger, D. J. (1967). Developing creativity and related attitudes. *The Journal of Experimental Education, 41 (2),* 63 - 69.

Tan-Willman, C. (1980). Fostering creativity and its effect on moral reasoning of prospective teachers. *Journal of Creative Behavior, 14 (4),* 258-263.

Torrance, E. P. (1972). Can we teach children to think creatively? *Journal of Creative Behavior, 6, (2),* 114-143.

Torrance, E. P. (1986). Teaching creative and gifted learners. In M. C. Wittrock (Ed.), *Handbook of Research on Teaching* (pp. 630-647). New York: MacMillan Publishing Company.

Torrance, E. P. (1987). Teaching for creativity. In S. G. Isaksen (Ed.), *Frontiers of Creativity Research: Beyond the basics* (189-215). Buffalo, NY: Bearly Limited.

Torrance, E. P., & Presbury, J. (1984). The criteria of success used in 242 recent experimental studies of creativity. *The Creative Child and Adult Quarterly, 9, (4),* 238-243.

Treffinger, D. J. & Ripple, R. E. (1970). The effect of programmed instructions on creative problem solving and attitudes. *Irish Journal of Education, 4,* 47-59.

Treffinger, D. J. & Speedie, S. M., & Brunner, W. D. (1974). Improving children's creative problem solving ability: The Purdue creativity project. *Journal of Creative Behavior, 8,* 20-30.

Tweet, C. C. (1980). *Effects of the implementation of creativity training in the elementary school social studies curriculum.* Unpublished master's thesis. Montana State University.

Waterstreet, M. A. (1977). *The effects of amount and spacing of creativity training sessions on immediate and enduring gains in the creative production of third grade children.* Unpublished master's thesis. University of Georgia.

Williams, R. E. (1977). Programmed instruction for creativity. *Programmed Learning and Educational Technology, 14,* 50-64.

Wilson, A. E. (1972). *A study of the effects of preservice creativity training on creative abilities and perceptions of prospective teachers and their pupils.* Unpublished masters thesis. West Virginia University.

Zelina, M. (1982). Pupils' creativity development program: Construction and results. *Ceskoslovenska-Psychologie, 26, (2),* 145-155.

Zelnick, J. (1972). *Effects of creativity training on reading performances of fourth-grade and fifth-grade children.* Unpublished master's thesis. Rutgers University.

◆ 9. CPS HAS BEEN WIDELY APPLIED

It is certainly worthwhile to have large amounts of conceptual, theoretical and empirical support for the usefulness of CPS. Reflection, inquiry and theory are important, but so are application and practice (Argyris & Schön, 1996). The acid test of the worth of CPS is the extent to which it has been successfully applied. There is evidence that it has been taught and applied within a variety of special populations. There is also case study evidence available.

Argyris, C., & Schön, D. A. (1996). *Organizational learning II: Theory, method and practice*. Reading, MA: Addison-Wesley.

SPECIAL POPULATIONS

One of the ways to document the impact of CPS is to examine the extent to which it has applied in a variety of populations. This is the issue of breadth of use. The following citations illustrate some of the various contexts within which CPS has been applied.

Avarello, L. L. (1993). *An exploratory study to determine the impact of a Creative Studies course on at-risk students*. Unpublished master's project. Center for Studies in Creativity, State University College at Buffalo.

Barnes, S. J. (1997). *Creativity in the workplace: The creativity professional's perspective*. Unpublished doctoral dissertation. The University of Nebraska.

Basadur, M. S., & Paton, B. R. (1993). Using creativity to boost profits in recessionary times. *Industrial Management, 35*, 14-19.

Bruce, B. (1991). *Impact of creative problem solving training on management behavior*. Unpublished master's project. Center for Studies in Creativity, State University College at Buffalo.

Burstiner, I. (1973). Creativity training: Management tool for high school department chairmen. *Journal of Experimental Education, 41*, 4, 17-19.

Callahan, C. M. (1973). *The effects of the Connecticut Mark I Creativity Program on the creative thinking of sixth grade students*. Unpublished master's thesis. University of Connecticut, Storrs.

Cartledge, C. J., & Krauser, E. L. (1963). Training first grade children in creative thinking under quantitative and qualitative motivation. *Journal of Educational Psychology, 54(6)*, 295-299.

Clapham, M. M., & Schuster, D. H. (1992). Can engineering students be trained to think more creatively? *Journal of Creative Behavior, 26, (3)*, 156-162.

Cohen, D., Whitmeyer, J. W., & Funk, W. H. (1960). Effects of group cohesiveness and training upon creative thinking. *Journal of Applied Psychology, 44, (5)*, 319-322.

Connolly, C. P. (1970). *An experimental investigation of the application of empirical program development procedure to instructional television programs on creative problem solving.* Unpublished master's thesis. Ohio State University.

Cramond, B., Martin, C. E., & Shaw, E. L. (1990). Generalizability of creative problem solving procedures to real-life problems. *Journal for the Education of the Gifted, 13,* (2), 141-155.

Curran, J. M. (1983). *Effects of CPS training on LD student's creative thinking and self-concept scores.* Unpublished master's thesis. Center for Studies in Creativity, State University College at Buffalo.

Elwell, P. A. (1986). *An analysis of the field testing of creative problem solving for teenagers using Torrance Tests.* Unpublished master's thesis. Center for Studies in Creativity, State University College at Buffalo.

Engelman, M. (1978*).* The response of older women to a creative problem solving program. *Dissertation Abstracts International, 38,* 7080A.

Engelman, M. (1977). *The response of older women to a creative problem solving program.* Unpublished doctoral dissertation (University Microfilms No. 7804854), University of Wisconsin-Madison, Madison, WI.

Engelman, M. (1981). The response of older women to a creative problem-solving program. *Educational Gerontology, 6,* 165-173.

Farrar, J. C. (1984). Effects of training in divergent thinking on learning mathematics by fourth grade children. (creativity, brainstorming, arithmetic). *Dissertation Abstracts International, 45,* 3351B.

Farrar, J. C. (1984). *Effects of training in divergent thinking on learning mathematics by fourth grade children.* Unpublished doctoral dissertation (University Microfilms No. DA8429002), North Carolina State University at Raleigh, Raleigh, N.C.

Fernald, L. W., & Nickolenko, P. (1993). The creative process: Its use and extent of formalization by corporations. *Journal of Creative Behavior, 27,* 214-220.

Flaherty, M. A. (1992). The effects of a holistic creativity program on the self-concept and creativity of third graders. *Journal of Creative Behavior, 26,* 165-171.

Heppner, P. P., & Reeder, B. L. (1984). Training in problem solving for residence hall staff: Who is most satisfied. *Journal of College Student Personnel, 25,* 357-360.

Geschka, H. (1993). The development and assessment of creative thinking techniques: A German perspective. In S. G. Isaksen, M. C. Murdock, R. L. Firestien & D. J. Treffinger (Eds.), *Nurturing and developing creativity: The emergence of a discipline* (pp. 215-236). Norwood, NJ: Ablex.

Gheen, W. L. (1970). *The adequacy of certain creative class methodologies in selected Texas industrial arts teacher training institutions.* Unpublished master's thesis. Texas A & M University.

Hackley, C. & Kitchen, P. J. (1997). Creative problem solving as a technology of expert behavior within marketing management. *Creativity and Innovation Management, 6,* 45-59.

Heppner, P. P., Baumgardner, A. H., Larson, L. M., & Petti, R. E. (1983). *Problem solving training for college students with problem solving deficits.* Paper presented at the annual meeting of the American Psychology Association. Anaheim, CA.

Huber, J. R., Treffinger, D. J., Tracy, D. B., & Rand, D. C. (1979). Self-instructional use of programmed creativity training materials with gifted and regular students. *Journal of Educational Psychology, 71,* 303-309.

Jaben, T. H. (1979). *The impact of creativity training on learning disabled students' creative thinking abilities and problem solving skills.* Unpublished master's thesis. University of Kansas.

Johnson, A. L. (1998). Teaching creative problem solving and applied reasoning skills: A modular approach. *California Western Law Review, 34,* 389-395.

Johnson, J. E. (1974). *Creative teaching: Its effects upon the creative thinking ability, achievement, and intelligence of selected fourth grade students.* Unpublished master's thesis. McNeese State University.

Jones, H. E. (1980). *The effects of a creativity training program for teachers upon the classroom responding behavior of teachers toward creative student behaviors.* Unpublished doctoral dissertation. West Virginia University.

Kalmar, M., & Kalmar, Z. (1980). Creativity training experiment with residential nursery school children. *Magyar-Pszichologiai-Szemle, 37, (1),* 21-37.

Kapusinski, A., Sutterlin, T., Hobbins, K. L., Wright, R. & Bendiksen, R. (1989). Problem solving sociology: Learning creative problem solving in an undergraduate sociology seminar. *Clinical Sociology Review, 7,* 178-197.

Kealy, J. R. (1977). A study of the effects of training in CPS on the creativity of student teachers of foreign languages and on the attitudes of their students. *Dissertation Abstracts International, 37,* 5053A.

Maciejczyk-Clapham, M., & Schuster, D. (1992). Can engineering students be trained to think more creatively? *Journal of Creative Behavior, 26,* 156-162.

Markewitz, D. A. (1982). *The influence of creativity intervention training on the adjustment potential of kindergarten children.* Unpublished doctoral dissertation. University of Saint Thomas.

Martin, D. F. (1971). *The effects of a creative problem solving workshop upon the cognitive operations of verbal classroom interaction in the primary school grades.* Unpublished master's thesis. University of Georgia.

Mathew, S. T. (1981). *The effectiveness of creative problem-solving in reducing the aggression of emotionally handicapped middle school children.* Unpublished doctoral dissertation, University of Florida.

McCluskey, K. W., McCluskey, A. L. A., Baker, P. A., & O'Hagan, S. (1996). Talent dormant - talent awake: A three-year summary of the Lost Prizes Project. *Creative Learning Today, 6,* 8-9.

McCluskey, K. W., Baker, P. A., O'Hagan, S. & Treffinger, D. J. (1995). *Lost prizes: Talent development and problem solving with at-risk students*. Sarasota, FL: Center for Creative Learning.

McCluskey, K. W., & Treffinger, D. J. (1998). Nurturing talented but troubled children and youth. *Reclaiming Children and Youth, 6*, 215-226.

Mijares-Colmenares, B. E., Masten, W. G., & Underwood, J. E. (1993). Effects of trait anxiety and the SCAMPER technique on creative thinking of intellectually gifted students. *Psychological Reports, 72, (3)*, 907-912.

Miller, J. H. (1974). *The effectiveness of training on creative thinking abilities of third grade children*. Unpublished master's thesis. University of Alabama.

Moreno, J. M. (1974). *The influence of race and social class level on the training of creative thinking and problem solving abilities of fifth and sixth grade students*. Unpublished master's thesis. St. Johns University, New York, NY.

Place, D. & McCluskey, A. (1995). Second chance: A program to support native inmates at-risk. In McCluskey, K. W., Baker, P. A., & O'Hagan, S. & Treffinger, D. J. (Eds.), *Lost prizes: Talent development and problem solving with at-risk students* (pp. 137-146). Sarasota, FL: Center for Creative Learning.

Place, D. J., McCluskey, A. L. A., McCluskey, K. W. & Treffinger, D. J. (In press). The second chance project: Creative approaches to developing the talents of at-risk native inmates. *Journal of Creative Behavior*.

Puccio, K. G. (1994). *An analysis of an observational study of creative problem solving for primary children*. Unpublished master's project. Center for Studies in Creativity, State University College at Buffalo.

Romaniuk, J. G. (1978). *Training creativity in the elderly: An examination of attitudes, self-perceptions and abilities*. Unpublished master's thesis. University of Wisconsin-Madison.

Romaniuk, J. G. (1979). Creative thinking in action: Reactions to a workshop designed for older adults. *Journal of Creative Behavior, 4*, 274-276.

Sharpe, L. W. (1976). The effects of a creative-thinking skills program on intermediate grade educationally handicapped children. *Journal of Creative Behavior, 10*, 138-145.

Shaw, J. M., & Cliatt, M. J. (1986). A model for training teachers to encourage divergent thinking in young children. *Journal of Creative Behavior, 20 (2)*, 81-88.

Shean, J. M. (1977). The effects of training in creative problem solving on divergent thinking and organizational perceptions of students of school administration. *Dissertation Abstracts International, 38*, 585A. (Northern Arizona University)

Sherief, N. M. S. (1978). *The effects of creativity training, classroom atmosphere and cognitive style on the creative thinking abilities of Egyptian elementary school children*. Unpublished master's thesis. Purdue University.

Sherrow, J. E. (1969). *The effect of a creative problem solving workshop on selected municipal recreation personnel*. Unpublished master's thesis. University of Illinois.

Steinmetz, C. S. (1968). Creativity training: A testing program that became a sales training program. *Journal of Creative Behavior, 2 (3),* 179-186.

Sullivan, T. (1969). Developing problem-solving ability in slow learning elementary students. *Journal of Creative Behavior, 3,* 284-290.

Talbot, R. J. (1993). Creativity in the organizational context: Implications for training. In S. G. Isaksen, M. C. Murdock, R. L. Firestien, D. J. Treffinger (Eds.), *Nurturing and Developing Creativity: The Emergence of a Discipline.* (pp. 177-214). Norwood, NJ: Ablex Publishing Corp.

Treffinger, D. J., & Parnes, S. J. (1980). Creative problem solving for the gifted and talented. *Roeper Review, 2,* 31-32.

CASE STUDIES

An alternative way to document and understand the impact of CPS is to dig deeper into how and why it was applied. Case studies provide a unique level of depth to help understand the results and context of specific applications.

Babij, B. (1999). A study in change: From bed sores to quality care. *Communiqué, 7,* 8-16.

Bingham, G. (1997). *Using task appraisal to examine CPS application within a business planning process: An instrumental case study.* Unpublished Masters project. Center for Studies in Creativity, State University College at Buffalo.

Conwell, J. C., Catalano, G. D., & Beard, J. E. (1993). A case study in creative problem solving in engineering design. *Journal of Engineering Education, 82,* 224-227.

Cougar, J. D., & Snow, T. A. (1990). *Case Study: Introducing a creativity improvement program in an information systems organization.* University of Colorado, Colorado Springs: Center for Research on Creativity and Innovation (CRCI Report 90-5).

De Schryver, L. (1992). *An impact study of creative problem solving facilitation training in an organizational setting.* Unpublished master's thesis. Center for Studies in Creativity, State University College at Buffalo.

Dewulf, S. & Baillie, C. (1999). *Creativity in art, science and engineering: How to foster creativity.* London: Department for Education and Employment.

Gordon, J., & Zemke, R. (1986). Making them more creative. *Training, 23, (5),* 30-34, 39-45.

Handley, C. (1990). Why Frito-Lay is crackling with new ideas: Use of the creative problem solving process is paying off at the snack food giant. *Purchasing, 108, May 3,* 84A2-84A3.

Hill, P. (1988). Innovation using creative problem solving techniques: A corporate case example. *Creativity & Innovation Yearbook, 1,* 106-111.

Hequet, M. (1992). Creativity training gets creative. *Training, 29, (2).* 41-46.

Isaksen, S. G., & Lewandowski, B. R. (1997). *An impact investigation: The CPS initiative in Bull UK & Ireland.* Unpublished research project. The Creative Problem Solving Group-Buffalo.

Isaksen, S. G., & Murdock, M. C. (1990). *Project Discovery evaluation report: A comprehensive quantitative and qualitative impact report on a program designed to introduce exploratory consumer research methodologies and develop new consumer products.* Unpublished research report. The Center for Studies in Creativity and The Creative Problem Solving Group - Buffalo.

Isaksen, S. G., Murdock, M. C., & De Schryver, L. (1991). *How continuous improvement and creative problem solving are impacting Exxon's marketing organization: A qualitative interview analysis documenting the impact of change following CPS training with continuous improvement facilitators.* Unpublished research project. The Center for Studies in Creativity and the Creative Problem Solving Group - Buffalo.

Isaksen, S. G., & Puccio, G. J. (1988). *The impact of training creative thinking skills: A quantitative and qualitative study of the impact of training on participants within the Procter & Gamble's two-day training course of Creative Thinking Skills.* Unpublished research project. The Center for Studies in Creativity and the Creative Problem Solving Group – Buffalo.

Kapusinski, A., Sutterlin, T., Hobbins, K. L., Wright, R., & Bendiksen, R. (1989). Problem solving sociology: Learning creative problem solving in an undergraduate sociology seminar. *Clinical Sociology Review, 7,* 178-197.

Lewandowski, B. R. (In preparation). *An internship experience in evaluation and qualitative analysis.* A report in preparation. Center for Studies in Creativity, State University College at Buffalo.

Lewis, W. (1996). Applying creative problem solving to a critical business problem. *Communiqué 2,* 1-4.

Morrison, D. (1988). Creative problem solving for a productivity consultant within Frito-Lay. In Gryskiewicz, S. S., D. Hills, & V. Barnebey (Eds.), *Creativity Week 10 – 1987 – Proceedings* (pp. 27-40). Greensboro, NC: Center for Creative Leadership.

Puccio, G. J. (1986). *Training effectiveness: The transfer and application of problem solving skills to the work setting.* Unpublished research project. The Center for Studies in Creativity, Buffalo, New York.

Reid, G. D. (1997). *A report on an internship experience: Evaluation and impact of facilitating CPS.* Unpublished masters project. Center for Studies in Creativity, State University College at Buffalo.

Reid, G. D., & Dorval, K. B. (1996). CPS-B tips the scales in Indiana. *Communiqué, 2,* 5-7.

Sensabaugh, S. J. (1985). *The Norfolk Southern innovative problem solving course.* An impact survey and case study documented by the Creativity Development Division of the Center for Creative Leadership. Greensboro, North Carolina.

Tanner, D. (1997). *Total creativity in business & industry: Road map to building a more innovative organization.* Des Moines, IA: Advanced Practical Thinking Training Inc.

Thamia, S., & Woods, M. F. (1984). A systematic small-group approach to creativity and innovation: A case study. *R&D Management, 14,* 25-35.

Thorn, D. (1987). Problem solving for innovation in industry. *Journal of Creative Behavior, 21(2)* 93-108.

AFTERWORD

A LOOK TO THE FUTURE

I hope that reading this book has been enjoyable and has been as much of a learning experience for you as it was for me in assembling it. We view facilitative leadership as a key concept for individuals, groups and organizations concerned with change and creativity. Through thirty years of developing my own facilitation skills, I have become aware that knowledge of, belief in, and sustained skilled performance in Creative Problem Solving (CPS) is not sufficient. Although expertise in process is necessary, making a real difference requires balanced consideration of the people and the environment, as well as, a clear focus on the desired results. As the old saying goes: "If you don't know where you're going, any road will get you there."

The role of process is one of the key differentiators between most people who view and use CPS more traditionally, and those who are now subscribing to a more flexible descriptive approach. This became very clear to me after attending an international conference on creativity and innovation. There were two major "camps" among the CPS practitioners involved in the master classes on facilitation. One group had already made up its mind about a process agenda before meeting with the client or knowing anything about the goal or method used prior to the meeting. They asserted that all clients need to begin at the same process starting point. Others were more concerned with using their newest or favorite tool. These facilitators had training and experience in a more traditional approach to CPS.

The other group sought a meaningful appraisal of the people involved, some possible choices regarding the methods to use, some information about the context and the needs the clients expressed. They saw the client's needs as essential for deciding whether they should use CPS, and, if so, where to begin. When these two groups of facilitators attempted to work together there was often a great deal of tension. This observation speaks to a real difference emerging within the field of creativity research and practice.

Much of our previous work was aimed at improving the traditional approaches. We had all done our share of process run throughs, and had observed some excellent intuitive practitioners. Now we are much more focused on the products and outcomes our clients want and need, and a lot less concerned with following a fixed process path or only using particular tools. We are now more concerned about qualifying and optimizing our process approach. We approach our work by focusing on the needs of the clients and the people they are working with, as well as the setting within which they are working.

I foresee the formation of a crossroads of those who engage in facilitative leadership and seek to make a difference with CPS. One pathway will involve the simple, clear and relatively easy approach of following a predetermined set of stages for all problems and opportunities. The other path may offer a little more complexity and require more deliberate decision making, but will allow greater rewards in terms of productivity. Those who choose the latter path will truly serve individuals, groups and organizations and be seen as integral to helping them respond to demands for change. You will need to decide which path you will walk down.

This book has been my first attempt to collect and organize a growing body of knowledge about facilitative leadership. Although its focus has been the method of CPS, most of the information will be relevant to any other change method you may be applying. My hope is that we will continue to pursue a rather steep learning curve and be able to share future insights through a variety of our publications and outlets.

Best of luck with all your facilitative leadership experiences!

Scott Isaksen